International Judicial Institutions

Is there a "system" of international justice? Or are the increasingly dispersed methods for its enforcement indicative of solely discrete "instances" of international justice?

Written by a former UN chief prosecutor and a leading international law expert, this book introduces this key debate in international humanitarian law. Analyzing the legal and political underpinnings of international judicial institutions, it provides the reader with an understanding of both the historical development of international judicial institutions and an overview of the differences and similarities between organizations.

The reader will come to see how newer institutions—both international courts and domestic providers of international justice—have responded to history and to their contemporary political environments. The inclusion of institutions' founding statutes allows the expert and student to compare the legal and political foundations of each iteration of international justice.

A fascinating book and a must buy for students, researchers, and the general reader interested in law and human rights.

Richard J. Goldstone is Visiting Professor of Law at Harvard Law School, former Justice of the Constitutional Court of South Africa, and former Chief Prosecutor of the United Nations International Criminal Tribunals for the former Yugoslavia and Rwanda.

Adam M. Smith is a Washington, DC-based international lawyer. He has written extensively on international law and has worked on justice in the Balkans, Asia, and Africa. Educated at Harvard, Oxford, and Brown, Smith has held posts at the UN and the World Bank and is the author of *After Genocide: Bringing the Devil to Justice*.

Routledge Global Institutions

Edited by Thomas G. Weiss
The CUNY Graduate Center, New York, USA
and Rorden Wilkinson
University of Manchester, UK

About the Series

The Global Institutions Series is designed to provide readers with comprehensive, accessible, and informative guides to the history, structure, and activities of key international organizations. Every volume stands on its own as a thorough and insightful treatment of a particular topic, but the series as a whole contributes to a coherent and complementary portrait of the phenomenon of global institutions at the dawn of the millennium.

Books are written by recognized experts, conform to a similar structure, and cover a range of themes and debates common to the series. These areas of shared concern include the general purpose and rationale for organizations, developments over time, membership, structure, decision-making procedures, and key functions. Moreover, current debates are placed in historical perspective alongside informed analysis and critique. Each book also contains an annotated bibliography and guide to electronic information as well as any annexes appropriate to the subject matter at hand.

The volumes currently published or under contract include:

The United Nations and Human Rights (2005)
A guide for a new era
by Julie Mertus (American University)

The UN Secretary General and Secretariat (2005)
by Leon Gordenker (Princeton University)

United Nations Global Conferences (2005)
by Michael G. Schechter (Michigan State University)

The UN General Assembly (2005)
by M.J. Peterson (University of Massachusetts, Amherst)

Internal Displacement (2006)
Conceptualization and its consequences
by Thomas G. Weiss (The CUNY Graduate Center) and David A. Korn

Global Environmental Institutions (2006)
by Elizabeth R. DeSombre (Wellesley College)

African Economic Institutions
by Kwame Akonor (Seton Hall University)

The United Nations Development Programme (UNDP)
by Elizabeth A. Mandeville (Tufts University) and Craig N. Murphy (Wellesley College)

The Regional Development Banks
Lending with a regional flavor
by Jonathan R. Strand (University of Nevada, Las Vegas)

Multilateral Cooperation Against Terrorism
by Peter Romaniuk (John Jay College of Criminal Justice, CUNY)

Peacebuilding
From concept to commission
by Robert Jenkins (University of London)

Transnational Organized Crime
by Frank Madsen (University of Cambridge)

Governing Climate Change
by Peter Newell (University of East Anglia) and Harriet A. Bulkeley (Durham University)

Millennium Development Goals (MDGs)
For a people-centered development agenda?
by Sakiko Fukada-Parr (The New School)

Regional Security
The capacity of international organizations
by Rodrigo Tavares (United Nations University)

Human Development
by Maggie Black

For further information regarding the series, please contact:

Craig Fowlie, Publisher, Politics & International Studies
Taylor & Francis
2 Park Square, Milton Park, Abingdon
Oxford OX14 4RN, UK

+44 (0)207 842 2057 Tel
+44 (0)207 842 2302 Fax

Craig.Fowlie@tandf.co.uk
www.routledge.com

International Judicial Institutions

The architecture of international justice at home and abroad

Richard J. Goldstone and Adam M. Smith

[handwritten inscription:] For Brett and Vianne, With warmest regards and appreciation for your friendship. And with much gratitude to Brett for his outstanding contribution to my class and ... Yew .

Routledge
Taylor & Francis Group

LONDON AND NEW YORK

First published 2009
by Routledge
2 Park Square, Milton Park, Abingdon, Oxon, OX14 4RN

Simultaneously published in the USA and Canada
by Routledge
270 Madison Avenue, New York, NY 10016

Routledge is an imprint of the Taylor & Francis Group, an informa business

© 2009 Richard J. Goldstone and Adam M. Smith

Typeset in Times New Roman by
Taylor & Francis Books
Printed and bound in Great Britain by
TJ International Ltd, Padstow, Cornwall

British Library Cataloguing in Publication Data
A catalogue record for this book is available from the British Library

Library of Congress Cataloging in Publication Data
Goldstone, Richard.
 International judicial pursuit : the architecture of international justice
 at home and abroad / Richard J. Goldstone and Adam M. Smith.
  p. cm. – (Global Institutions series)
 Includes bibliographical references and index.
 1. Justice, Administration of–International cooperation. 2.
 International law. 3. Humanitarian law. 4. International courts. I.
 Smith, Adam M. II. Title.
 K7051.G65 2008
 341–dc22   2008008361

ISBN 978-0-415-77645-5 (hbk)
ISBN 978-0-415-77646-2 (pbk)
ISBN 978-0-203-89203-9 (ebk)

Contents

Boxes

Foreword

The current volume is the twenty-eighth in a dynamic series on "global institutions." The series strives (and, based on the volumes published to date, succeeds) to provide readers with definitive guides to the most visible aspects of what we know as "global governance." Remarkable as it may seem, there exist relatively few books that offer in-depth treatments of prominent global bodies, processes, and associated issues, much less an entire series of concise, and complementary volumes. Those that do exist are either out of date, inaccessible to the non-specialist reader, or seek to develop a specialized understanding of particular aspects of an institution or process rather than offer an overall account of its functioning. Similarly, existing books have often been written in highly technical language or have been crafted "in-house" and are notoriously self-serving and narrow.

The advent of electronic media has helped by making information, documents, and resolutions of international organizations more widely available, but it has also complicated matters. The growing reliance on the Internet and other electronic methods of finding information about key international organizations and processes has served, ironically, to limit the educational materials to which most readers have ready access—namely, books. Public relations documents, raw data, and loosely refereed web sites do not make for intelligent analysis. Official publications compete with a vast amount of electronically available information, much of which is suspect because of its ideological or self-promoting slant. Paradoxically, the growing range of purportedly independent web sites offering analyses of the activities of particular organizations has emerged, but one inadvertent consequence has been to frustrate access to basic, authoritative, critical, and well researched texts. The market for such has actually been reduced by the ready availability of varying quality electronic materials.

For those of us who teach, research, and practice in the area, this access to information has been particularly frustrating. We were delighted when Routledge saw the value of a series that bucks this trend and provides key reference points to the most significant global institutions. They know that serious students and professionals want serious analyses. We have assembled a first-rate line-up of authors to address that market. Our intention, then, is to provide one-stop shopping for all readers—students (both undergraduate and postgraduate), negotiators, diplomats, practitioners from nongovernmental and intergovernmental organizations, and interested parties alike—seeking information about the most prominent institutional aspects of global governance.

International judicial institutions

International attempts to regulate the laws of war and grotesque human rights abuses have a longish history in global governance. The consequences of technological advances in weaponry and the character of attacks on human beings led a Swiss businessman named Henry Dunant to start what is now called the International Committee of the Red Cross.[1] He was appalled that in the battle of Solferino in 1859, in what is now Italy, wounded soldiers were simply left on the battlefield. In 1864, the first Geneva Convention for Victims of War was concluded, providing legal protection to soldiers disabled in international war and the medical personnel who cared for them. These laws of war were refined in the Hague Conventions of 1899 and 1907, which, most notably, banned the use of certain types of technology in war.

The development of international humanitarian law continued with the 1925 Geneva Protocol to the Hague Convention and, after the conclusion of World War II, the four 1949 Geneva Conventions (and their three additional protocols in 1977 and 2005). Critical to the post-war legal regime were the war crimes tribunals in Nuremburg and Tokyo, which established the doctrine of individual responsibility for crimes against peace, war crimes, and crimes against humanity, and which paved the way for the eventual creation of a permanent international criminal court.

In addition to the development of international humanitarian law, the development of human rights ideas, conventions, and machinery have been a prominent part of the post-war effort, and several books in this series concentrate on this crucial development in international relations.[2] At the signing of the Universal Declaration of Human Rights in 1948, Eleanor Roosevelt predicted "a curious grapevine" would spread the ideas contained in the declaration far and wide.[3] The last six decades have been quite a ride and form part of the story from the Universal Declaration through the tortuous debate and negotiation of the two conventions on economic, social, and cultural as well as civil and political rights, in the 1950s and 1960s, and the later developments in the rights of special groups and the right to development in the 1980s, to the World Conference on Human Rights in Vienna and the establishment of the Office of the High Commissioner for Human Rights in the 1990s. The most recent chapter deals with the establishment of the UN Human Rights Council, the first session of which took place in June 2006, though it may not be a real step forward from the UN Commission on Human Rights.

In the post–Cold War era, several types of non-consensual activities have been authorized by the Security Council, and it is in this context that the current book on international judicial pursuit is crucial. Although much more attention has been paid to the growing use of international military forces and of economic sanctions,[4] international criminal prosecution is another type of intervention that, for the first time since the immediate aftermath of World War II, is employed to bring to justice those who have committed crimes against humanity. A number of legal decisions suggest considerable erosion of the rules relating to the immunity of states and their leaders. These have long provided that leading officials (including retired ones) of a state cannot be tried in courts in another country for acts committed in their own state and in the exercise of their official duties. Although the Genocide Convention specifically calls for punishing perpetrators "whether they are constitutionally responsible rulers, public officials or private individuals," state practice over decades overwhelmingly supported the notion of sovereign immunity. This is one reason why states—and in particular the United States under the Clinton administration—avoided labeling the Rwandan bloodbath "genocide."

The fight to establish limits to impunity received a boost with the establishment of the International Criminal Tribunal for the former Yugoslavia (ICTY) and for Rwanda (ICTR) in 1993 and 1994, respectively. Subsequent violence in Burundi, the Democratic Republic of Congo, East Timor, and Sierra Leone led to calls for additional ad hoc tribunals, as did, two decades later, the Khmer Rouge's atrocities of the 1970s. While the tribunals for the former Yugoslavia and Rwanda are entirely international, the ones for Cambodia, East Timor, and Sierra Leone are a mix of local and foreign judges and an international prosecutor. If we fast forward to 2006, the death of Slobodan Milosevic during his trial in The Hague instead of in a luxury suite on the French

Riviera made it seem as if a new era was perhaps dawning, especially when Charles Taylor was captured shortly thereafter and indicted for his crimes in West Africa. At a minimum, dictators were on notice that on occasion there could be international juridical consequences for abusive conduct.

Dissatisfaction with early institutional shortcomings for both the ICTY and ICTR demonstrated to many observers the need for a permanent court. The Rome Statute of the International Criminal Court was established in 1998, when 120 states participating in the United Nations Diplomatic Conference of Plenipotentiaries on the Establishment of an International Criminal Court adopted the statute, which entered into force only four years later after the requisite 60 ratifications. Anyone who commits crimes under the statute after this date is liable for prosecution. While some important states are not parties (including the United States, which under George W. Bush has made non-membership a cornerstone of the National Defense Security Strategy), international agreement on the independence of the prosecutor and the court's jurisdiction over internal conflicts and disturbances suggests that criminal prosecution could become a common, rather than ad hoc, form of intervention as a response to large-scale atrocities.

To do justice to the historical sweep of these efforts at international criminal pursuit and current efforts to move ahead, we needed someone with an acute knowledge not only of the broad legal and political developments but also of the nuts and bolts of post–Cold War experiments. We were delighted, then, when Justice Richard Goldstone and Adam Smith agreed to write this book for us, which continued a collaboration that began on a shorter version of the argument.[5]

Richard Goldstone is one of the world's most formidable authorities on this topic, having served as a justice of the Constitutional Court in South Africa and at The Hague (at the United Nations international criminal tribunals for the former Yugoslavia and Rwanda), as well as on several international commissions. He has taught a course on this topic at numerous universities since "retiring" (at Harvard Law School, New York University Law School, Fordham Law School, and, most recently, Georgetown Law School). His young partner, Adam Smith, has extensive global political, economic, and cultural knowledge gained via experiences working with foreign governments, multilaterals, academia, and the private sector in more than 80 countries, and has published on a range of international affairs, legal, political economy, and public policy issues.

The book exudes authority yet is accessible. As readers will quickly become aware, the book is an invaluable resource and clearly deserves to be read by all interested in the history, politics, and law of global governance. We heartily recommend it; and, as always, we welcome comments from readers.

Thomas G. Weiss, the CUNY Graduate Center, New York, USA
Rorden Wilkinson, University of Manchester, UK
August 2008

Acknowledgment

Parts of Chapters 1 and 5 first appeared in Chapter 26 "International Criminal Court and Ad Hoc Tribunals" by Richard Goldstone pp. 463–478 from *Oxford Handbook on the United Nations* edited by Weiss, Thomas G. and Daws, Sam (2007). Used by permission of Oxford University Press.

Parts of the Introduction and Chapters 1 and 5 are based on material that first appeared in "From Nuremberg to the Hague: The Future of International Criminal Prosecution – Review Essay," by Adam M. Smith, pp. 563–575 in *Harvard International Law Journal*, vol. 45(2), Summer 2004. Copyright (c) 2004 The President and Fellows of Harvard College, and the Harvard International Law Journal. Used with permission.

Abbreviations

ASP	Assembly of States Parties (to the ICC Treaty)
CIL	Customary International Law
CPA	Coalition Provisional Authority (in Iraq)
ECCC	Extraordinary Chambers in the Courts of Cambodia
ICC	International Criminal Court
ICJ	International Court of Justice
ICRC	International Committee for the Red Cross
ICTR	International Criminal Tribunal for Rwanda
ICTY	International Criminal Tribunal for the former Yugoslavia
IHL	International Humanitarian Law
IJP	International Judges and Prosecutors (in Kosovo)
ILC	International Law Commission
IMT	International Military Tribunal (in Nuremberg)
IMTFE	International Military Tribunal for the Far East
IST	Iraqi Special Tribunal
NATO	North Atlantic Treaty Organization
NGO	Non-Governmental Organization
SCSL	Special Court for Sierra Leone
STL	Special Tribunal for Lebanon
TRC	Truth and Reconciliation Commission
UN	United Nations
UNGA	United Nations General Assembly
UNMIK	United Nations Interim Administration Mission in Kosovo
UNSC	United Nations Security Council
UNTAET	United Nations Transitional Administration for East Timor
UNWCC	United Nations War Crimes Commission

Introduction

"International justice" is as much a term of art as it is a tangible goal. Susceptible to numerous potentially incompatible definitions, and steeped in religious, political, economic and social, let alone judicial overtones, a key barrier to any pursuit of international justice has been the obfuscation and equivocation inherent within the concept itself. Despite this, and perhaps because of it, recently international justice has achieved a critical mass of global support, with surveys of domestic polities and actions and statements by states indicating a near universal desire for some sort of enforceable mechanism to appropriately punish those who commit grievous crimes in violation of international humanitarian law (IHL).[1] Indeed, while attempts to establish tribunals to prosecute other areas of international law, such as drugs and human trafficking, have met with little success, those focused on IHL violations have become a global phenomenon.

In a sense there is little new about such widespread support for international justice. After all, the basis of many of the world's major faiths rests on some idea of divine justice; it has long been natural for practitioners to bring the holy into the profane, the church, mosque and synagogue into the street. However, for most of recorded history this desire to impose a universal order on global disorder, and to hold those who thwart society's will to account, has remained firmly in the religious canon, venturing into the secular only in the halls of academia. Differences regarding how best to pursue international justice, and more pointedly, who belongs in the dock in such a system, hampered any widespread emergence.

It is untrue that concerted efforts to enforce international justice never appeared. Rather, until recently, such efforts have done so but only in the wake of unique global political circumstances, and even then have only been ephemeral. That is, institutions like those that emerged after World War II at Nuremberg and in Tokyo to try members of the Axis, and even those UN courts created in 1993 and 1994 to deal with bloodshed in the former Yugoslavia and Rwanda, were aberrations, and explicitly so. Each arose in an era of unprecedented consensus, with those after World War II emerging in the fleeting unity that joined the Allies from East and West between the end of 1945 and the start of the Cold War, and those in the 1990s coming about in the immediate post–Cold War era and the similarly short-lived consensus that emerged under *Pax Americana* and the "end of history." Even with the backdrop of consensus, the architects of these institutions were cabined, which resulted both in the 1940s and then in the mid-1990s in the creation of temporary institutions, designed with specific, limited remits. They were not intended to form a perennial system of international justice, but rather solely to provide instances of it.

The changes in this regard since the middle of the 1990s are seismic and threefold. First, there has been a proliferation of further, ad hoc, limited tribunals in several parts of the world. In nations including Sierra Leone, Cambodia, and Lebanon, states have returned to the "Nuremberg" model, creating international courts for specific, time- and subject-limited purposes. However, so common have these tribunals become that they can no longer be viewed as aberrations on the world stage. Rather, resort to such courts is now a recognized option on the menu of choices faced by states wishing to address mass crimes.

The second significant change over the past decade has been a simultaneous and unprecedented movement toward establishing a *permanent* institution of international justice. The Hague-based International Criminal Court (ICC), which developed out of the Treaty of Rome in 1998 and became officially operational on 1 July 2002, two months after the end of the month in which the 60th state deposited its instruments of ratification,[2] is no doubt the most well known player in this regard.

Despite the well deserved attention placed on the ICC, an arguably even more vibrant location for the "permanent" practice of enforceable IHL is on the domestic plane. Many of the limited international tribunals founded since the mid-1990s in Sierra Leone, Cambodia, and Lebanon are at least partly domestic institutions that have been "internationalized." However, the phenomenon of international crimes in international or internationalized courts is not limited to these endeavors; rather, states throughout the world have begun practicing international law, and pursuing international justice, in the confines of their own domestic judicial systems. Using the controversial assertion of "universal jurisdiction" (which gained fame due to the events surrounding the attempted extradition of former Chilean leader Augusto Pinochet from the United Kingdom),[3] or the much more widely accepted right of states to use international law to punish the criminal excesses of prior regimes (as seen in Iraq, Ethiopia, and elsewhere), more "international" justice is practiced at the domestic level than in the strictly international arena. Indeed one of the paradoxes of the twenty-first century's movements toward universal justice is that criminal law is being simultaneously internationalized *and* localized. This has further complicated the institutional picture as states have progressed down remarkably different paths in dispensing domestic, international justice.

The third change has come along with this localization, and is another important feature of the diversity in dealing with mass violations: the rise of nonjudicial bodies to "legally" address mass crimes. While the Nuremberg model, manifest after World War II and then in the UN criminal tribunals of the early 1990s, was singularly focused on the rectitude of prosecutions to achieve justice, there have always been dissenters to this approach. They have been concerned that the necessarily punitive and retrospective focus of trials limits the ability for states to move forward toward the hopeful end of such process: ensuring accountability, deterring repetition and reconciling societies. Indeed, trials have always been only one of an array of tools states can use to these ends.[4]

In today's world in the states where international justice has emerged, the potential counterproductivity of a strictly "Nuremberg" model of imposed, international justice has become even clearer. At Nuremberg, whether or not the justice the Allies dispensed was "victors' justice," it most certainly was an instance of victors imposing justice on the vanquished; this is an impossibility in many current transitions where there is no wholly defeated side, let alone no occupied state that would allow for such a solution. Consequently, the situation in modern post-conflict environments is usually more ambiguous. In such cases, partially vanquished factions often see trials as unjust retribution rather than as re-establishment of law. Effective post-conflict transitions become even more difficult if certain groups feel maligned by the process itself.

Truth commissions and other instruments short of criminal penalties—but very much within the temple of IHL enforcement—have arguably done a superior job than traditional criminal justice in achieving reconciliation in certain countries. The South African Truth and Reconciliation Commission played a substantial role in post-apartheid reconciliation,[5] and similar commissions in Guatemala, reunified Germany, El Salvador, and nearly two dozen other locales, have potentially been more successful in rebuilding their states than would have been large-scale criminal prosecutions.[6] Far from prosecutions, a key component of the South African commission was its offer of amnesty to witnesses in exchange for truth.[7] While some have bemoaned the fact that broad allowances of immunity result in perpetrators being allowed freedom, many louder voices have insisted that the delivery of truth—far from guaranteed in an adversarial criminal proceeding[8]— is valid compensation to victims. Even then, at least in the South African case, it was the threat of prosecution that induced many of the applications for amnesty.

Circling back, the institutional environment, though enriched by these nonjudicial bodies, is evidently further complicated by them. Not only are they bona fide tools to provide international justice, if not enforce IHL, but in many instances they exist alongside more traditional judicial organizations aiming to prosecute. Such a relationship existed in Sierra Leone, which played host to both a court and a truth commission; while both professed the same goal of repairing the country, at times the institutions were at odds regarding how best to achieve this aim.

Layout of the book

As this brief description of the changes seen since the mid-1990s makes clear, the clarity and simplicity of international justice provided by the Nuremberg model has long since dissipated. In its stead has emerged an institutional landscape of IHL enforcement that is rich, multifaceted, fluid, and, for the layperson and expert alike, confusing. This book's primary aim is to provide some order amidst this apparent entropy. It will do so in a few steps.

First, a baseline supposition upon which all institutions claiming to pursue international justice rests is that there is an international legal code ripe for enforcement. Chapter 1, detailing the slow, historical development of IHL, demonstrates that such a code exists. While we will discuss the very real fact that there are thinkers who question this conclusion—with some continuing to doubt the validity, if not existence, of an international legal code—the book's focus is not on any existential issue surrounding the reality of the concept. There is a body of IHL that exists and is currently being enforced in the motley institutions described above. However, we are the first to admit that international law is unique, and not only because there is no legislature that passes that law for implementation. Rather, unlike almost any domestic legal system, international law has a codified aspect and an uncodified part. The latter, unlike the American or British common law, often has little to do with law developed by judges ("case law"). Rather, as will be discussed, defining uncodified international law—so-called customary international law (CIL)—is a contentious process in which law can only be found if it is shown that a certain course of behavior is followed by states over a significant period of time *because* the states believed it was their legal obligation to do so. A consequence of this malleability has been that, as practitioners at Nuremberg and other tribunals have admitted, the process of prosecuting international crimes has often involved as much making law (or finding law) as it has enforcing it.[9]

Though the once-vague contours of IHL have become clearer with its extensive practice since the end of the Cold War, defining exactly what crimes fall under its purview remains a moving target. The treaty of the ICC would seem to exhaustively define which crimes are included—the most infamous including genocide and crimes against humanity.[10] Yet, not only does the treaty leave undefined a key crime that was actually prosecuted at Nuremberg—the definition of waging an "aggressive" war has been left to be defined at a later juncture—but, as will emerge from later chapters, the world of international justice has perhaps moved on from the static language of the Rome Treaty.

The bounds of what crimes are rightly adjudicated before an "international" tribunal have expanded. It is no longer only war crimes or even "mass" crimes like genocide that receive such attention. Rather, international institutions are increasingly called into service to confront "smaller" crimes, and even those focused on individual harms. The UN's international tribunals in East Timor (the "Special Panels"), for instance, had jurisdiction over simple murder as defined by the East Timorese criminal code[11] (i.e. "murder" outside of its commission in conjunction with a war crime or larger infraction). And the international tribunal recently established to prosecute the assassination of Lebanese politician Rafiq Hariri is explicitly concerned with a crime (the murder of a single individual and those in his entourage) the limited circumstances of which would usually have been thought to render it outside the purview of international justice.[12]

With the nature of IHL described, the bulk of this book will discuss the institutional choices pursued to enforce it. Though there are several logical ways we could divide this analysis (for instance looking at purely international bodies, followed by domestic and "hybrid" institutions), proceeding chronologically provides the reader with a much clearer sense of exactly how we arrived at the current stage and state of international justice. Indeed, the taxonomy of "international" or "hybrid" is inexact and potentially raises more questions than it answers. We feel it important to realize that no institution developed in a vacuum or ignorant of its predecessor institutions and contemporaries. Nor has the emergence of any institution been the product of random thought. Rather the development and redevelopment of enforcement mechanisms has occurred over time, a product of a fragile and perpetual dialectic between political and legal action and reaction, with the pendulum swinging between the international and the domestic, the local and the global. By examining each instance as it emerged, the political and legal forces that have held sway at different times become much clearer, as do the distinct, half-dozen eras that have defined international judicial institutions.

Six institutional periods

The history of the institutional structures of IHL enforcement can be divided into six time periods.

Chapter 2 discusses the initial two stages in this development. First, in the centuries before World War I, there were discrete instances of enforcement of what looked like international justice. Such instances could be said only to "resemble" international criminal justice because the idea of an enforceable IHL is of comparatively recent vintage. Rules of war applicable to armed forces, and enforceable internally within the specific armies have been present, in some senses, for millennia.

However, it was not until the late nineteenth century and the turn of the twentieth century that a body of written rules that we would recognize as being proto-modern even appeared. Still, we would be remiss if we were not to mention the prosecution of such notables as Charles I in 1649 or various minor leaders in the European Middle Ages (such as Peter von Hagenbach and Conradin von Hohenstaufen), under charges that would not appear out of place if heard before a modern court trying infractions of IHL. The law under which such prosecutions were based was often the undefined, and perhaps indefinable "laws of nations," an unbound set of rules (broadly related to the logic of inviolable national sovereignty) that set out what nations and their leaders could or could not do. The "nation" focus might explain why it was solely heads of state (or their proxies) who were found liable, if anyone was, in this early period.

The sea change in IHL occurred in the late nineteenth and early twentieth centuries, with the brisk development of codified international law. In this fervent period, the first international treaties on the subject were signed limiting (and indeed, making illegal) certain behaviors on the battlefield, so that by the time World War I began all players at least putatively agreed on the contours of what was to be permitted. During the Great War all sides were scrupulous in maintaining records of charges of the other side's wrongdoings during the war. Thus when the war ended in German and Ottoman defeat, it was not surprising that the treaties at Versailles and Sèvres explicitly mentioned trials of those who had transgressed these newly agreed upon rules.[13] For a variety of political reasons, and a few legal ones, the trials were wracked with difficulties. Despite their problems, they remain an important guidepost in the development and enforcement of modern IHL. They also served to develop a basic doubt still present in modern proceedings that the prosecution of mass crimes can rarely be left to the states responsible for their commission.

Chapter 3 covers the third era which emerged after World War II, when after a contentious political debate between the Allies it was finally agreed to try several of the major leaders from Germany and Japan, with prosecutors adopting and legalizing the neologism "crimes against humanity" (a term which was actually first used in descriptions of the Turks' crimes against the Armenians 30 years earlier[14]) to describe the scope and content of the legal violations committed. These trials were, until the 1990s, the quintessential international prosecutions under IHL—and, as will be argued, continue to reverberate today. Each post–World War II court was multinational in structure and process, with prosecutors and judges from various countries. Despite this seemingly global support for the prosecutions, the political realities of the brewing Cold War played a determinative role in the proceedings, limiting the number and nationality of defendants, restricting the scope of the trials (concluding them relatively quickly), and, in the end, even commuting the sentences of many of those convicted.[15]

Though it encountered difficulties, the Nuremberg model excited many and in the spirit of multinational partnership that existed in the early days of the United Nations (UN), the world community quickly asked the UN's International Law Commission "to study the desirability and possibility of establishing an international judicial organ for the trial of persons charged with [grave violations]."[16]

The Cold War stunted any development on this measure, but as Chapter 4 argues, the fourth era of international justice enforcement proceeded apace. With work on the international plane frozen through Security Council intransigence, the era of Cold War prosecutions moved to the states. This era saw the rise of domestic prosecutions for international crimes, which in a sense was a continuation of such prosecutions from before Nuremberg; the primary difference was that now such prosecutions often used the full weight of the Nuremberg precedent to justify their actions. These domestic trials have proven strong precedents for the current rise of similar domestic prosecutions. Throughout the Cold War, states such as West Germany and Israel, and to a lesser degree others including France, Canada, and Australia, engaged in prosecuting (or attempting to prosecute) international crimes. Convictions often involved the de jure and/or de facto assignment of *international* criminal responsibility in the confines of *domestic* systems.

Chapter 5 picks up the re-internationalization of international justice, allowed once the Cold War ended—stage five. The fall of the Berlin Wall allowed international organizations to retake the mantle of IHL enforcement. Negotiations for the creation of an ICC resumed almost immediately. The laborious diplomatic discussions took place against a backdrop of continued domestic interest in prosecution (with countries often unwilling to give up the legal sovereignty they had asserted on this measure since 1945), and the re-emergence of destructive ethnic forces that led to the wars in the former Yugoslavia and in Rwanda. No doubt with the negotiations toward an ICC in mind, the world community acted, initially creating the International Criminal Tribunal for the former Yugoslavia (ICTY) in 1993,[17] and then providing it a sister institution 18 months later in the form of the International Criminal Tribunal for Rwanda (ICTR).[18] Each of these "ad hoc" courts was mandated to prosecute "serious" violations of IHL. The institutional hallmark of these organizations, clearly in line with the lessons of World War I, was that they were subsidiary bodies of the UN Security Council, and thus each had the enforceable right to remove cases from local jurisdiction.

Chapter 6 covers the sixth stage of such enforcement, bringing us into the present, an era marked by both the continuation of domestic prosecutions and the establishment of international institutions reacting to what some see as the excesses of the ICTY and ICTR. On the one side, the UN-backed "hybrid" courts that have emerged in Sierra Leone, East Timor, Cambodia, and Lebanon have been a response to the financial and institutional excesses of the ICTY and ICTR. At some points in their operations the ad hocs have accounted for nearly 10 percent of the UN's entire operating budget.[19] The hybrid courts are designed to be local institutions with international components and were thought far more cost effective and judicially efficient solutions. As we shall see, the reality of their operations has led to some doubt in their abilities to provide streamlined justice. The hybrid courts and the persistence (and intensification) of domestic prosecutions for violations of IHL, were also a reaction against the institutional over-reaching that many saw in the ICTY and ICTR in that they were courts with unquestioned jurisdictional supremacy in the Balkans and Rwanda. In the eyes of some this improperly removed not just cases, but also the perception that justice was being done.

The ICC, which is a prime feature of this modern era, was similarly designed, at least partly, as a reaction to the Nuremberg model. Indeed, ironically, it will likely promote the continued diversity of modes of prosecuting international law. One of the key differences between it and its predecessor international bodies, and the leitmotif of the modern enforcement era, is that it does not have jurisdictional pre-eminence. Its jurisdiction is governed by the principle of "complementarity" which, in simplified terms, permits the ICC to prosecute only if states prove unable or unwilling to do so themselves.[20]

Conclusion

The modern diversity of international and domestic efforts to hold individuals to account for violations of IHL is an exciting development and certainly, for supporters of human rights, an optimistic one. It represents a global coalescing around the inviolability of certain universal axioms of behavior and the protection of fundamental rights. Despite these hopeful signs, this book is written against the backdrop of an unfortunate acknowledgment: as both the means to prosecute international crimes and the will to do so have proliferated, so too have violations. The end of impunity is not nigh.

The future prognosis for international criminal justice, with which this book will conclude in Chapter 7, takes this sad fact into account. The chapter provides a list of questions that need to be answered in order to establish effective international judicial institutions, but notes that such institutions are not a panacea and the world can ill afford to view them as such. Yet, the chapter will argue that despite the existence of travesties such as Darfur, the institutions arrayed to address such crimes send an important message, not just to the perpetrators but also to the victims: the world is watching and will not be silent.

1 International humanitarian law

A short review

The history of enforceable IHL is both extensive and surprisingly brief. This dichotomy is illustrated by examining the conclusions of two leading thinkers on the topic. Writing in 2003, Antonio Cassese argued that the concept is "relatively new," pointing to its development in the years after World War II.[1] Yet, writing in 1947 Georg Schwarzenberger disagreed with the then-popular claim that post–World War II enforcement of IHL was "of a totally unprecedented character;"[2] Schwarzenberger traced such instances of enforcement as far back as 1268 and found elements of what was claimed to be uniquely modern international justice throughout history, from antiquity to the present.[3] The confusion is complete once one recognizes that both scholars are accurate.

It is a primary aim of this chapter to explain how both impressions of IHL are true, with each illuminating a different, equally important aspect of the topic.

What is it that international justice is enforcing?

In its least adorned guise, IHL is the branch of international criminal law concerned with international crimes committed in armed conflict and includes genocide and crimes against humanity, whether committed in times of war or in times of peace. It is also concerned with the trial and punishment of those who have committed such crimes. As such it would seem similar to criminal law that exists on the domestic plane in every state. However, to understand the differences between IHL and its domestic (or in the parlance of international lawyers "municipal") cousins, one has to retreat to first principles. The domestic plane is the perfect place to do this.

When one breaks a domestic criminal law, what has that person actually done? Putting aside the specifics of the action, what he or she has accomplished is a violation of a code or norm established by a sovereign state. That violation is the crime. There are usually two classes of victims to the crime: the individuals to whom the malfeasance was directed *and* the state itself whose hegemony, power, and sovereignty was illegitimately challenged by the violator's conduct. In most states legal redress for crimes is similarly split: the individual citizen who has been affected can sue the violator for the harm suffered. This is usually dubbed a "civil" suit, with the result of such suits, if successful, "civil" penalties, the often-stated goal of which is to make the victims once again "whole." However, the sovereign or state victim also has redress, and the legal action states take falls into the rubric of "crimes." The sovereign files a "criminal" suit against the individual, the result of which is *criminal* penalties (such as incarceration or a fine), the goals of which can be motley and include having the violator "pay for" the harm done to the state or to deter or incapacitate the violator from committing further bad acts.

Transposing this system onto the international level, we encounter a pair of related issues that simultaneously illustrate how different IHL is from its closest analogs: domestic criminal law and non-criminal, international law. There are two questions in this regard: who "owns" international law? And who, or what, is the appropriate subject of such law? Regarding the first question, in the international system, as in the domestic, one can inquire that if an IHL violation has occurred, what has actually happened? And, as in the domestic realm, a violation reflects conduct against codes recognized by a "legitimate sovereign." Yet, in a world of 192 states—literally, 192 "sovereigns"—and one in which international law has traditionally been governed by consent of states rather than fiat from above, who is the sovereign to whom unquestioned fealty is owed regarding IHL? Put more pointedly, whose will is actually being violated?

In many respects, it is the answer to this question that lends credence to those like Georg Schwarzenberger who see ancient remnants in modern IHL. The "sovereign" in international criminal law is not the leadership of any particular state, but rather some notion of a collective, or even universal will. In centuries past, this "will" was often equated with the divine,[4] which in turn propagated the idea that certain acts were simply beyond the pale. These acts, many of which became known to international lawyers as peremptory norms, or *jus cogens*, are "fundamental principles" of international law from which no derogation is ever permitted. That is, states not only do not need to consent to be bound by *jus cogens*, they cannot refuse to consent. Though the exact composition of the peremptory norm category remains in flux, a brief analysis of one of the oldest, and most universally agreed upon, members manifests the dual rationale behind the existence of *jus cogens*, and the consequent agreement of states to cede some aspects of their sovereignty both to each other and some higher goal. That international crime is piracy.

"Piracy" consists of committing various crimes—robbery, kidnapping, rape, etc.—at sea (though this definition has now been modernized to include such acts committed aboard other vessels, such as aircraft). It has long been the scourge of nations, at times devastating commerce and exploration. The means employed by pirates have often been horrifying, and the universal revulsion to their behavior has led to one of more enduring identifiers of international crimes: such crimes are "heinous." Indeed, the "heinousness" principle applied to piracy was used in the past, and continues to be employed today, to justify its placement in the pantheon of peremptory norms.[5] In short, to perpetrate the act of piracy is to be an enemy not just of the victim vessel or its occupants, but to become an "enemy of humanity" (*hostis humani generis*).

However, the other driver behind piracy's placement on the list came from the geography and scope of the violation. More often than not, piracy takes place in international waters, outside the jurisdictional reach of states. Consequently, as no state exercises sovereignty over international waters and law derives from the notion of sovereignty, it could be argued that there was no proper law on the high seas. And, indeed, that is what pirates seem to take advantage of. Yet, well before any treaties on the subject clarified law in international waters, states implicitly and often explicitly agreed to *all* exercising joint jurisdiction over the acts of pirates. All states had the right to punish pirates, and even the obligation to do so, for the sake of themselves and other members of the international community. In the language of international lawyers, assuming jurisdiction over crimes in which "all states can be held to have a legal interest," can be viewed as an "obligation *erga omnes*. ['in relation to everyone']."[6]

This understanding of joint jurisdiction for crimes that were too big, too unwieldy, and too heinous for any single state to address reflected a subtle limitation in the notion of unquestioned state sovereignty. It was evidence of supra-national duties that states owed to the international community by simple virtue of their being in the community. Thus was set the precedent for finding the "sovereign" in international crimes.

This process of looking above the state to a multinational "sovereign" has taken time, and is related to the second difference mentioned above, that between IHL and international law writ large. Ironically, this second difference concerns not looking above the state, but rather below, down to the individual. Prosecuting for violations of IHL requires the assignment of individual criminal liability for violations against international norms. Though viewed through the prism of domestic criminal law it might seem odd if IHL did not focus on the individual, from the perspective of international law this "piercing the veil" of the state is a watershed. The state was always the subject of international law, not the individual. This can be illustrated by reference to the weight of treaties and other international agreements that impose state responsibilities—compared with the relative paucity of such treaties and agreements that focus on individual responsibilities— and by reference to the concept's strong philosophical and historical base. Ever since its "birth" the state has enjoyed a hallowed place in international law. First on a de facto basis, and then enshrined de jure by the Treaty of Westphalia in 1648, the "state" was the sole, legitimate actor on the world stage. More importantly for IHL, there was a limit to what foreign states, let alone the amorphous "international community" could do to a state's citizens. After all, citizens of states owed allegiance to their particular sovereigns, and its laws governed, not those of some absent, supranational entity.

This monolithic structure both imperiled individuals—as there was little, legally that could be done by the international community if a sovereign wished to abuse his people—*and* protected them—as, if their sovereign was untroubled by their behavior, there was little, legally that the international community could do to seek redress for crimes committed by individuals against citizens of other states. Today's IHL fundamentally questions the inviolability of the state by placing individuals at its center, rather than states. It is in this sense, that Cassese and others, who speak of the "new," post–World War II IHL, are right. Assigning international responsibility to individuals and *not* their states (indeed, often explicitly, exonerating the state itself for such acts), is a relatively recent phenomenon. Such a practice was considered after World War I, and only began in earnest following World War II.[7]

Students of history may question this account, pointing to various instances in the more distant past where individuals seem to have been made the subject of international outrage regarding their actions. One of the more famous (in international law circles) of such cases occurred in the late fifteenth century when Charles the Bold, Duke of Burgundy, appointed Peter von Hagenbach governor of Breisach, a fortified town on the Upper Rhine. The citizens of Breisach had no desire to be ruled by the duke and initially proved troubling to Governor von Hagenbach. In response, the governor introduced a regime of arbitrariness, brutality and terror in order to reduce the population of Breisach to total submission. Murder, rape, illegal taxation and the wanton confiscation of private property became generalized practices. All these violent acts were also committed against inhabitants of the neighboring territories.[8]

When he was finally deposed in 1474 after five years of terror, he was put on trial before a panel of 28 judges from a coalition of states and independent towns—it was undoubtedly a "real international court."[9] His charges were many, and it remains unclear under what body of law he was tried. However the fact that an international diversity of 28 judges made up the tribunal suggests that it was by reference to norms above those of any single sovereign that served as the basis for the charges. Indeed, among other "malefacta," von Hagenbach was charged with "trampl[ing] under foot the laws of God and man."[10] He was convicted and executed.

Though there are aspects of von Hagenbach's trial that find echoes in modern IHL (not the least of which that the defendant refused to recognize the legality of the court, a charge regularly heard from the dock in modern international tribunals), there is an important distinction between the "individual" responsibility assessed on von Hagenbach, and that seen in today's prosecutions for IHL violations. The difference reduces to the fact that though von Hagenbach was a man, he was not convicted solely as an individual, but rather as the representative of the state (ruled by the hated duke). He lived at the height of the era of absolute monarchy, *l'état c'est moi*. Thus, to a significant degree, it was the state that his prosecutor so despised, as it was in the state's name that von Hagenbach had engaged in his violence.

The difference to today's IHL is thus evident. While von Hagenbach may have been the legal personification of the Duke of Burgundy, Hermann Göring was not Nazi Germany, Slobodan Milosevic was not Serbia. Instead of stopping at the state, ever since the end of World War II, IHL goes through the state, prosecuting individuals for their actions. Under today's international law, the state provides little legal protection for its citizens, if their acts are "heinous" enough. This has required a radical reassessment of state sovereignty.

Thus, the story of IHL is the tale of changing notions of sovereignty, of where law comes from, who has the legitimate authority to enforce it (in legal terms, who has jurisdiction), and over whom it can be enforced. With this structure in mind we can turn to the content of the law. This part of the story takes place, at least initially, not in the courtroom, but on the battlefield.

The laws of war

What has become modern day enforceable IHL is the end result of a steady march toward limiting excesses, initially just those on the battlefield and increasingly those that occur during peacetime.

However, this end result was hardly contemplated by those who began this process. To succeed, it had to overcome a powerful, underlying axiom of national behavior: in war, especially if the survival of the state was at stake, it was long thought that there was no legal limit to what could be done to advance its interests. In the words of Thucydides, uttered in the fifth century, BC: "to a king or commonwealth, nothing is unjust which is useful."[11] Or, as Cicero more famously put it 500 years later, "Inter arma, silent leges"—law is silent amidst the clash of arms.[12]

Though Cicero's and Thucydides' pronouncements were never entirely accurate—as there are comparatively ancient rules and regulations, often emanating from religion, that had long governed at least types of warfare—such maxims effectively served as justification for gruesome wartime behavior well into the seventeenth century when the first robust, perennial, battlefield rules were developed. It is true that more informal, ephemeral rules and limitations on certain battlefield behaviors had existed for millennia—these included promulgations by Roman Emperor Maurice in the sixth century and various penitential decrees issued in conjunction with specific battles (such as at Soissons in 923 and Hastings in 1066).[13] There were even more established rules of conduct, such as those embodied in various chivalric codes, which were arguably the first examples of "international criminal law" as they could be enforced by any commander into whose hands an offender might fall.[14] These codes, however, were not only intermittently enforced, and then only among the "knightly" class (leaving non-knights without similar protections), they were also supplanted in the seventeenth century, the era that marked the birth of longstanding, effectively enforced rules of battle, peace, and conquest. That such law would wait until then to make its appearance is not surprising given that the first major spate of intellectual work on the subject occurred only in the sixteenth century, the halcyon days of the grandfathers of international law: Pierino Belli, Alberico Gentili, and Hugo Grotius, amongst others.

On the eve of his entry into the Thirty Years War in 1618, the Swedish king Gustavus Adolphus issued his Articles of War. His Articles were also not the first such code to regulate soldier conduct on the battlefield (the code instituted by the Dutch Republic in the 1590s likely holds that distinction[15]), but his would prove the most resilient; parts of it can still be seen in modern military doctrine throughout the world.[16] Among its 167 articles, it barred pillaging and established rules to protect children, women, and the infirm who were in the way of war; the result was that "compared to his, other armies of the time were barbarians."[17] It was at least partly from these initial prohibitions during war that the concept of "war crimes" would emerge, a term that for many would come to be synonymous with IHL. Gustavus was hardly the humanitarian; he realized that a disciplined fighting force was critical to success, and would surely outfight the undisciplined, mercenary forces of his enemies. His military successes suggest that he was right.

Despite its historical base in military necessity rather than human rights or criminal law, the Articles of War set the stage for further refinements and limitations on what could be done on the battlefield. Through its "export" into armies throughout Europe, and through Europe's colonial exploits, to armies further afield, the notion that a state could do as it pleased when in conflict began to recede. This did not mean that war became civilized; rather excesses still existed and European military history, let alone that of other regions, is full of bloody examples in which Gustavus' pronouncements were clearly not heeded. Still, law was no longer silent.

With the exception of the British Articles of War supplanting Gustavus' as the gold standard for fighting forces, the core of such articles remained largely unaltered for more than 200 years. The impetus for change, and for strengthening and expanding the Articles again only had partly humanitarian roots. By the 1850s technological advances made war more violent and more immediate even to those far from the frontlines. The violence of war was exacerbated by advances in strategy and munitions. Gone were the set pieces of battle, and in their stead were fast moving, chaotic maneuvers. Gone was the limited fall out of cannonballs and buckshot; in its stead were expanding bullets and "explosive projectiles," soon to be followed by attacks from the air and poison gas. War became an ever more fearsome enterprise. It was the dawn of the "total" war, and the birth of war fighting that could directly, and quickly involve (and devastate) an entire people.

Battlefield technology dovetailed with another set of advances that allowed "witnesses" to battlefield carnage the ability to be present at the war even if not physically so. Starting during the Crimean War in 1854, with the development of war journalism—aided by the telegraph— the home front was given center seats to the mounting devastation of conflict. The impact of such a "broadcast" war was immediate and far reaching. During the Crimean War (1853–56), dispatches from the first war correspondent, William Howard Russell, moved some to action (such as Florence Nightingale who, the story goes, credited such reporting for instigating her entry into war time nursing),[18] and others to revulsion. Indeed, Russell's reporting, and the immediacy with which the home front received his reports, played a not insignificant role in turning the tide of popular opinion against British involvement in Asia Minor.[19]

A similar set of observations regarding the growing savagery of war were made by Henry Dunant in 1859 when he was witness to the Battle of Solferino. His recounting of that conflict,[20] and especially the manner in which the dead on the battlefield were neglected and abused, directly led to the creation of the International Committee of the Red Cross (ICRC), the organization which, to this day, remains the "keeper" of IHL.

Thus, it was logical that the first wave of major developments in IHL occurred immediately on the heels of these first "public" and immediately "publicized" wars. Beginning in the 1860s, such law developed briskly on many fronts, in many parts of the world. North America saw the development of the Lieber Code, which was released on 24 April 1863 as General Order No. 100 by President Abraham Lincoln to the Union troops during the Civil War (1861–65). The Code, officially known as the "Instructions for the Government of Armies of the United States in the Field," explicitly mandated that Union soldiers treat enemies and occupied populations "ethically." A key development in the code was that it was the first such document to expressly forbid the theretofore common understanding that "no quarter" be given to an enemy.[21] The example set by the United States in the Lieber rules was soon followed by other governments, which proceeded to issue ordinances or manuals of instruction for the guidance of their military commanders. Such manuals were issued by Prussia in 1870, the Netherlands in 1871, the French in 1877, Serbia in 1879, Spain in 1882, Portugal in 1890 and Italy in 1896.[22] The first Red Cross Treaty came in 1864, based in large part on Dunant's observations of the Battle of Solferino four years prior; unsurprisingly, given Dunant's concerns, this first treaty concerned the treatment of those wounded in the field.[23] In 1868, Czar Alexander II became seized of the matter, issuing the St Petersburg Declaration;[24] this document is arguably the first truly modern exposition of IHL. The declaration was the end product of the first international convention on the laws of war and included a set of principles closely resembling modern conceptions of

IHL. In particular, they concentrated on limiting the use of specific weapons during war in order to limit "needless suffering." This declaration was expanded, in large part by elements in the Lieber Code, six years later and in 1880 the Institute of International Law brought various strands of development together under its "Oxford Manual on the Laws of War on Land."[25] While a significant accomplishment, the Manual suffered from many limitations, not the least of which the fact that the "laws of war" only dealt with inter-state conflicts, leaving civil wars untouched by international law. Though many claimed that civil wars were covered under "customary international law" (CIL) (see below) this omission would not explicitly be corrected until a century later and the adoption (by most, but not all, states) of the Second Additional Protocol of the Geneva Conventions in 1977.[26]

The momentum of these developments led to the 1899 and 1907 Hague conventions, concerning limits on the practice of war, which would in turn serve as the basis for "Geneva" law addressing humanitarian principles that emerged 20 and 40 years later (in the 1929 and 1949 Geneva conventions).

Enter the courtroom

The growing body of laws from 1860 provided some structure to the category of "international crimes." And these crimes were, at times, prosecuted. They were not done so by international courts, but rather by military courts; many national militaries had incorporated the new international rules into their "Articles of War." Consequently, their violation led to the laying of military, criminal charges. It was in large measure due to internationally informed domestic codes that, for example, war crimes trials (courts martial) were conducted following violations that occurred during the Boer War and during the American occupation of the Philippines, both at the turn of the twentieth century.

Though domestic military enforcement of "international crimes" did not dissipate (and indeed has not dissipated), there were two further developments that needed to occur before modern IHL could emerge. First, the prosecution of such crimes had to be seen as no longer the sole province of military justice—it became a civilian judicial process. And, second, civilian domestic prosecutions had to give way to the international civilian tribunals that have come to personify the pursuit of today's international justice. A full discussion of the vicissitudes of political and legal realities that led to these decisions and developments is outside the scope of this book; however, an understanding of IHL requires a brief overview of the key points in this development. In short, the process was a slow movement that began prior to World War I, progressed through the interwar period, and finally led to the establishment of the Nuremberg and Tokyo trials after World War II.

There are several key points of this development, with the first appearing on the eve of World War I. The growing body of IHL and permeation of Lieber-like codes throughout the world, meant that each side began the Great War wielding law alongside their weapons. World War I was the first major combat in which all sides expended significant effort to document the legal wrongs of the others during the waging of battle.

The result was one of the first media war campaigns, with each side proudly claiming its devotion to international law,[27] refuting all accusations, while making counter-claims. "Atrocity propaganda" had been born. Many celebrated investigations were conducted, with the Bryce Report on German Activities in Belgium the most famous, but certainly not alone.[28] Barely a week after the hostilities began in 1914 a special Belgian commission was set up, producing a "Grey Book" recounting various crimes committed by the German invaders. The French were also very quick to start gathering evidence of German war crimes, made all the easier once German troops began operating in France.

The Allies were not alone, and in October 1914 the Prussian war ministry established the *Militäruntersuchungsstell für Verletzungen des Kriegsrechts*, the Military Bureau of Investigation of Violations of the Law of War. Notably, its official brief was "to determine violations of the laws and customs of war which enemy military and civilian persons have committed against the Prussian troops and to investigate whatever accusations of this nature are made by the enemy against members of the Prussian Army."[29] One of the first acts of this bureau was to refute the Belgian "Grey Book" and through the autumn of 1914 German military judges and court officers traveled through Belgium taking depositions. Belgian claims were countered by a mass of 73 collected depositions, which along with other investigative material was soon to be compiled into a German "White Book" which attempted to justify Berlin's actions.[30]

Given the vibrant legal activity that had occurred during the war it became clear that the victors would wish to use their research in trials after the conflict. There were two sets of trials the Allies hoped to establish, based on two different sets of war crimes. First, regarding the Germans, the Treaty of Versailles explicitly demanded that the defeated powers recognize the Allies' right to "bring before *military* tribunals persons accused of having committed acts in violation of the laws and customs of war."[31] While the desired prosecution of Kaiser Wilhelm was hindered by the fact that his Dutch hosts in exile refused to sur-render him, trials against other Germans were similarly soon lost to political will and concern about the stability of the German state. Thus, due to a set of circumstances described later in this book, instead of military tribunals, the compromise forced on the Allies was to try Germans before domestic, German courts in Leipzig.

Interestingly, the same basic machinations occurred in regard to the second set of trials the Allies wanted, those against the Ottomans for crimes committed against the Armenians during World War I. One of the more horrific aspects of the entire war involved the 1915–17 slaying of more than 1.5 million Armenians by the Ottomans in what is widely considered the twentieth century's first genocide. Once these events were publicized the Triple Entente was evidently disgusted and in May 1915, France, Russia, and Great Britain released a statement "publicly inform[ing] … [Constantinople] that [it] would be h[e]ld personally responsible for the said crimes."[32] It was unclear what such "personal responsibility" entailed, but there was clearly the notion that the acts of which the Ottomans were accused comprised crimes against more than just the Armenian victims. Heinousness was again the calling card of these crimes, and Woodrow Wilson's secretary of state, Robert Lansing, clearly illustrates the tension between the old model of state inviolability and the new understanding that some crimes merit intervention from outside. Lansing stated that he thought that the Turkish government's deportation of Armenians was "more or less justified." But he said,

> [i]t was not to my mind the deportation which was objectionable but the horrible brutality which attended its execution. It is one of the blackest pages in the history of this war, and I think we were fully justified in intervening as we did on behalf of the wretched people, even though they were Turkish subjects.[33]

Despite this, it was not until after the war that the thought of interna-tional trials against the Ottomans was broached. Yet here too, though the Treaty of Sèvres, which ended the Ottoman part of World War I, contained similar language to Versailles regarding trials,[34] political realities on the ground in Turkey quickly forced the Allies to abandon not just the idea of bringing Turks before Allied military courts, but even of their prosecution at all. The Treaty of Sèvres was never ratified and was quickly superseded by the Treaty of Lausanne, which far from mandating trials actually contained provisions providing amnesty for Turks.[35] It was international pressure, and no doubt the presence of more than a million British troops in the country, that led to the Turks "agreeing" to pursue their own trials, again of Turkish perpetrators before civilian Turkish courts.

Thus, the emergence of civilian trials for such crimes was a function not of international will toward that end, but rather of specific political circumstances that provided those wishing for trials no other options. Even with their imperfections, the post–World War I trials provided the needed bridge from the purely military courts that were once thought central to prosecuting "war crimes" to the civilian courts of today. Both the Leipzig and Constantinople trials were civilian enterprises (though the latter actually came to be called the Turkish Courts Martial). It was in large measure their failures that allowed the final push to international, civilian tribunals that were erected after World War II, and then again after the Cold War in the 1990s.

As will be discussed in the next chapter, after World War II, there were similar debates and pressures to erect tribunals. Similar to World War I, there was a longstanding assumption held throughout the war that "regular" war crimes trials would be conducted, perhaps within the military justice system for crimes of war such as torturing prisoners of war, or refusing to assist survivors of sunken ships. The idea to prosecute the architects of such crimes (like the attempt to try the Kaiser in World War I) was not considered until late in the conflict. Once the debates between the victorious Allies had subsided and it became clear that trials were to take place, it is instructive that the more famous of the trials were deemed "military" tribunals (the International Military Tribunal at Nuremberg, and the International Military Tribunal for the Far East), under the still surviving assumption that all such trials are properly the military's province. However, though aspects of the Far East tribunal were indeed military in structure if not operation, the overall military description was in name only, as the vast majority of the trials' components were civilian, with, for the most part, civilian lawyers and judges.[36] Though here too, the Nuremberg and Tokyo processes included not just the prosecution of the senior German and Japanese officials prosecuted at the main tribunal, but also the trials of thousands more who were prosecuted under more traditional military systems of justice.

The seeming success of these civilian-qua-military tribunals set the stage for true international civilian courts, which became the working hypothesis for how such "war crimes" courts were to be established in the future, and indeed which were established in the 1990s.

With this history of institutional development in mind—extending from the battlefield to the domestic courtroom—the last piece to understanding modern international criminal law is a brief overview of its contents.

What is the law of international humanitarian law?

Though there is vigorous debate regarding the contents of such law (let alone its validity, see below), and by its very nature a definitive list of the crimes it covers is difficult to construct, there are some broad agreements on the basic architecture of IHL. Article 38 of the Statute of the International Court of Justice (ICJ) is a logical starting point for finding the content of modern IHL. There, the statute finds four separate sources for international law:

1   international conventions, whether general or particular, establishing rules expressly recognized by … states;
2   international custom, as evidence of a general practice accepted as law;
3   the general principles of law recognized by civilized nations;
4   … judicial decisions and the teachings of the most highly qualified publicists of the various nations, as subsidiary means for the determination of rules of law.[37]

There are important differences between the law "found" for the purposes of the ICJ's inter-state jurisdiction and that applicable to individuals under IHL; still, Article 38 provides a good template and starting point.

Applying the ICJ's model, it can be said that there are two initial building blocks of IHL, broadly corresponding with Article 38 (1) and (2), and which reflect the lengthy history of the concept (in line with the ancient history described by Schwarzenberger above). First, there are the peremptory norms, the *jus cogens* violations that have been brought into IHL as central offenses. The prohibition of piracy, slavery, mass atrocities, and "wars of aggression" are widely agreed to play key roles in this body of law. Each of these crimes has been further solidified in the international legal canon by their explication in international treaties, such as the 1948 Convention on Prevention and Punishment of the Crime of Genocide. Despite this, note that at least in regards to "wars of aggression"—the prohibition of which was included in a more recent convention—debate still exists regarding its definition.

The second building block of the concept reflects the military roots of much of international criminal law. These are the more explicit "war crimes," defined as violations of the "laws of war." These laws, which were found initially in the Articles of War of various states, were legally "internationalized" with the first Geneva and Hague conventions in the late nineteenth and early twentieth centuries. The Hague conventions of 1899 and 1907, which emanated from the first and second

Hague peace conferences, included broad understandings about the waging of war and the securing of peace—such as articles detailing the laws and customs of war on land, the legal "Opening of Hostilities" and the modes of "Pacific Settlement of International Disputes." The conventions also included specific prohibitions including the use of "expanding" bullets, the laying of automatic submarine contact mines, and "Launching of Projectiles and Explosives from Balloons." Enduring features of the 1907 convention include the notion of "proportionality," which provides militaries the right to fight only so far as their actions do not cause unnecessary suffering.

Also included are the four Geneva conventions, starting in 1864 with the Henry Dunant-inspired treaty concerning the "Amelioration of the Condition of the Wounded and Sick in Armed Forces in the Field."[38] The third and fourth conventions, both passed in 1949, have provided further constraints to military practice, with the Third Convention regulating the treatment of prisoners of war, and the Fourth Convention "relative to the Protection of Civilian Persons in Time of War."

In addition to these codified aspects, IHL content also derives from CIL, the construct of which has often been controversial. The nature of CIL is based on the notion that even if uncodified, there are certain "international" codes to which states almost by definition subscribe; in the language of the statute of the International Court of Justice, these are roughly akin to the "principles of law recognized by civilized nations."[39] The notion of *jus cogens* is a good example of such laws. No treaty or convention is needed to hold a state or individual responsible for the commission of some of these acts.

Though the world community evidently recognizes that some laws are customary, outside the peremptory norm category the landscape of what rules are included becomes far less clear. In international law, a legal custom is defined as "a widespread practice accepted by states as law" (known as *opinio juris*),[40] or "the principles of the law of nations, as they result from the usage established among civilized peoples, from the laws of humanity, and the dictates of the public conscience."[41] Despite the inexactness inherent in such a definition, states by and large recognize the requirements for law to become customary. As Rosenne notes, CIL

> consists of rules of law derived from the consistent conduct of states acting out of the belief that the law required them to act that way.[42]

However, there is no consensus as to how long a practice must be in evidence before it is deemed "consistent conduct," nor is there definitive guidance regarding how one determines that such conduct was under-taken *because* of supposed legal obligations, rather than for any other reason.[43] Given this uncertainty, there exists a wide range of laws that could give rise to international liability that some have claimed fit into this category. In 2005, the International Committee of the Red Cross, for instance, published a 5,000-page study identifying what it deemed to be 161 rules that have become "customary."[44] Many of the rules they found to be customary, for instance the majority of the provisions in "Common Article Three" of the Geneva conventions, are also included in treaties to which the majority of the world belong; thus some "customary" rules are also binding under other legal instruments. However, one of the more controversial parts of the ICRC's findings included its conclusion that non-international conflicts are also custo-marily included under the protections afforded in the Geneva conven-tions (which are explicitly written with reference to international conflicts). A similar finding was made in the first prosecution before the International Criminal Tribunal for the former Yugoslavia; in *Prosecutor v. Tadic* the Appeals Chamber found that including domestic conflict within the protections provided under the Geneva conventions was "generally accepted customary law."[45]

The controversy over both the ICRC's finding and that of the ICTY comes from the fact that there is a treaty addressing the very issue that both of these bodies found to be "customary": the Second Additional Protocol to the Geneva Conventions. Some states have explicitly refused to sign or ratify this treaty. If these rules are customary, they would bind states that have explicitly found them objectionable. This would be a fundamental departure from a basic tenet of international treaty law: apart from peremptory norms, consent by a state is required before treaty provisions can be enforced on it.[46]

A fourth foundation for IHL derives from the fourth part of Article 38. As will be seen later in the book, even if not officially binding, judicial decisions made at Nuremberg, the more recent international tribunals, and even in national courts, have directly impacted the definition and content of IHL. Moreover, Article 38(4) recognizes that the development of international law at large has, since the time of Grotius and Puffendorf, long been guided by leading practitioners and thinkers in the field (the "most qualified publicists"). Some of these thinkers have posited their own lists of international delicts which have acquired broad levels of acceptance. For instance, in 1986 M. Cherif Bassiouni canvassed 312 international conventions and concluded that there were 22 categories of international crime.[47] His list is extensive—it includes typical mem-bers such as crimes like genocide and crimes against humanity and adds to them crimes such as environmental degradation and bribery of foreign public officials—and is consequently controversial. Indeed, "not all legal scholars agree with [his] ... list of ... crimes or even agree that such acts fall within the scope of international law."[48]

There are an unknown number of such "publicists" from which law can derive, but there are some leading organizations—essentially groups of publicists—that have proven determinative. The International Law Commission (ILC) is the first among equals in this regard; established by the United Nations General Assembly (UNGA) in 1947 for "promotion of the progressive development of international law and its codification"[49] the ILC is a rotating membership group of nearly three dozen leading scholars and practitioners in international law from around the world. Though the ILC has been involved in codifying international law of all types, it has long been particularly active in IHL; in 1948 it was the organization to which the General Assembly turned "to study the desirability and possibility of establishing an international juridical organ for the trial of persons charged with [grave crimes],"[50] it was the body to first draft the ICC statute (from which the final version was negotiated), and it has twice released its own drafts detailing the codification of international crimes (in 1954 and 1996).[51] Its most recent promulgation, the ILC's Draft Code of Crimes against the Peace and Security of Mankind, includes violations such as crimes against UN personnel, persecution on political and religious grounds and institutionalized discrimination.[52]

A final, and often determinative, source of IHL departs from the ICJ's rubric, and speaks to the unique role institutions play in not just enforcing IHL but also in defining it. In any given proceedings, a key definition of IHL comes from the institutions established to prosecute it—the tribunals and courts with which this book is centrally concerned. Such institutions have, since the Versailles Treaty first broached the topic, been founded on statutes. In addition to describing the physical makeup of tribunals, these statutes have included references to the crimes that are to be under examination. The first such statute to result in an actual tribunal (unlike the statutory components mentioned at Versailles) was the London Charter, the legal basis for the Nuremberg trials.[53] That charter broadly limited the crimes under review to three categories: war crimes, crimes against humanity, and crimes against peace.[54] As we will see in the next chapters, more recent courts, such as the UN ad hoc courts, the Special Court for Sierra Leone, and others have been far more explicit in their listing of subject crimes. The Rome Statute which forms the legal foundation for the International Criminal Court follows the London Charter's model of listing the broad categories of crimes in its remit (genocide, crimes against humanity, war crimes, aggression), but then proceeds to devote Articles 5 through 8 to describing, in fairly exhaustive detail, the first three of these crimes.[55]

The amorphous contours of IHL aside, it is the statute of a given institution that governs the law it applies. Indeed, more so than almost any other branch of law, the content of international law has been intimately shaped by the institutions within which it has been prac-ticed. This has become even more evident with the recent emergence of international criminal tribunals that appear to be concerned with crimes thought outside the scope of the concept. The Special Tribunal for Lebanon, established by the UN in May 2007, is expressly limited to trying those associated with the assassination of former prime min-ister Rafiq Hariri. The prosecution of crimes directed at specific per-sons has rarely played a part in similar international tribunals. Despite this, the statute will govern.

The controversy: is it law?

As the disagreements over the contours of CIL suggest, there is far from universal agreement regarding the "existence" of enforceable IHL, let alone its make-up. Understanding where this controversy comes from is the final part of this brief overview. Such controversy has become an important part of both existing IHL and its future devel-opment. Two criticisms have pervaded this controversy, the first heard largely prior to the 1990s' reemergence of IHL, and the latter a more recent creation. The first set of criticisms may seem odd in an increas-ingly legalized world, in which numerous international courts exist prosecuting defendants for violations of IHL. Yet, even in the wake of the Nuremberg and Tokyo trials, there remained leading scholars who claimed that "international criminal law in any true sense [did] ... not exist."[56]

These critics usually relied on the seemingly unequal circumstances in which IHL was practiced. On the one hand, the international rela-tions "realists" could point to the anarchy that is the global commons and the fact that all too often might makes right, with powerful coun-tries able to do as they please with little consequence. Thus, when such "law" is practiced in the wake of conflicts, most clearly at Nuremberg and Tokyo, it is not justice practitioners have been after, but revenge, albeit sanitized by judicial robes.

Even a brief analysis of IHL prior to the 1990s provides some credence to these claims. It certainly seems that the peoples who wound up on the wrong side of the armistice lines were more likely to end up in the dock. After all, there were no Soviet or American defendants at Nuremberg or Tokyo, despite the evident horrors of the Dresden firebombing and the cataclysms that were Hiroshima and Nagasaki.

A corollary to this selective practice often pointed to was that while victors' justice defined IHL when it was practiced, IHL was actually enforced with such irregularity it may well belittle the concept of "law" to call IHL a component part. Some have asked, noting the absence of Hitler, Hirohito and others from the respective post–World War II tribunals, that "[i]f law is synonymous with justice and justice means that violators are punished [and victims are provided justice], then what kind of law is international [humanitarian] law?"[57]

While these arguments held sway prior to the end of the Cold War, more recently, critics of IHL have become more concerned with other features of the process. For instance some have pointed to the "democratic deficit" inherit in IHL; there is no legislature that passes international law and thus its imposition on individuals who did not have a representative say in the promulgation of the law is invalid.[58] Indeed, for some this lack makes IHL not only invalid, but also a clear violation of national sovereignty to allow citizens of a state to be subjected to an international legal order. This is also a colorable claim; states and not people have a say in the formation of IHL and it has been true of IHL practiced post–World War II and since the 1990s that it can be mandated, and applied to states that may not recognize its validity. This is unlike general international legal obligations stemming from treaties which often leave open the ability for a state to opt out of certain provisions by asserting a "reservation" which can qualify a state's full acceptance of an agreement.

Other recent critics have questioned how IHL could be "law" when so much of it is "customary" and is thus uncodified. This too is a forceful observation; while increasingly IHL has been codified—most recently and completely in the statute of the International Criminal Court— several of the crimes for which defendants have been prosecuted before international tribunals, ranging from Nuremberg to today's UN tribunal for the former Yugoslavia, were "found" by the court rather than "legislated" by statute.[59] The "crime" of encouraging genocide via the media is a leading example.[60] How can IHL be law if it is unclear just what the term covers?

What is interesting about this progression of criticisms is that critics have by and large moved from a criticism that IHL is not "law" because it is practiced too little, to one that posits that IHL is not "law" because it is practiced too much.

As Anupam Chander has argued:

> [t]here was a time when the critics of international law denounced it for its irrelevance, its masquerade of power. ... [T]he critique has shifted. Today, international law is denounced not for its weakness, but for its vigor, specifically its transfer of authority from [the] local to [the] international.[61]

And, indeed, the overview of IHL above demonstrates the basic facts that underlie these criticisms. For the bulk of recorded legal history, any IHL enforcement was fleeting and if it existed at all was practiced in a way that could only fairly be described as "victors' justice." Yet, "in large part this [criticism] has lost its poignancy" over time[62] as international and national courts have made the practice of IHL far from transient. Indeed, as will become clear in the following chapters, the phenomenon of international criminal justice has since the 1990s emerged in a far less tentative manner and though international justice has its flaws and "victors" tend to remain absent from the dock, the system is becoming fairer, more inclusive, and, perhaps most noteworthy, more permanent.

2 The pre-dawn of international justice

Through World War I

Institutions have played determinative roles in how international justice has been defined and dispensed. For much of recorded history, the absence of clearly codified international law arguably meant that institutions occupied an even more central place in the law of international justice than the "law" itself. As such, it is not surprising that the quality, let alone quantity, of international justice practiced has differed markedly over time, dependent largely on the make-up of institutions erected to prosecute violations and the political, legal, and social support they have received from both their constituents and sponsors.

As discussed in Chapter 1, there have been two broad categories of institutions charged with international justice. The first, and more self-evident, are those truly international, independent bodies established by multinational entities, staffed by citizens from various countries and specifically mandated to prosecute international crimes. It has only been through fits and starts that the international community has consented to the establishment of such institutions. Interest in doing so has historically risen at times of great crisis or disgust, only to quickly recede. The years following World War I saw an initial desire for such proceedings, only to founder under political pressures and eventual lack of interest. Twenty years later, the assassination of King Alexander of Yugoslavia in 1934 led the League of Nations to draw up a statute for an international criminal court primarily to prosecute "terrorism."[1] It was only ratified by the Empire of India, and the proposal, along with the entire League, was soon lost to history. Immediately after the end of World War II and the establishment of the United Nations, the world community asked the International Legal Commission to begin working on such a court; due primarily to the Cold War, interest quickly waned for that endeavor as well. Similarly, in the immediate aftermath of the massacre of Israeli athletes at the Munich Olympic Games in 1972, there was some talk of a world court to address such international crimes.[2] Yet, enthusiasm for that enterprise also quickly depleted.

Rather than international institutions, even the conventions describing international crimes have historically had decidedly more domesticated and domestic goals. It is these domestic "institutions" that have historically done much of the groundbreaking work when it comes to prosecuting international crimes. This eventuality has been somewhat according to plan, and is an outcome of much of the primary treaties laying out international law. For instance, the Genocide Convention, describing perhaps the prototypical international crime, makes no specific allowance for an international court to try this international crime. Though the convention mentions that prosecutions for the crime could be "by such international penal tribunal as may have jurisdiction with respect to those contracting parties which shall have accepted its jurisdiction" the true gravity for prosecutions was always thought to be individual states who are mandated under the convention to pass "the necessary legislation to give effect to the provisions of the present convention, and, in particular, to provide effective penalties for persons guilty of genocide" and to prosecute violations of the convention "in a competent tribunal."[3]

It is important to keep in mind these two, often competing institutional forms that have been created to deal with international crimes—the international and the domestic. As will become evident, the clarity of two, discrete forms has in recent years receded with the rise of hybrid bodies that take on characteristics of both international and domestic institutions.

"Absent" international institutions and the era of the domestic through the end of World War II

Until the treaties of Versailles and Sèvres ended the First World War, and made concrete calls to try violators of "international justice" (as discussed below, described in varying manners), it is fair to say that international justice, let alone international judicial institutions, was ephemeral if it existed at all. This does not mean that trials of individuals for crimes that would fit in the modern canon of IHL did not exist; far from it. There are cases from at least the thirteenth century in which leaders have been tried for "international" crimes that would not look out of place in the modern international criminal courtroom.

In 1268, Naples, Italy was host to the trial of Conradin von Hohenstaufen, the Duke of Suabia.[4] Sixteen-year-old von Hohenstaufen was tried, convicted, and executed for "waging an unjust war"—one of the crimes that would play a central role in the debates leading up to Nuremberg and still occupies and perplexes supporters of the ICC today. In 1305, Scottish nationalist Sir William Wallace was tried before an English court, accused of what would today be certainly described as "war crimes": Wallace's revolt against the Crown involved his undertaking a horrific rush of violence against English civilians, "sparing neither age nor sex, monk nor nun."[5] And, as discussed in Chapter 1, the late fifteenth century saw the trial and execution of Peter von Hagenbach, also convicted of seemingly modern crimes— essentially arbitrary violence, brutality and terror that would likely amount to "crimes against humanity" if he were tried before a modern tribunal.[6]

These three trials are noteworthy, and have become favorites of international law scholars, not just because of their direct ties to modern international humanitarian law, but also for the fact that they were unique. Rather than the von Hohenstaufen, Wallace or von Hagenbach proceedings catalyzing a series of such trials and giving birth to effective institutions of international justice, they were aberrations, and existed in a time when Cicero's pronouncements were more or less heeded. Law was indeed silent as battle raged. Forward-looking thinkers, and perhaps those who wished to exact a specific sort of vengeance on a vanquished enemy, from time to time, raised the issue of (and even pursued) prosecutions for certain violations. But all too often legal desires gave way to political pragmatics. Such was the case when the European powers met at the Congress of Vienna in 1815 in the aftermath of the Napoleonic Wars.

Since his 1799 coup d'état and self-aggrandizement to become "Emperor of the French," Napoleon Bonaparte had set Europe ablaze. His territorial ambitions knew no bounds, and in the first decade of the nineteenth century Napoleon had led his forces against almost all major European powers. In 1814, after his disastrous adventures into the Russian winter, he was defeated, forced to abdicate, and under the Treaty of Fontainebleau banished to Elba, a tiny island in the Mediterranean off the coast of Italy, where he could keep his title of "Emperor" with his sole possession being the 90 square mile island. His exile was short-lived and he returned to France in March 1815, governing for the "Hundred Days" and in the process waging further battles, before finally and definitively being defeated by Wellington at Waterloo in June 1815. None of Napoleon's wars were defensive conflicts; they were fundamentally expansionist and in modern parlance Napoleon would likely to be said to have committed the crime of "waging aggressive war."

Thus, when the European powers met at the Congress of Vienna, they convened not just to carve up post-Napoleonic Europe in a fashion that would encourage stability and peace, but also to devise an appropriate set of consequences for the man who had instigated the conflagration. In a debate that would replay itself more than a century later after World War II, various powers argued for different solutions. The Prussians, ironically playing the role that the British would assume in the 1940s, argued for the most simple: shooting Napoleon was the best option. Britain refused and ardently argued for Napoleon to be tried for his misdeeds, by French courts, sitting under the command of the now-restored Bourbons. In the end there was to be no trial, and stuck amidst the extremes of Prussian desires for revenge and British desires for measured recompense, the Congress settled on the ignominious "solution" of exiling Napoleon for a second time. This time they wisely chose a location further afield: St Helena in the southern Atlantic Ocean.

There was no trial of Napoleon, and in the views of some the "Napoleonic precedent" to this day refers to "the use of extralegal means to get rid of an enemy."[7] However, there were some trials after the Napoleonic wars, and they were in line with the British desires to see the Bourbon courts in action. Two senior Bonapartists, Michel Ney and Charles de la Bedoyere, were tried and though their convictions were difficult for some to stomach, there is evidence that the trials were actually quite fair. Thus, the precedent from the Napoleonic wars may well be not the absence of trials, but rather the presence of limited, domestic trials. The crimes of which Ney and Bedoyere were convicted were not "international crimes" per se, but that may solely be due to the absence of nomenclature. They were each tried for "treason," shorthand for a whole range of misdeeds ascribable to Napoleon's armies both inside and outside France. In the last act of "post" Napoleonic Europe, they were both executed, Bedoyere in August, and Ney in December 1815 a few months after the conclusion of the Congress of Vienna.

With these trials in mind, the Napoleonic precedent from an institutional perspective may more accurately be described as the first pangs of domestic institutions conscripted to prosecute international crimes. Unsurprisingly, this became more common during the course of the nineteenth century as international law (and in particular international humanitarian law) became more defined. It is important to note that for many in the nineteenth century, and still in many cases today, a trial for "war crimes" may not have been thought as a trial to correct international wrongs, but rather to right domestic delicts. Even in today's world we see the similar equivocation in domestic prosecutions for clearly international crimes. This is a function of two phenomena:

the explicit domestication of aspects of international law (for instance the ICC implementing legislation, inter alia, has often required adopting states to incorporate the international crimes listed in the Rome Statute into their *domestic* code); and, as will be discussed, the difficulty some states and peoples have in accepting judgments of truly international bodies or laws. These states and peoples are more apt to accept such judgments if the veneer of domestic accountability is laid atop whatever international prosecution arises.

Good examples of these domestic "international" prosecutions were courts martial held in two different parts of the world at the turn of the twentieth century: the Philippines and South Africa.

In the former, the early 1900s saw the United States engaged in a violent pacification battle throughout the Philippines against insurgent groups. The United States had been ceded the islands by Spain as a result of the 1898 Spanish-American War and was having a difficult time establishing control. There were numerous attacks by insurgents and increasingly violent counter-attacks by American soldiers. A particularly brutal reprisal against Filipino insurgents occurred in September 1901 after an ambush by factions that left 59 Americans killed and 23 wounded.[8] Once the American reprisals against the insurgents—which included torture, arbitrary killings and a host of other crimes—were publicized, pressure mounted in the United States until one of the generals, Littleton Waller, was brought before a court martial to explain.[9] This war was the first protracted international conflict the United States engaged in both under the Lieber Code and since the late nineteenth century's impressive build up of international law.

The Lieber Code was technically domestic US law, but it is an early example of the often free flow of law and precedent between the international and the domestic realms; after all, as discussed in the prior chapter the Lieber Code served as inspiration for parts of the "Oxford Manual"—a document describing international law—as well as catalyzing the development of similar codes of conduct in various militaries around the world. Consequently, especially viewed from the standpoint of history, charging Waller under the Lieber Code—which served as the basis for his court martial—was both a domestic and international act. He, and nearly 50 other officers and soldiers were tried for "cruelty, looting and like crimes" during the conflict.[10]

Meanwhile in South Africa, the British were engaged in an equally violent conflict against the descendants of Dutch settlers, the Boers. The Boer War saw no explicit Lieber Code in place for the British, let alone their adversaries, but given that the Boer War was the first such conflict after the Hague conventions that clarified many of the rules of war, it is interesting that British courts martial, of even its own soldiers, often spoke directly to requirements under international law and the "rules of war." In one of the more famous of such trials, against Henry "Breaker" Morant and two other lieutenants fighting with the British, the defendants were brought before a British army court on charges of violating the rules of war in making various reprisal killings. In many ways, the trial that occurred in 1902 has been replayed countless times since then when war crimes and international justice have been at stake. The same arguments and counter-arguments were raised. There was the claim that despite the rules of war, certain actions contrary to them were necessary due to the flagrant abuses of the rules of war by the enemy.[11] And, there was the argument that liability cannot lie with Morant as he was merely following orders of a superior. In the end, Morant's defense did not succeed, and though some have been rightly troubled by the potentially "sham" justice that emerged from the trials, these trials, like those in the Philippines, demonstrated that international law was finding a home, albeit not yet in the international sphere. It was being adopted and co-opted into domestic proceedings, a process that has continued to this day.

This does not mean that the era before World War I was devoid of ideas and proposals about international courts erected for international crimes. In 1870, for example, there was a proposal to form an international criminal court to hear cases relating to atrocities committed during the Franco-Prussian War. A lack of interest by European parties saw this proposal fade. However, what it does mean is that the world was not yet ready for international institutions directed toward international crimes.

It was only during the Great War that such an idea first gained real traction.

Post–World War I

Though often grouped together, there were two separate attempts to wage international justice at the end of World War I: one against the Germans, and the other against the Turks.

Germany

In the German context, talk of post-war trials was common on both sides of the front throughout World War I, with each side making bold claims that the other would be brought to trial at the conclusion of the hostilities. Less than two weeks after the cessation of hostilities the first official statement to back up their wartime bluster was made. British prime minister David Lloyd George announced that he wanted to try the Kaiser on the basis of his "waging an aggressive war;" and, "he pledged the entire influence of the British government at the [Versailles] Peace Conference to see that justice [would be] done."[12]

Lloyd George's argument was the first move in what would become a heated debate amongst the Allies that took place both before and during the Versailles Peace Conference. There was a broad-based desire shared by each of the Allies to "bring to justice the German criminals who had committed so many war crimes on the land, on the sea and in the air."[13] The discord existed regarding exactly who would be charged, what crimes they would be charged with, and before what tribunal they would be brought.

The British and French initially argued that they wished to see the prosecution of anybody involved in war crimes, "of high and of low degree, from the Kaiser to the private."[14] This was quickly deemed quixotic and the Allies began to focus their attention on a smaller number of higher ranking and supposedly more culpable parts of the Kaiser's government. Regarding the specific charges, the political groundwork had already been laid. In December 1918, the Allied leaders had convened in London and issued a joint statement calling for the Kaiser's trial for "his crimes against humanity."[15] This was never fully debated at Versailles, with many in the Allies' camp instead opting to try the Kaiser for committing a war of aggression. The American representatives refuted this proposal, arguing that such a charge would lead to a "meticulous examination of the history of European politics for the past twenty years."[16] In essence, what wars could *not* be deemed as such? More analytical heads prevailed and the resulting crimes agreed upon focused on the Kaiser's particular strategies, rather than the overall determination that his instigated conflict was "aggressive." Thus, the Kaiser's violation of Belgian neutrality and pursuit of unrestricted submarine warfare became the legal underpinnings for any potential charges.

There was also eventual agreement on what sort of courts the victors wished to establish. The treaty actually refers to several courts. The first, and most interesting and important, is a distinctly, and uniquely, international body, though only composed of Allied-nominated judges. The Kaiser and perhaps some other senior officials would be brought before that institution. However, the treaty also provided for trials before national military tribunals, or multinational military tribunals, distinct from the "special tribunal." Here too we see the mixing of international justice with both multinational and domestic organizations.

In broad, unapologetic language, Articles 227–30 of the Versailles Treaty established the legal basis for both the "special tribunal," as well as national/multinational military tribunals, and demanded German compliance with any trials of their citizens. Under the heading "Penalties," the relevant articles are as follows:

Article 227

The Allied and Associated Powers publicly arraign William II of Hohenzollern, formerly German Emperor, for a supreme offence against international morality and the sanctity of treaties.

A special tribunal will be constituted to try the accused, thereby assuring him the guarantees essential to the right of defence. It will be composed of five judges, one appointed by each of the following Powers: namely, the United States of America, Great Britain, France, Italy and Japan.

In its decision the tribunal will be guided by the highest motives of international policy, with a view to vindicating the solemn obligations of international undertakings and the validity of international morality. It will be its duty to fix the punishment which it considers should be imposed.

The Allied and Associated Powers will address a request to the Government of the Netherlands for the surrender to them of the ex-Emperor in order that he may be put on trial.

Article 228

The German Government recognises the right of the Allied and Associated Powers to bring before military tribunals persons accused of having committed acts in violation of the laws and customs of war. Such persons shall, if found guilty, be sentenced to punishments laid down by law. This provision will apply notwithstanding any proceedings or prosecution before a tribunal in Germany or in the territory of her allies.

The German Government shall hand over to the Allied and Associated Powers, or to such one of them as shall so request, all persons accused of having committed an act in violation of the laws and customs of war, who are specified either by name or by the rank, office or employment which they held under the German authorities.

Article 229

Persons guilty of criminal acts against the nationals of one of the Allied and Associated Powers will be brought before the military tribunals of that power.

Persons guilty of criminal acts against the nationals of more than one of the Allied and Associated Powers will be brought before military tribunals composed of members of the military tribunals of the Powers concerned.

In every case the accused will be entitled to name his own counsel.

Article 230
The German Government undertakes to furnish all documents and information of every kind, the production of which may be considered necessary to ensure the full knowledge of the incriminating acts, the discovery of offenders and the just appreciation of responsibility.[17]

The treaty was groundbreaking, and in some aspects strikingly modern (e.g. its stated concern for protecting defense rights). However, problems with these aspects of the Versailles Treaty quickly emerged, not the least of which the unheeded request in Article 227 to the Netherlands to deliver the Kaiser for trial. The Dutch refused to surrender their "guest." There were also problems on the home front, and German citizens began to agitate against the treaty's punitive aspects; the potential trials proved an especially sensitive issue.

Thrown quickly into political and logistical disarray, the trials began to proceed on two separate tracks: one involved the steady calls from London and Paris for the prosecution of Kaiser Wilhelm II; the other track actually resulted in trials and involved proceedings against "other" war criminals. These "others" originally numbered more than 1,500 and included figures such as Paul von Hindenburg and Karl Dönitz. The publication of such an extensive list produced immediate political repercussions in Weimar, with British and French diplomats reporting that the rickety German government might actually collapse if all of the suspects were forcibly brought before a war crimes court. The Allies were shaken and quickly ceded to a compromise floated by Berlin which suggested trying suspects in Germany, before a German court. The number of potential suspects was also quickly reduced, often radically; in the French case, an initial, internal list of 2,000 names was whittled down to 11, a process that in itself raised the ire of many French. In the end, the Allies agreed to accept an offer by Germany to try 45 accused before the Criminal Senate of the Imperial Court of Justice of Germany.[18]

The Germans were evidently strategic in their wish to try their citizens. That the German government had established its own German State Tribunal—designed to investigate and adjudicate German-committed war crimes—a full year before the Leipzig proposal was offered to the Allies, suggests that the government viewed the tribunal as decidedly advantageous.[19] Once the Germans took control the proceedings quickly descended into shambles. German authorities claimed inability to find suspects, let alone defendants. As a result, many viewed the Allied post–World War I prosecution effort in Germany a failure, publicly doubting the ability of a "defeated state" to impartially apply international law to its servicemen.[20]

Turkey

World War I saw the culmination of a program of annihilation perpetrated by the Ottomans against the Armenian populations of the empire; in all 1.5 million Armenians were murdered in what many have come to describe as the twentieth century's first case of genocide. The 1915 massacres, following up on more "minor" episodes of slaughter that occurred during 1894–96 and 1909—which combined resulted in more than 200,000 Armenian deaths[21]—led to the Turks being included in the list of suspected war criminals to be tried following World War I.

Though the Allies initially knew comparatively little of the Armenian massacres—save frequent reports by their legations in Constantinople and elsewhere[22]—the lobby for such prosecutions proved strong. In the British context, Viscount James Bryce, the same man who authored the Bryce Report on German actions in Belgium, was a prime actor in the movement, establishing an Anglo-Armenian Association and fomenting support by both publishing graphic descriptions of the crimes and making frequent references to the fact that the Armenians were also Christian (unlike their Turkish murderers).[23] The other major powers—France and Russia—also proved supportive. While French support was always muted, the Russians were vociferous in their demands for prosecution, if only to placate their own substantial Armenian population, a large number of whom served in the Red Army.

Ironically, there were components within Turkey that also supported prosecution. Representatives of the Ottoman royal household were desperate to hold on to power and fearful of not just Allied strength but also of the political competition of the "Young Turks" who all but ran the post-war government and were the most implicated in the Armenian matters. At the Paris Peace Conference these royal representatives capitulated to the Allies, but threw the entire blame onto the Young Turks, many of whom had fled to Germany—further obviating any sympathies the Allies may have had.[24]

Britain took the lead in pushing for the Turkish trials and by 1919, on the back of two Ottoman commissions that had been collecting evidence and holding hearings, pushed for the arrest of suspects. The Ottoman interior minister drew up a list of those responsible for the Armenian killings and, over a period of four months, had them arrested. By April 1919, the Ottomans held 107 suspects.[25] However, the nationalist backlash among the Turkish people was substantial, and the British were soon stymied. The British encountered problems ranging from trying to find sufficient evidence and testimony from displaced Armenian witnesses and obtaining documentary evidence hidden in Ottoman archives, to outright retaliatory violence by nationalists.[26]

As a result of these difficulties, a compromise solution was found, remarkably similar to the Leipzig *modus vivendi*. At the peace signed between the Allies and the Ottomans at Sèvres in 1920, the Turkish government recognized the right of the Allies to conduct trials and determine punishment; however, the treaty was never ratified by any of its signatories and it would soon be replaced by the Treaty of Lausanne, which not only contained no such provisions, but also was accompanied by a declaration of amnesty for crimes committed during World War I.[27]

But, to the credit of the British, despite the formal amnesties, they pushed for trials in Turkey. The Ottomans finally conceded and erected the first special courts martial, which, over the 10-month period between March 1919 and January 1920 tried 36 people in five groups of trials.[28] However, the most senior indictees, all in exile in Germany, were not prosecuted; despite arguments to insert the requirement of their extradition into the Versailles Treaty (which was signed in the middle of this period), no demand was made. Similarly, Turkish requests for extradition were unheeded by Germany.

In years following, both of these trials assumed the title of "failed justice," with officials choosing to all but forget Constantinople and pledging to avoid any repeats of Leipzig when the next war crimes arose. Some have taken to calling the proceedings a "judicial farce."[29] When World War II ended and the Allies were once more contemplating the disposition of German criminals, memories of the First World War's "failed" trials ran high. "On the British side Anthony Eden cringed at 'that ill-starred enterprise at the end of the last war.' For the Americans, John Pehle of the War Refugee Board thought it 'abominable,' and Henry Morgenthau, Jr. a 'fiasco.'"[30] The post–World War II efforts would be drastically different.

3 International justice following World War II

Nuremberg and Tokyo

For many of those outside the legal community, the grainy, black-and-white pictures of defendants sitting before judges at Nuremberg remain *the* images of international justice. Even if they have been closed for more than six decades, and at least half a dozen other international tribunals have been established in the past 15 years, the post–World War II trials—at Nuremberg and to a lesser extent at Tokyo—maintain a hold on the popular conscience that subsequent proceedings have been unable to match.

From the perspective of modern IHL the outsized importance of the post–World War II proceedings is largely justified. Nuremberg and Tokyo represented not a simple evolution in dealing with crimes of war, but a revolution in the way the world community sought to address humanity's worst violators. However, despite their popular image and their significance in the development of IHL and IHL enforcement, a closer examination of these proceedings demonstrates not only that they almost failed to occur, but also that far ranging political and legal forces combined to provide the courts decidedly mixed legacies.

This chapter will argue that while their successes and failures may be debatable, the post–World War II tribunals continue to serve as fundamental signposts to the modern pursuit of justice. Almost every aspect of modern IHL enforcement can be traced to some aspect of the Nuremberg and Tokyo trials, with subsequent institutional designers closely examining the courts, adopting and adapting elements that were deemed successful and equally relying on the trials to learn from their institutional shortcomings. To some degree all modern institutions seeking to enforce IHL are the progeny of these post World War II "judicial experiments" and this heritage includes not just the legal machineries of justice, but also the very same judicial and political forces and pressures that made Nuremberg and Tokyo far more (and less) than the cursory eye of the public was able to see.

The Nuremberg baseline: a legal institution or a political one?

Despite its well deserved fame and its continuing impact, Nuremberg was an inauspicious start to "modern" international criminal justice, and it was a start that almost did not happen. In 1942, under the auspices of the inter-Allied Conference on the Punishment of War Crimes, the representatives of nine occupied countries—Belgium, Czechoslovakia, France, Greece, Luxembourg, Norway, The Netherlands, Poland and Yugoslavia—met at St. James' Palace in London and signed a declaration placing "among their principal war aims the punishment, through the channel of organized justice," those responsible for acts of violence against civilian populations.[1] However, despite Winston Churchill's 1941 assertion that "[r]etribution for [German] crimes must ... take its place among the major purposes of the War,"[2] contemplations about such trials, let alone support for them on behalf of the primary Allied powers, were slow in coming even after the 1942 conference. Indeed for the major Allies, the idea of any sort of tribunal to try the German leadership as war criminals emerged only at the very end of World War II, and backing for such proceedings was mixed, at best. As late as 1943, the British government's official policy was to summarily execute war criminals "[t]he guilt of such individuals [being] so black that they [fell] outside and [went] beyond the scope of any judicial process."[3] The Americans, still under an ailing Franklin Delano Roosevelt, agreed with the British position, concerned not so much with the judicial difficulties of a trial but rather with the risk that a "fair" trial might allow the accused a way out. While there was disquiet in some parts of the American administration, notably on behalf of Secretary of War Henry Stimson, White House policy until almost the end of the war was explicitly against the establishment of trials for captured German leadership.

Ironically, it was the Soviets who first bucked the trend and demanded trials. Yet it was not true legal process that the Soviets desired. The Soviets made it clear that the German leadership was guilty and would be executed. However, Moscow had learned from its experiences with the Stalin purges and show trials of the 1930s that public acceptance for such a penalty could only be assured if trials preceded executions. Roosevelt's death in 1945 provided an opening for American supporters for trials, and an "unlikely alliance of Communist leaders and American liberals was mobilized ... to insist on a judicial tribunal."[4] Secretary of War Stimson survived Roosevelt, and working under President Truman drafted the American proposal: "Trial of European War Criminals." Unsurprisingly, the Americans and Soviets diverged when it came to the scope of the fair process the Germans deserved; the French and the British, who were finally compelled into supporting the process, also had their own notions for what trials should look like.

The structure of the Nuremberg judicial institutions was finalized over the course of three meetings between the "Big Three" (the United States, the United Kingdom and the Soviet Union)—Tehran in 1943, Yalta and Potsdam, both in 1945, and a final drafting meeting among non-heads of government representatives in London. Robert Jackson, the United States Supreme Court justice who would be asked to serve as the lead Nuremberg prosecutor, was a key element in the final process that led to the 8 August 1945 release of the London Charter of the International Military Tribunal. The London Charter was signed by the Big Three, who had agreed to concede an equal role to the provisional French government (the only major Allied power occupied during the war; thus it signed the document as the Provisional Government of the French Republic).

The brief document, composed of six sections and 30 articles, set out the basics for what the tribunal would look like, the laws and procedures under which it would operate, and its available judgments and sentences. This document remains the blueprint for war crimes trials, and as such it is worthy of quoting at length, remarking on the specific components that have proven long-lasting, particularly controversial, or, in the case of very few aspects, ephemeral:

Box 3.1   Highlights of the London Charter leading to Nuremberg

Following a contentious meeting in London between the four victorious allied powers, the London Charter of the International Military Tribunal Article called for the "just and prompt trial and punishment of the major war criminals of the European Axis." The tribunal claimed jurisdiction over three main crimes, each of which encompassed novel charges that, in many instances, had never before been laid, or, in some cases, even defined. The tripartite charges consisted of: (1) "Crimes Against Peace," which included the planning of, or participation in a conspiracy for the planning/ waging of, "aggressive war"; (2) "War Crimes," which included the enslavement of civilian populations, the ill treatment of prisoners of war and the destruction of civilian property "not justified by military necessity"; (3) "Crimes Against Humanity"—a legal neologism that quickly entered the popular vernacular—which included "inhumane acts" and "persecutions on political, racial or religious grounds" regardless whether such acts were "in violation of the domestic law of the country where perpetrated." Importantly, the Charter forbade the use of superior responsibility as a defense.

I. CONSTITUTION OF THE INTERNATIONAL MILITARY TRIBUNAL

Article 2
The Tribunal shall consist of four members, each with an alternate. One member and one alternate shall be appointed by each of the Signatories. ...

This article defines the tribunal's judiciary, a four-member body with judges appointed by each of the charter's signatories; as such there was an American (Francis Biddle), a Briton (Lord Justice Lawrence), a Frenchman (Donnedieu de Vabres) and a Soviet (Iona Nikitchenko) jurist.

Article 3
Neither the Tribunal, its members nor their alternates can be challenged by the prosecution, or by the Defendants or their Counsel. ...

Article 3 addresses one of the longest-standing and most often heard criticisms of any international tribunal. As von Hagenbach made clear in the 1400s when he stood before his accusers, Charles I repeated when arraigned before Parliament at the end of the English Civil War in 1648, and Slobodan Milosevic, Charles Taylor, Saddam Hussein and others have repeated in the modern era, there is a long tradition of defendants arguing that their prosecuting courts were unlawfully established, a fact rendering any resulting conviction illegitimate.[5] The drafters of the London Charter likely feared that such a claim would be raised and realized that the legitimacy of the institution might be built on hollow ground unless the institution itself had the power to justify its own existence. This is not legal double talk, but rather has a long history in international law; the idea of "competence de la competence," in which an international tribunal has the authority to determine its own competence and jurisdiction, was already longstanding.[6] And

Justice Jackson in his drafting paid heed to this notion, while trying to thwart what he thought, it turns out presciently, would be key criticisms of the Nuremberg enterprise.

Interestingly, at the International Criminal Tribunal for the former Yugoslavia, one of the first issues faced by the tribunal was a challenge made by a defendant regarding the tribunal's legal legitimacy. In a lengthy proceeding that culminated in the Appeals Chamber of the court ruling on the matter, it was held in *Prosecutor v. Tadic*, that the tribunal had the definitive power to determine the propriety of its own jurisdiction.[7]

II. JURISDICTION AND GENERAL PRINCIPLES

Article 6
The Tribunal established by the Agreement referred to in Article 1 hereof for the trial and punishment of the major war criminals of the European Axis countries shall have the power to try and punish persons who, acting in the interests of the European Axis countries, whether as individuals or as members of organizations, committed any of the following crimes.

The following acts, or any of them, are crimes coming within the jurisdiction of the Tribunal for which there shall be individual responsibility:

(a) *Crimes Against Peace*: namely, planning, preparation, initiation or waging of a war of aggression, or a war in violation of international treaties, agreements or assurances, or participation in a common plan or conspiracy for the accomplishment of any of the foregoing ...

Note again, the "waging of aggressive war," seen in the initial prosecution desires of the Allies after World War I, makes another appearance here. As will be discussed below, the exact meaning of "aggression" remains undefined and is a source of significant discord in the international community, even among those who wish to prosecute the crime.

(b) *War Crimes*: namely, violations of the laws or customs of war. Such violations shall include, but not be limited to, murder, ill-treatment or deportation to slave labor or for any other purpose of civilian population of or in occupied territory, murder or ill-treatment of prisoners of war or persons on the seas, killing of hostages, plunder of public or private property, wanton destruction of cities, towns or villages, or devastation not justified by military necessity;

(c)   *Crimes Against Humanity*: namely, murder, extermination, enslavement, deportation, and other inhumane acts committed
against any civilian population, before or during the war; or
persecutions on political, racial or religious grounds in execution of or in connection with any crime within the jurisdiction
of the Tribunal, whether or not in violation of the domestic
law of the country where perpetrated.

Part (c) explicitly internationalized the crimes under review by the tribunal. The key here was that defendants would be liable for their actions
even if those actions were not in violation of the law of the country
where they were perpetrated. International law could deem something
impermissible that domestic criminal law left untouched. Perhaps sub-
consciously, what the London drafters were doing was speaking to the
notion of both *jus cogens* and customary international law, arguing that
no matter the neglect of a municipal judicial system to criminalize certain
wrongs, the international system had the power *and* obligation to do so.

Leaders, organizers, instigators and accomplices participating in
the formulation or execution of a common plan or conspiracy to
commit any of the foregoing crimes are responsible for all acts
performed by any persons in execution of such plan.

The "conspiracy" element of the charter was critical. One of the difficulties many foresaw with Nuremberg was the ascribing of specific evidence
to leaders that directly implicated them with acts that amounted to
violations. At times the chain of command was long and complicated,
a factor that could have left it impossible to directly establish a violation
committed by a higher-ranking official. The conspiracy rule allowed a
much looser link between a defendant and the acts. "Conspiracy" in
such a broad notion is primarily a common law concept—the type of
law practiced in the United States and the United Kingdom; as such
there was some dissent (and continues to be in its current usage) from
those civil law states which generally employ a much narrower definition of conspiracy. In the civil system, the type and quality of evidence
needed to convict for a conspiracy is much closer to the type and
quality of evidence needed to convict a defendant directly.

Article 7
The official position of defendants, whether as Heads of State
or responsible officials in Government Departments, shall not be

considered as freeing them from responsibility or mitigating punishment.

Article 8
The fact that the Defendant acted pursuant to order of his Government or of a superior shall not free him from responsibility, but may be considered in mitigation of punishment if the Tribunal determines that justice so requires.

To those outside the legal field, and perhaps to those inside it, these two articles are among the most well known and celebrated contributions provided by Nuremberg. Taken together, they make clear that there is no immunity from prosecution for certain crimes; claims of immunity by virtue of government position or by virtue of acting pursuant to superior orders are equally illegitimate. Though the margins of the standard remain controversial, and indeed with slightly convoluted facts the International Court of Justice found that an individual who was a sitting foreign minister was immune to a foreign court's charges of crimes against humanity,[8] the basics of this rule have been maintained and it has grown stronger and more universally accepted over time. For most modern international tribunals, along with the domestic and hybrid courts prosecuting international crimes, the position of defendants as sitting leaders while crimes commenced is among the precise grounds upon which prosecution is based. The trial against Japanese general Tomoyuki Yamashita (see below) is a good, early example of such a prosecution. It was in large part his senior position that made him liable, rather than provided him protection.

Article 9
At the trial of any individual member of any group or organization the Tribunal may declare (in connection with any act of which the individual may be convicted) that the group or organization of which the individual was a member was a criminal organization.

This Article introduces the concept of a "criminal organization," the notion that not just individuals, but the organizations to which they belong can be adjudged, as a whole, "criminal." During the Nuremberg trials several institutions affiliated with the Nazi state were so found, including the Gestapo and the Schutzstaffel (SS), the latter of which was deemed as such in the tribunal's first case, against Hermann Göring. Interestingly, there was no definition of "criminal organization" until the Tribunal's hearings began. And it was only after Case No. 1 had found that the SS fit the description that prosecutions of subsequent defendants both at Nuremberg and at various subsidiary proceedings, for instance in the "Doctors' Trial", also included this charge.

Article 9 has proven over time to be one of the more controversial components of the London Charter,[9] and it has not been included in any subsequent international tribunal. As one such recent court addressing international crimes held:

> This Tribunal agrees with the rulings issued by international courts whereby mere membership in a state agency, even if that state is known to be repressive, or in a criminal organization, is not sufficient in itself to say that a member thereof has participated in the commission of a crime.[10]

Article 12
The Tribunal shall have the right to take proceedings against a person charged with crimes set out in Article 6 of this Charter in his absence, if he has not been found or if the Tribunal, for any reason, finds it necessary, in the interests of justice, to conduct the hearing in his absence.

Whether international justice is served by prosecuting defendants in absentia has long been debated. Historically absentia prosecutions have often been held. After World War I, for example, in the wake of the unsatisfactory legal responses in Germany and Turkey, some states chose to mount their own prosecutions in absentia. The French were particularly enthusiastic in this regard. The drafters of the London Charter followed this trend explicitly in allowing absentia prosecutions, some of which occurred. However, subsequent international tribunals have shied away from absentia trials. The result has been both positive—ensuring the presence of the indicted to hear and contest the charges against him, and negative—witness the immediate cessation of the war crimes trials of Slobodan Milosevic and Foday Sankoh upon their untimely deaths.

Article 13
The Tribunal shall draw up rules for its procedure. These rules shall not be inconsistent with the provisions of this Charter.

Other than in respect of the ICC which has adopted a different process, this has been a common aspect of tribunals that followed Nuremberg. The tribunal itself is charged with designing its rules of procedure.

III. COMMITTEE FOR THE INVESTIGATION AND PROSECUTION OF MAJOR WAR CRIMINALS

Article 14

Each Signatory shall appoint a Chief Prosecutor for the investigation of the charges against and the prosecution of major war criminals.

The Chief Prosecutors shall act as a committee for the following purposes:

(a) to agree upon a plan of the individual work of each of the Chief Prosecutors and his staff,

(b) to settle the final designation of major war criminals to be tried by the Tribunal,

(c) to approve the Indictment and the documents to be submitted therewith,

(d) to lodge the Indictment and the accompany documents with the Tribunal,

(e) to draw up and recommend to the Tribunal for its approval draft rules of procedure, contemplated by Article 13 of this Charter. The Tribunal shall have the power to accept, with or without amendments, or to reject, the rules so recommended.

Article 14 sets up the other pole of authority in the Nuremberg system, and one that has, more or less, been maintained in the modern incarnations of international tribunals. The prosecutor was designed to be a powerful part of the process and is given a great degree of deference on each of the five tasks assigned to him. The only difference in the modern tribunal, that existed de facto at Nuremberg in its "secretariat," was that some of the administrative tasks of the prosecutor have been officially moved to the tribunal's "registry," the third part of most modern international courts' hierarchy: the judges ("chambers"), the prosecutor, and the registry.

IV. FAIR TRIAL FOR DEFENDANTS

Article 16

In order to ensure fair trial for the Defendants, the following procedure shall be followed:

(a) The Indictment shall include full particulars specifying in detail the charges against the Defendants. A copy of the Indictment and of all the documents lodged with the Indictment, translated into a language which he understands, shall be furnished to the Defendant at reasonable time before the Trial.

(b) During any preliminary examination or trial of a Defendant he will have the right to give any explanation relevant to the charges made against him.

(c) A preliminary examination of a Defendant and his Trial shall be conducted in, or translated into, a language which the Defendant understands.

(d) A Defendant shall have the right to conduct his own defense before the Tribunal or to have the assistance of Counsel.

(e) A Defendant shall have the right through himself or through his Counsel to present evidence at the Trial in support of his defense, and to cross-examine any witness called by the Prosecution.

Article 16 may appear unobjectionable, but it was amongst the hardest negotiated aspects of the London Charter. In its drafting it had to balance numerous competing notions and realities. First, there was the debate regarding how much fair process to provide the Nazi defendants. As mentioned, for the Soviets, the requisite process was more limited than that desired by the other parties. Second, there was a contentious debate between the civil law states (particularly France) and the common law states (the United States and the United Kingdom) which have different, and at times opposing, concepts of fairness in the dispensation of justice. Some of these differences were addressed in their absence from Article 16 (such as whether judges would have inquisitorial roles in the process, as in civil law countries, or whether they would solely have passive, adjudicatory roles, as in common law states). Finally, there was the concern primarily on behalf the British and the Americans about the outcome of "too much process." The nature of a "fair trial" is that defendants at least theoretically have the chance of exoneration. The British were concerned that prosecution teams would be unable to collect "solid forensic evidence" linking defendants to crimes.[11] As such, the Tribunal may well have been forced to acquit the majority of the defendants.

The American version of this concern related to the question of whether to extend Constitutional protections to defendants. Such a move would, inter alia, provide them the ability to assert a privilege against self-incrimination (as provided by the Fifth Amendment). Internally, the Americans concluded that such rights could not extend to war criminal defendants.[12]

Though the British concern was heeded, and was likely alleviated somewhat by Article 19 (below), the ability of the Allies to obtain the necessary evidence and witnesses was greatly eased by the military and political realities of post–World War II Germany.

V. POWERS OF THE TRIBUNAL AND CONDUCT OF THE TRIAL

Article 17
The Tribunal shall have the power
(a) to summon witnesses to the Trial and to require their attendance and testimony and to put questions to them,
(b) to interrogate any Defendant,
(c) to require the production of documents and other evidentiary material,
(d) to administer oaths to witnesses,
(e) to appoint officers for the carrying out of any task designated by the Tribunal including the power to have evidence taken on commission.

Section V made law what was already clear on the ground in Germany after VE Day. The Allies were in control and could exert their will in whichever fashion they chose. Consequently, it was somewhat superfluous, even if legally necessary, to say that the tribunal—an arm of the Allied occupation—had the power to summon witnesses and require the production of documents and other evidence. All of Germany was open to the Allied forces, with the only difficulty usually being the amount of evidence available, not the ability to obtain it.

Language akin to Section V exists in the statutes of some of the modern day tribunals, but the difficulties in acquiring evidence and witnesses in many of these cases make the words more aspirational than superfluous. It may be unnecessary to provide a tribunal, with the full power of an occupier behind it, the right to all evidence and other materials located in the occupied state. However, it is a far more difficult task to assure a tribunal of the same access if it is located in or is forced to deal with recalcitrant states unwilling to give up evidence or material to the tribunal *and* with no occupying power to enforce the tribunal's will. This has proven a significant difficulty in some of the trials of the ICTY and ICTR, and already appears to be a significant obstacle for the new ICC.

Article 19

The Tribunal shall not be bound by technical rules of evidence. It shall adopt and apply to the greatest possible extent expeditious and nontechnical procedure, and shall admit any evidence which it deems to be of probative value.

As mentioned, Article 19 partly placated British concerns that the provision of too much "fairness" in the tribunal process could result in mass acquittals of Nazi criminals. By removing "technical rules of evidence," which would perhaps have greatly constrained the tribunal in its use of defendant and witness testimony and other second-hand reports, the tribunal became open to almost anything that could be presented that had "probative value"—this is a very low standard.

Other than speaking to the concerns of some of the charter's drafters, there is good legal justification for dispensing with such technical rules. One of the primary reasons for an assiduous commitment to follow rules of evidence comes from the common law system, in which evidence is often heard by a jury of laypeople. It is thought that laypeople are not trained in the skill of determining "good" evidence, and consequently the law protects them (and thus the defendant) through a complex web of rules that limit what evidence can be presented and how it may be presented. Yet, once juries have ruled and the case goes to the appellate stage (where it is heard solely before judges), or even in first instance cases in which only judges hear the evidence, technical rules of evidence are, if not entirely removed, significantly relaxed under the assumption that judges know the law and can determine whether specific items make for legal evidence or not.

This relaxation of evidentiary rules has played a role in almost all prosecutions of international criminal law since Nuremberg, from domestic proceedings to modern international criminal tribunals.

Article 24

The proceedings at the Trial shall take the following course:
(a) The Indictment shall be read in court.
(b) The Tribunal shall ask each Defendant whether he pleads "guilty" or "not guilty."
(c) The prosecution shall make an opening statement.
(d) The Tribunal shall ask the prosecution and the defense what evidence (if any) they wish to submit to the Tribunal, and the Tribunal shall rule upon the admissibility of any such evidence.

(e)   The witnesses for the Prosecution shall be examined and after that the witnesses for the Defense. Thereafter such rebutting evidence as may be held by the Tribunal to be admissible shall be called by either the Prosecution or the Defense.

(f)   The Tribunal may put any question to any witness and to any defendant, at any time.

(g)   The Prosecution and the Defense shall interrogate and may cross examine any witnesses and any Defendant who gives testimony.

(h)   The Defense shall address the court.

(i)   The Prosecution shall address the court.

(j)   Each Defendant may make a statement to the Tribunal.

(k)   The Tribunal shall deliver judgment and pronounce sentence.

With some exceptions and alterations in specific situations, this basic, 11-part process describes the phases of a trial in a modern tribunal as much as it did at Nuremberg. Note that part (f), which allows the tribunal to interrupt a proceeding to ask a question is in line with the activist judges of civil law states, and indeed this activism when it has been exercised in some cases in modern tribunals has led to some concern and frustration on behalf of common law lawyers.[13]

VI. JUDGMENT AND SENTENCE

Article 26
The judgment of the Tribunal as to the guilt or the innocence of any Defendant shall give the reasons on which it is based, and shall be final and not subject to review.

Modern tribunals have definitively rejected parts of Article 26. Whereas there existed no appeal for Nuremberg convicts, the appellate system is now an active part of international tribunals. The appeals process has also played an important role in the various domestic proceedings that have sought to prosecute international crimes.

The outcome and criticisms of Nuremberg

It was much to the credit of the tribunal's chief prosecutor, United States Supreme Court Justice Robert Jackson, for managing the process and balancing the political demands made on him by all sides. At each stage in the process, from the initial drafting of the Charter to the final prosecutions, he was forced to balance his desire for effective due process and blind justice, with the overpowering dictates of politics.

Nowhere was the delicacy of this balance more clear than in the determination of who the trials were to prosecute. The answer was far from evident, and was based as much on arbitrary political needs as on questions of criminal culpability. As an English participant in the trials characterized the issue: "The test should be: do we want the man for making a success of our trial? If yes, we must have him."[14]

Initially, the nationality of defendants was thought immaterial, and Germans, Italians, Hungarians and other accomplices to the Third Reich were on the list. However, as the post-war reality shifted, and the Cold War started to seem inevitable, the nationality of prospective defendants became critical. The Americans insisted on removing all Italians, for want of upsetting a potential ally against the Soviets, and the Soviets, in turn, removed Hungarians and others within their sphere. Consequently, within a few months of its commencement, it was agreed that only a select few Germans were to be tried. This meant that no members of the Arrow Cross party, the Nazi offshoot that ruled Hungary at the end of the war, nor any members of Mussolini's Black Shirt brigade that not only were complicit with the Germans but authored their own well established war crimes during the invasion of Ethiopia in 1935, were to be prosecuted.

The 22 Nazi officials who were eventually indicted were charged with a broad ranging conspiracy to "wage aggressive war," war crimes, and crimes against humanity—almost all indictments never before issued. Even the terminology was new: "crimes against humanity" were given operational legal definition by the indictments in which they were first used.

There were two prime problems with the prosecution's theory of conspiracy. Such an argument, backed up with evidence as varied as Adolf Hitler's *Mein Kampf* and the Kellogg-Briand Pact (in which nations of the world offered a "frank renunciation of war"[15]) was met with concern by the Soviets, who worried that such a broad conspiracy may implicate them, via the Molotov-Ribbentrop Soviet-German Non-Aggression Pact.[16] Consequently, the nature of the conspiracy charge was very limited; any mention of Soviet-Nazi cooperation was stricken from the proceedings, as was any charge related to Nazi bombing campaigns of civilian centers. Once thought to be a prime element in the prosecution case, these bombings were dropped for fear that equally horrific Allied attacks on Dresden and other cities would be brought up by the defense.

There was an additional concern that the defendants' acts, at the time of their commission, were not illegal; it was only through the lens of hindsight—and new standards like "crimes against humanity"—that they could be deemed against the law.[17] Retrospective justice was required to criminalize these acts, and such a course was almost entirely alien to the Anglo-Saxon system. Still, Jackson managed this tension, adroitly appealing to common law principles predating any Third Reich legislation: he claimed that the acts charged were always criminal, and any resort to their legalization via Nazi rulings provided no safe harbor.

It is noteworthy that this legal maneuvering failed to placate one of Justice Jackson's colleagues from the United States Supreme Court, Justice William O. Douglas. He complained at the time and for years after that

> no matter how finely the lawyers analyzed it, the crime for which the Nazis were tried had never been formalized as a crime with the definiteness required by our legal standards, nor outlawed with a death penalty by the international community. By our standards that crime arose under an ex post facto law. Goering *et al.* deserved severe punishment. But their guilt did not justify us in substituting power for principle.[18]

This political gamesmanship, which served as the backdrop to the tribunal and was largely masked from the public at large, continued even after defendants had become convicts. Notably, the vast majority of those convicted—including those tried at the much larger Dachau Trials (a simultaneous set of trials held at the former concentration camp which dealt with almost 1,700 mid-level German functionaries, concentration camp officials, and military officers)[19]—were released after serving a short sentence, or even no prison time. These commutations were often effected without the knowledge of the trials' judges, and were based on larger political considerations. The importance to the West of securing West German support in the Cold War trumped the requirements of justice. Despite some ex post complaints from the US Congress[20] the occupying US Army was convinced that winning German hearts and minds was not possible so long as so many Germans were being tried and punished. This troublesome aspect of the trials' outcome—and the final point at which politics and justice met at Nuremberg—is a key legacy of the trials. This conflation of political and judicial ends serves as an uneasy building block of modern international criminal justice.

This mixing of politics and justice led to some vigorous hand-wringing after the fact, with none so notable as a fiery speech given by United States Senator Robert Taft of Ohio in October 1946. His concerns included not just Justice Douglas' anxieties about ex post facto law, but about whether Nuremberg would "discourage the making of aggressive war" and whether there was more vengeance than justice in the Nuremberg results.

About this whole judgment there is the spirit of vengeance, and vengeance is seldom justice. The hanging of the eleven men convicted will be a blot on the American record which we shall long regret.[21]

Intriguingly, John F. Kennedy, writing in his Pulitzer Prize winning *Profiles in Courage*, posited that Senator Taft's and Justice Douglas' "conclusions are shared, I believe, by a substantial number of American citizens today. And they were shared, at least privately, by a goodly number in 1946."[22]

Some commentators found this legacy of Cold War politics and the potential for ex post facto law even more troubling, likening Nuremberg to the botched prosecutions after the First World War. George Finch, then president of the American Society for International Law, intoned that:

Political expediency frustrated the efforts to punish war crimes following World War I. Similarly, novel legal concepts and considerations of expediency were interjected into the work of ... the London agreement establishing the Nuremberg Tribunal. As a result, much criticism of the value of that Tribunal's judgment as a precedent in international law has been invited—criticism which might and should have been avoided.[23]

But along with the criticism there were some remarkable successes that moved international law into new and important territory. The very fact that Nuremberg existed at all is cause for some celebration; after the abortive attempts following World War I and discord amongst the Allies regarding the best course of action, the establishing of the tribunal was a testament to the unwavering desire of some actors to see international justice finally receive its due. In addition to its existence, some of the tribunal's findings have proven critical to the development of war crimes and a wider understanding of international justice. For instance, up until Nuremberg there remained the overhang of Westphalian logic that states, rather than citizens, were the only true focus of international law. But, the

International Military Tribunal at Nuremberg settled this question by declaring in the judgment that "crimes against international law are committed by men not by abstract entities and only by punishing individuals who commit crimes can the provisions of international law be enforced".[24]

Other findings have proven less definitive, if no less important. For instance the tribunal's findings on the prosecution of a war of aggression were important, yet, as mentioned above, the understanding of what such a war actually looks like remains elusive.

Still, in one of the first acts of the new UN, the entire judgment of the Nuremberg tribunal was adopted by the body, giving life to an international criminal code, standing apart from the statute of any particular tribunal, for the first time. The Nuremberg precedent was subsequently an important step toward some of the major treaties and conventions that continued to define and refine international humanitarian law after World War II:

- The Genocide Convention, 1948
- The Universal Declaration of Human Rights, 1948
- The Geneva Conventions on the Laws and Customs of War, 1949
- The Convention on the Abolition of the Statute of Limitations on War Crimes and Crimes against Humanity, 1968

In the end, though its criticisms have been numerous they have not obscured its successes and its stature has only grown. Still, Nuremberg, which was convened in November 1945 and closed four years later, can be said to have been a momentous, even if somewhat uncomfortable and far from perfect or universally supported, start to international enforcement of international criminal law.

The Tokyo trials

The lesser known cousin to the Nuremberg trials were those proceedings held in Tokyo convened to try leaders of the Empire of Japan for various crimes committed during World War II against the Allies and in the process of Japan's brutal occupation of much of East Asia. Coming on the heels of Nuremberg, and involving each of the four powers that convened the Nuremberg trials, it was logical that the trials had many similarities to their European counterpart. The intention of the major powers to prosecute Japanese war criminals was first publicly articulated in July 1945 when the Soviet Union, the United Kingdom and the United States issued the joint Potsdam Declaration, which laid out the Allies' demands for Japan's surrender. Three quarters of the way through the document, the Allies proclaimed that they

> [did] not intend that the Japanese shall be enslaved as a race or destroyed as [a] nation, but *stern justice* shall be meted out to all

war criminals, including those who have visited cruelties upon our prisoners.[25]

The Tokyo trials were governed by the Charter of the International Military Tribunal for the Far East (CIMTFE), proclaimed on 19 January 1946 and modeled closely on the London Charter, but with some important differences that reflected differences between post-war Japan and post-war Germany.

The key difference between the two poles of the Axis after their respective surrenders was the degree in which their occupations were internationalized and militarized. In post-war Germany, the political environment that emerged was under the control of the four Allied powers, each charged with a separate zone of the state, and each holding sway in a sector of Berlin. The Allies ostensibly worked together in administration through an Allied Control Council. Though this quad-partite arrangement would soon disintegrate, leading to the amalgamation of the western zones into the Federal Republic of Germany (West Germany) and the Soviet's cleaving of the eastern sector to form the German Democratic Republic (East Germany), during the Nuremberg trials all four exercised a measure of power in the still-unified country. Consequently, the Nuremberg trials, starting with their statute in the London Charter, to decisions regarding process, prosecutions and commutation, were forced to contend with pressures from each of the controlling powers, resulting in various compromises and bows to political and diplomatic needs throughout.

Post-war Japan was a study in contrast. Though 11 states signed the Japanese instrument of surrender it says much about what would emerge in Japan that the document was signed on board the USS *Missouri*, an American battleship. The Americans would come to almost unitarily occupy and control Japan. Some outlying territories both of Japan and those regions which had been under Japanese occupation were split between various Allied powers. For instance, the Soviet Union was assigned Sakhalin and the Kuril Islands to administer, while the Republic of China was mandated Taiwan and the Pescadores. However it was the supreme commander of the Allied powers, the chief military officer of the United States forces in Japan, who was given unilateral control over the country's four main islands: Honshu, Hokkaido, Shikoku and Kyushu. By the end of 1945, 350,000 Americans were occupying the country.

In addition to its American face, the occupation of Japan was also far more "militarized" than the German occupation. In Germany the Allied Control Council began as a military occupation, but quickly took on civilian aspects when military governors were replaced by civilian commissioners. This was not the case in Japan, and for the entirety of its occupation the country was directly administered by military governors, first General Douglas MacArthur and then General Matthew Ridgeway.

The result of this was reflected in the Tokyo trials which were both more American *and* more akin to a military trial—in particular an American court martial—than was seen in Nuremberg. Touches of American law and military procedure were present throughout the trial, no more noticeably than in the tribunal's statute—the Charter of the International Military Tribunal for the Far East (IMTFE). For instance, Article 1 in the Nuremberg statute proclaimed that establishment of the tribunal under the agreement of the four powers; Article 1 of the Tokyo statute provides only that the tribunal is established, paying heed solely to its American authors, not any others. Moreover, Article 9 of the Tokyo statute proclaims that only English and the language of the accused would be the working languages of the tribunal. There was no requirement for French or Russian, or any other translation, as in the Nuremberg trials. This is perhaps somewhat odd because under Article 2, judges at the Tokyo tribunal were to hail from each of the countries that signed the Japanese instrument of surrender (which included the Soviet Union and France), plus India and the Philippines.

Turning to its similarities with modern US courts martial, it is important to note that the key institutional player in American courts martial is not the judge or the prosecutor, but the commanding officer of the region in which a court martial is to take place. It is under his authority that a court martial is convened and it is at his discretion to act upon decisions rendered by a court martial. The IMTFE charter follows this model closely. The commanding officer in this case was the supreme commander for the Allied powers, General MacArthur. The statute makes clear that the tribunal was convened under his authority; indeed at its conclusion under its final Article 17, the drafters wrote "By command of General MacArthur." To make the point even clearer, two of his aides were also mentioned, Major General Richard J. Marshall, MacArthur's chief of staff, and Brigadier General B. M. Fitch, the adjutant general.

As the convening authority, much as he would if convening a court martial in the US army, MacArthur controlled the appointment of almost all players in the trial and even much of its procedure. For instance, Article 2 of the IMTFE charter held that the "Tribunal shall consist of not less than six members nor more than eleven members … from the names submitted by the Signatories to the Instrument of Surrender, India, and the Commonwealth of the Philippines." However, the proviso was that any of these members had to be "appointed by the Supreme Allied Commander of the Allied Powers."

Article 8 described the role of the prosecutor, pointedly using the Americanized term "chief of counsel" instead of the more internationalized "chief prosecutor." Here too General MacArthur was a primary player. Article 8 mandated that

> The Chief of Counsel designated by the Supreme Commander for the Allied Powers is responsible for the investigation and prosecution of charges against war criminals within the jurisdiction of this Tribunal, and will render such legal assistance to the Supreme Commander as is appropriate.

MacArthur chose an American, and a former military lawyer, Joseph B. Keenan, as his chief of counsel.

Article 17 mimics the modern American rule regarding the disposition of a court martial trial after a decision has been rendered by the judge. Article 17 mandated that

> The judgment will be announced in open court and will give the reasons on which it is based. The record of the trial will be transmitted directly to the Supreme Commander for the Allied Powers for his action thereon.

It was General MacArthur, not the court, who had final say as to the disposition of any defendant in any trial.

Other than the militarized aspects of the tribunal, there were other key distinctions between Nuremberg and the Tokyo trials. For instance, in the realm of evidence, perhaps learning from the experience of Nuremberg, the drafters of the IMTFE charter went even further than their peers in London, setting out in exhaustive detail the scope of material that was to be admissible before the tribunal.

Article 13: Evidence.
(a) Admissibility. The Tribunal shall not be bound by technical rules of evidence. It shall adopt and apply to the greatest possible extent expeditious and non-technical procedure, and shall admit any evidence which it deems to have probative value. All purported admissions or statements of the accused are admissible.

(b)   Relevance. The Tribunal may require to be informed of the nature of any evidence before it is offered in order to rule upon the relevance.

(c)   Specific Evidence Admissible. In particular, and without limiting in any way the scope of the foregoing general rules, the following evidence may be admitted:

(1)   A document, regardless of its security classification and without proof of its issuance or signature, which appears to the Tribunal to have been signed or issued by any officer, department, agency or member of the armed forces of any government.

(2)   A report which appears to the Tribunal to have been signed or issued by the International Red Cross or a member thereof, or by a doctor of medicine or any medical service personnel, or by an investigator or intelligence officer, or by any other person who appears to the Tribunal to have personal knowledge of the matters contained in the report.

(3)   An affidavit, deposition or other signed statement.

(4)   A diary, letter or other document, including sworn or unsworn statements which appear to the Tribunal to contain information relating to the charge.

(5)   A copy of a document or other secondary evidence of its contents, if the original is not immediately available.

While these procedural differences were important, the London Charter and the IMTFE Charter were alike in establishing a tripartite structure for defining war crimes. Article 4 of the IMTFE closely followed the London Charter's Article 6:

Jurisdiction Over Persons and Offenses. The Tribunal shall have the power to try and punish Far Eastern war criminals who as individuals or as members of organizations are charged with offenses which include Crimes against Peace.

The following acts, or any of them, are crimes coming within the jurisdiction of the Tribunal for which there shall be individual responsibility:

(a)   *Crimes against Peace:* Namely, the planning, preparation, initiation or waging of a declared or undeclared war of aggression, or a war in violation of international law, treaties, agreements or assurances, or participation in a common plan or conspiracy for the accomplishment of any of the foregoing;

(b) *Conventional War Crimes:* Namely, violations of the laws or customs of war;

(c) *Crimes against Humanity:* Namely, murder, extermination, enslavement, deportation, and other inhumane acts committed against any civilian population, before or during the war, or persecutions on political or racial grounds in execution of or in connection with any crime within the jurisdiction of the Tribunal, whether or not in violation of the domestic law of the country where perpetrated. Leaders, organizers, instigators and accomplices participating in the formulation or execution of a common plan or conspiracy to commit any of the foregoing crimes are responsible for all acts performed by any person in execution of such plan.

Unlike at Nuremberg, these three categories came to define the Tokyo trials, with various criminals brought before the tribunal labeled as Class A, B or C defendants. While nearly 6,000 Japanese were charged with B and C crimes (mostly related to prisoner abuse), the focal point of the tribunals were on the Class A suspects. Eighty Class A suspects (which included the most senior officials) were detained; 28 of them were brought before the tribunal.[26] Of these, 25 were convicted, the most famous of whom was Hideki Tojo, who served as prime minister and war minister of Japan during the war. He, along with six others, were sentenced to death. Sixteen other defendants received life sentences and two received incarceration for shorter periods.

Tojo's convictions were emblematic of many of the trials held before the tribunal, which, perhaps again due to its comparatively military style, placed a heavy focus on the waging of aggressive war. Indeed, of the dozens of charges allayed on him, he was in the end only convicted of the following:

Count 1   (waging wars of aggression, and war or wars in violation of international law)
Count 27   (waging unprovoked war against the Republic of China)
Count 29   (waging aggressive war against the United States)
Count 31   (waging aggressive war against the British Commonwealth (Hong Kong))
Count 32   (waging aggressive war against the Netherlands (Indonesia))
Count 33   (waging aggressive war against France (Indochina))
Count 54   (ordering, authorizing, and permitting inhumane treatment of prisoners of war (POWs) and others).

There were several criticisms of the Tokyo trials that emerged both immediately after their conclusion and that have become more evident as time has passed. The key criticism was shared with the Nuremberg trials. Both post-war proceedings, even if conducted in different environments and paying heed to different occupation masters, were creatures of the post–World War II world and would quickly become players in the nascent Cold War. Much as at Nuremberg, the types of crimes under the Tokyo trials' purview, the listing of potential defendants, and the final disposition of convicts were controlled, at least in part, by political concerns. General MacArthur, perhaps familiar with the difficulties the Americans had encountered with pacifying the Philippines 50 years earlier, was very concerned that the trials would lead to such discord from the Japanese that the Americans would lose the ability to erect the Japanese state as a bulwark against Soviet expansionism in East Asia.

This accounts for some of the more flagrant absences from the dock at the Tokyo trials. MacArthur became convinced that the only way he could be assured of Japanese support was if the Japanese people remained unified under the emperor and the imperial household. Emperor Hirohito would not only not be forced to abdicate, but neither he nor any member of his family would be forced to face judgment, no matter how implicated they had been in the war effort. MacArthur went even further than merely ensuring that Hirohito remained off the list of defendants. According to historians John Dower and Herbert Bix, MacArthur actively worked to protect Hirohito: MacArthur ensured that testimony provided before the Tokyo trials was often slanted to divert any culpability from Hirohito; at times, US forces holding defendants awaiting trial required them to pledge to support their sovereign during their trials and not to implicate him or his family in any misdeeds. In a sense, in order to protect Hirohito, and with him the unity of Japan, the prosecution team was charged to function not just to prosecute the accused but to simultaneously defend the emperor.[27] The resulting implicit exoneration of the royal family was a gross distortion of the truth; later evidence revealed that Hirohito was most certainly not a "pacifist pawn" in the Showa government's expansionism and violence, but an eager and active participant in it. It was largely Hirohito's absence from trial that led American diplomat George Kennan to declare that the trials were "profoundly misconceived from the start."[28]

The second absence at the Tokyo trials were many of the members of the notorious Unit 731, the medical "research" arm of the Imperial Army that undertook gruesome human experimentation during World

War II. Unit 731 was implicated in using live, human subjects for germ and biological weapons testing, conventional arms testing, and vivisection. General MacArthur, again due to Cold War realities, secretly granted the unit immunity from prosecution before the tribunal, both in exchange for the knowledge they had accrued during their experiments and in order to ensure that the Soviets did not receive such knowledge—"The value to the US of Japanese BW [biological warfare] data is of such importance to national security as to far outweigh the value accruing from 'war crimes' prosecution."[29]

The disposition of Unit 731 relates to a further lasting criticism of the Japanese trials, rather different from those at Nuremberg. Due to a constellation of factors, many of which remain in play in modern Japan, the Tokyo trials did not instigate a bout of soul searching on behalf of Japanese citizens. As such, war criminals, even those who were convicted and executed, remain for many bona fide national heroes. To this day it is an important political gesture for Japanese leaders to pay homage at the Yasukuni shrine, the final resting place of 12 Class A convicted war criminals and at least two other suspected Class A criminals. Further, many war criminals who were not executed were fully rehabilitated into society. For instance, the head of Unit 731 became president of the Japanese Medical Association, while four years after he was paroled from his war crimes conviction Mamoru Shigemitsu returned to his post as foreign minister of Japan (which he had held at the end of World War II).

While these criticisms are serious, the most famous and trenchant of criticisms of the Tokyo trials actually came from within the tribunal itself. The Indian judge appointed to serve as one of the 11 jurists was Justice Radhabinod Pal, a 60-year-old former Calcutta High Court judge who, by his own admission, arrived in Tokyo with scant knowledge of international law.[30] His contribution to the tribunal came in his voluminous dissent, refusing to find any of the defendants guilty of Class A war crimes. He wrote:

> I would hold that each and every one of the accused must be found not guilty of each and every one of the charges in the indictment and should be acquitted of all those charges.[31]

Unwittingly following the lead of Senator Taft and Justice Douglas in their rebukes of the Nuremberg trials, Pal conceded that the evidence that atrocities were perpetrated was overwhelming. His complaint, however, was with the tribunal itself, rather than whether or not evil had been conducted. He was concerned with the structure of the tribunal, the absence of any judges sharing the same citizenship as the defendants, and the lack of the tribunal's jurisdiction over any crimes committed by the Allies (notably the atomic bombing of Hiroshima and Nagasaki). He was dubious that the trial was anything but the victors exercising judicial revenge on the vanquished, and thus he was certain that the trials would not contribute to lasting peace.[32] For his words, Pal posthumously received the auspicious tribute of being honored, alongside the dozen Class A war criminals, at the Yasukuni shrine in Tokyo.

Some of Justice Pal's criticisms were likely politically, rather than judicially, informed; he was "an Asian nationalist [and] saw things very differently from the other judges."[33] He was a well known intellectual agitator for Indian independence and opposed to colonialism or anything that smacked of Western influence over Asia, which he saw in the American occupation of Japan. Thus it might be possible to legally discount Pal's more extreme conclusions, such as his refusal to concede that any aspect of the Japanese war effort was offensive and that the United States somehow baited Japan into launching its December 1941 surprise attack on Pearl Harbor. However, some of Pal's complaints were on much firmer legal grounding, and some of the criticisms continue to hold true in modern tribunals. It is rare for any judge sitting in a tribunal to share the nationality of any defendant; it is rare for the crimes of all sides to be under equal examination in a tribunal, especially if some crimes were committed by outside "Super Powers"; and it is uncertain whether such tribunals always contribute to lasting peace in a conflict-scarred region. However, these criticisms have been taken seriously, especially more recently, with the domestication of war crimes trials and the addition of non-punitive, truth commission processes either augmenting or replacing punitive justice.

4 The Cold War and the rise of domestic international justice

While in recent years globalization has rendered the line between the domestic and international increasingly hard to discern, law has long been seen as at least partly resistant to the trend. As sectors of society ranging from the economy to the academy have been busily, and often willingly, universalizing, law has been a comparative bastion of particularism. After all domestic law has unique characteristics and inherent frictions that can serve to shield local regulation from internationalizing pressures. For instance, there is the fact that in most cases it is a domestic legislature charged with passing laws and lawmakers are usually responsive to their local constituents rather than an international clientele. Consequently, municipal laws will only be as "international" as domestic constituents demand.

On the more extreme end of the spectrum, it must be noted that unlike with the increasingly arguably anarchical global flows of information and other goods, those who rail against the globalization of domestic law often have significant powers to actually enforce their concerns. Though there is some question whether they are effective, laws can be written to limit the encroachment of internationalism, and domestic judicial thinkers who welcome globalization in their work can even potentially be removed from public legal roles.[1]

Despite this, and the fact that many major states appear to be entering an era of guarded interactions with the world, if not isolationism, it is evident that the divide between international and domestic law is receding, even if not as fast as the rest of society is globalizing. The reach of transnational European Union regulations into the domestic laws of its member states is a powerful instance of this, but so too is the increasing internationalization of domestic law itself. For instance, a justice from the US Supreme Court—which is charged with the interpretation of the US Constitution—noted that in recent years the court's docket has included cases concerning Ecuadorian plaintiffs, Dutch defendants, the Warsaw Convention, and the "European cartel authority."[2] Similarly global dockets have appeared throughout the world. This internationalization has led judges, even when faced with complicated, yet seemingly strictly "domestic" matters, increasingly to look to other jurisdictions for ideas, if not precedent.[3]

IHL has not been immune from this trend, and the adoption, if not legal incorporation, of IHL (or IHL-like laws) into municipal codes has been marked. This chapter will begin the examination of the cross-fertilization of international and domestic law as it relates to IHL, and will demonstrate that while "globalization" may be a new trend, aspects of such legal globalization in the IHL arena have been present for decades, if not longer.

The international in the domestic; the domestic in the international

An initial explanation is in order regarding domestic pursuit of international justice, which began in earnest after World War II and has continued today. One could reasonably ask: "are not domestic courts practicing domestic law; and, if so, how can these trials be included in an analysis of prosecutions under international law?" Indeed, the separation between domestic and international law maintains and is an important analytical, if not practical, buffer. L. C. Green, the great international legal theorist, goes even further in arguing what domestic courts are actually allowed to do when dealing with international law:

> if a country uses in its national criminal law a definition that only partly meets the conditions of international law ... , the courts of that country would only be entitled to try those whose actions fall within its own definition, although it might well be that the country concerned might have breached its international obligations by adopting so narrow a definition.[4]

In short, domestic law trumps and a trial in any domestic institution will pay heed to domestic law which may or may not fall in line with relevant international codes.

This observation is accurate for some but not all nations, and arguably increasingly less so for those states to which it has not applied. First, some jurisdictions have always included international law in their domestic law; such states, like Belgium, are known to international lawyers as "monist" states and are defined by the fact they automatically incorporate international law into national law.[5] Monists see no distinction between international and domestic laws; the two bodies of law are part of the same whole. Contrarily, "dualist" states are more in line with those described by Green, and it is in those states that international law is only a part of domestic law "to the extent that national measures so provide."[6]

However even in famously dualist states, such as the United States, the United Kingdom, and Australia, the line between international and domestic law is not as clear as Green suggests. As Australian High Court justice Michael Kirby has noted, there is a growing "rapprochement between international and national law."[7] Some of this "rapprochement" is actually centuries old; for instance in the United States, despite the supremacy of the Constitution, Congress is given power (under the Constitution's Article 1, Section 8) "to define and punish ... offenses against the laws of nations." The federal "Alien Tort Claims Act," passed by the first Congress in 1789, relies explicitly on this power.[8] Though 200 years of jurisprudence has not definitively determined what the framers meant by "laws of nations," a commonly, and long-stated view is that the "laws of nations" refers to some sort of code above domestic laws, ranging from the will of the global populace—that which has been "universally proclaimed by all nations"[9]—to the "laws of nature."[10] More recently, the stated goal of some US domestic legislation has been to further domestic jurisdiction over defined international crime. For instance, the 1998 International Crime Control Act was designed to "substantially improve the ability of US law enforcement agencies to investigate *and prosecute* international criminals."[11]

The allowance of the international into the domestic criminal code is also evident in jurisprudence. Much to the chagrin of some, US courts have regularly cited foreign domestic and international cases in their decisions,[12] and US courts have at times consented to handling strictly international criminal claims. Thus, when United States Supreme Court justice Frank Murphy issued his dissent in *Yamashita* (see below), he stated that the case was "not dealing with an ordinary tort or criminal action [but with] an international crime";[13] importantly his disagreement with the majority was not due to a lack of jurisdiction to hear the "international" matter but with substantive elements of the trial below.

More recently, some US courts have gone even further. In the 2003 case *Talisman of Sudan v. Talisman Energy*, a federal court relied on international jurisprudence in its conclusion, citing to "international law," the statutes of the ICTY, ICTR and ICC, and noted that "jurisprudence of the ICTY and ICTR is increasingly being consulted by [US] courts."[14]

As much as the international has been incorporated into the domestic, we see a similar incorporation of the domestic into the international. For instance, as Cassese notes regarding the ICTY case *Furundžija*:[15]

In that case, after surveying international treaties and cases to establish whether there existed any rule of customary international law defining rape, [the] Trial Chamber … embarked upon an examination of [various] national legislation[s] in order to identify a possible common definition of that offense.[16]

In essence, the tribunal was searching for guidance on international law in domestic codes.

The second difficulty with the supposed strict separation between the domestic and the international is that some international law is explicitly designed to be enforced, at least in part, by national courts. Mentioned earlier is the Genocide Convention, which, though an international regulation, places the primary burden of its enforcement on domestic tribunals.

And, finally, Green's criticism does not recognize that domestic courts and laws are increasingly becoming internationalized. Many of the nations that ratify the Rome Statute for the ICC, for example, incorporate the international crimes mentioned in that statute into their *domestic* codes. Indeed, one of the goals of the International Criminal Court is to have domestic entities be the primary prosecutors of these crimes, and for the international body to only step in on a "complementary" basis—hence the principle of "complementarity" discussed in greater detail below in reference to the ICC. This internationalization has occurred not just as a result of Rome; as will also be discussed, some states have chosen to more fully embrace international law in the domestic canon, while others have been slowly compelled and cajoled by international pressure to incorporate piecemeal aspects of international law and procedure into their domestic criminal codes.

The result is that domestic courts have long been, and continue to be, one of the most vibrant and active locations for the furtherance of international justice. But, this does not mean that domestic trials have been without difficulties or controversies of their own. Domestic international justice brings with it different problems than internationalized proceedings, but problems nonetheless.

Domestic trials for international crimes after World War II and before the Cold War (1945–50)

While the Nuremberg and Tokyo trials are more famous, the majority of defendants prosecuted for war crimes after World War II were tried in other countries, by either regular domestic judiciaries or specially convened bodies charged with addressing the international (and at times domestic) crimes charged. Historically, in some respects it could be said that the mass, unprecedented international trials at Nuremberg and Tokyo were originally conceived as afterthoughts. The main avenue for prosecutions, planned throughout the war, was always going to be domestic judiciaries.

Evidence for this comes from the United Nations War Crimes Commission (UNWCC), an organization that bore the "United Nations" name some two years before the UN was even established at the San Francisco conference. The UNWCC was formed in October 1943 and arose out of a meeting held at the British Foreign Office in London. Seventeen nations were represented: Australia, Belgium, Canada, China, Czechoslovakia, France, Greece, India, Luxembourg, the Netherlands, New Zealand, Norway, Poland, South Africa, the United Kingdom, the United States of America, and Yugoslavia. These member states charged the new agency with "receiving information about war crimes, developing and recording evidence, identifying the persons responsible, and referring cases to the *Governments* concerned for legal action."[17] There was no talk of international tribunals.

Though the UNWCC would also come to aid in the work of the Nuremberg and Tokyo trials, the quantity of material it amassed in its six short years of operations, and the appetite among many of the major and minor Allies to prosecute as many as possible, meant that the majority of the UNWCC material would come to aid domestic trials prosecuting violations of international law, rather than the international trials. The official record for the UNWCC files held at UN archives illustrates how much evidence the body obtained:

> Records consist of minutes of the Commission and its committees, 1943–48, published by the Commission and its committees; records of the Research Office, 1944–49, primarily reports, bulletins, and other printed documents, including photographs, about war crimes, and books and documents collected by the Research Office for use in investigation; files of charges submitted by member governments against ca. 40,000 German, Italian, Bulgarian, Albanian, Hungarian, Romanian, and Japanese war criminals, suspects, and material witnesses.

The UNWCC prepared "80 lists, naming war criminals, suspects and material witnesses, some 36,529 persons and 281 groups—about a quarter of them (an estimated ten thousand persons) were brought to trial"[18] for crimes committed in Europe and the Far East in the era immediately following World War II (1945–50). Again the vast majority were held outside the confines of the international tribunals. Some noteworthy highlights of such trials include the American military tribunals which held 809 trials in both Germany and Japan involving 1,600 defendants; the British held 524 trials involving 937 defendants; and the French tried 2,107 individuals; the Soviet Union and the Chinese communist forces also held an unknown number of trials against Japanese war criminals.[19] Others were tried before Belgian courts, as well as courts in Denmark, Luxembourg, the Netherlands, Norway, Greece, Yugoslavia and the Philippines (which included the famous *Kuroda v. Jalandoni* trial[20]). Indeed, few countries involved in the war failed to have any trials.

Some of the most momentous of the war crimes cases arguably came out of the domestic prosecutions, rather than the international ones. The "Hostage Case,"[21] noteworthy in part for its clear definition of what an international crime is, was a case held by a US military tribunal in "subsequent" hearings to Nuremberg. The "Yamashita Standard" which marked an important evolution in defining command responsibility emerged from the war crimes trial of Japanese general Tomoyuki Yamashita (see below), a trial held by US military forces, not the international tribunals.[22] It was a Dutch court sitting in Batavia, Indonesia that provided the only post-war convictions of Japanese soldiers regarding the forced prostitution of "comfort women,"[23] a precedent that helped shape later international law regarding rapes and forced pregnancy. And due to General MacArthur's grant of immunity from prosecution before the Tokyo trials, the primary legal retribution exacted on the Imperial Army's notorious Unit 731 was in domestic trials, notably at the hands of the Soviet Union's December 1949 Khabarovsk war crime trials.[24]

The domestic trials were of such scope, and recorded such relative success, that some commentators even used them as levers to criticize the international efforts at Nuremberg and Tokyo. One observer argued that the success of the domestic war crimes trials suggested that "adequate law existed for the punishment of atrocities committed during the war" without resort to novel legal theories and institutions.[25]

While there certainly were successes, the diversity of models for prosecuting war criminals on the domestic plane makes it somewhat difficult to assess how fair or just the trials actually were. And there remains some concern that at least some of the trials were more about securing convictions than any true concern for "justice." The *Yamashita* case is often mentioned in this regard. Yamashita was a successful Japanese field commander during World War II, who had managed to lead Japanese forces in the capture of Malaya and Singapore before being assigned to defend the Philippines during the last days of the war. Yamashita's men, in their occupation of captured territories, exercised a brutal regime which included mass executions (such as the Sook Ching Massacre and the Manila Massacre, which together took the lives of as many as 150,000 civilians), starvation, clubbing, burning alive and other indignities amassed on Allied troops and citizens on the ground.

Yamashita surrendered with his forces in September 1945 and was taken into US custody. A US military tribunal was convened in Manila under the direction of General William Styer, the US commander for the Western Pacific. During the last three months of 1945 the tribunal tried General Yamashita, accusing him of war crimes associated with the actions of men under his command. The end result of *In re Yamishita*, as the case came to be known, was the general's conviction and the development of a much higher standard for command responsibility than had theretofore been accepted. What was unique about *Yamishita*, from the perspective of war crimes, was that not only did the defense not contest that the war crimes were committed, but the prosecution did not actually charge the general with having committed any war crime or crime against humanity. Instead, he was charged with an omission of action to prevent his men's behavior, rather than any commission. Yamashita protested that not only did he not participate in the actions that underlay his charges, but also he was unaware that his men were undertaking them. The judges chastised him for his ignorance, holding that if

> there is no effective attempt by a commander to discover and control ... criminal acts [of his subordinates], such a commander may be held responsible, even criminally liable.[26]

The case was appealed to the US Supreme Court, which further fleshed out the standard. The court argued that international law, through the law of war, "presupposes that [violations of the law of war] are to be avoided through the control of the operations of war by commanders who to some extent are responsible for their subordinates."[27] The court believed that absent such a duty upon commanders, nothing would prevent occupying forces from committing atrocities upon the civilian population. The court held that General Yamashita was, by virtue of his position as commander of the Japanese forces in the Philippines, under an "affirmative duty to take such measures as were within his power and appropriate in the circumstances to protect prisoners of war and the civilian population."[28]

It is noteworthy that vociferous dissents were filed by two justices, Murphy and Rutledge, who protested about the process of the trial, and procedural irregularities throughout.[29]

In addition to some questions about the fairness of domestic trials, it is telling that even domestic judges and leaders were not immune to the wider global political realities that plagued their international judicial brethren. In its quest for completeness, the UNWCC had collected information on not just more war crimes and war criminals than could possibly be convicted, but also on more war crimes and criminals than many wished to see in the dock. Such was the case regarding the UNWCC's tense relationship with the government of Ethiopia. The UNWCC refused to invite the Ethiopians to be full members of the commission but agreed to accept a large dossier of files amassed concerning Italian war crimes committed in Ethiopia. These files contained information about the use of poison gas, the maltreatment of political prisoners, and other flagrant violations, along with testimony from survivors and witnesses, and the smoking gun of telegrams between Mussolini and his minister in Ethiopia and other recorded Italian orders implicating Rome and Italian troops in motley crimes. The Ethiopians had established, and the UNWCC concurred, that a prima facie case could be made against at least two senior Italian leaders, Pietro Badoglio and Rodolfo Graziani.[30] Ethiopia requested their extradition, but the request was never heeded; both marshals were protected by the West's desire to placate the Italian population and maintain a strong bulwark against the Soviet expansion seen across the Adriatic and rising domestically in the increasingly powerful Italian Communist Party. The same Cold War concerns that limited the scope of the Nuremberg and Tokyo trials thus served to limit the possibility of domestic proceedings. This problem of absent or unavailable defendants would prove deleterious to domestic prosecutions throughout the Cold War; though, as will be seen in the case of Adolf Eichmann, some states used extreme means to solve this difficulty and allow trials when the wider world community was seemingly content not to.

Cold War trials (1950–89)

Even though the UN, in General Assembly Resolution 95 "[a]ffirmed the principles of international law recognized by the Charter of the Nuremberg Tribunal and the Judgment of the Tribunal," and asked the International Law Commission to proceed with its examination of the potential for a permanent international criminal court, the Cold War stalled the international process. Despite this, domestic prosecutions continued after 1950, both in states that had prosecuted international crimes in the immediate aftermath of World War II, and, even more noteworthy, in other states who saw fit to pursue perpetrators of World War II crimes. Important additions in this regard were prosecutions (and stalled prosecutions) in Israel, Canada, Australia, France, and perhaps most notably, in West Germany.

Different states recorded different kinds of success and failure in their trials; the institutions used were various and the problems encountered ranged from the prosaic to the crucial. Outside political forces played important roles in many countries, as did the unique experiences of the various states that embarked on prosecutions. For instance, in France the Vichy occupation would prove an impenetrable overhang to its trials, while in Israel the Holocaust survivors who made up much of its judiciary when it undertook trials would prove destabilizing to the notions of a detached, dispassionate judicial system. The West Germans, meanwhile, had a difficult time converting their trials into educational tools for forcing the German populace to come to terms with the then recent past. While the World War II experience played a central role in domestic trials throughout the Cold War (and even today), toward the end of the Cold War other states, often inspired by Nuremberg, became active in pursuing justice for other international crimes that occurred after 1945; the junta trials in Argentina and the beginnings of such trials in Chile are seminal aspects of this trend.

Israel

The most celebrated of the domestic Cold War cases was that of Adolf Eichmann, a senior Nazi figure who escaped Europe after World War II. Eichmann's storied trial began in Jerusalem in April 1961. The proceedings were noteworthy not just for the substantial role that the defendant had played in committing crimes and thus the light that the prosecution shed on the mechanics of the "Final Solution," but also for the manner in which his attendance at the trial was assured. Eichmann had not been captured by the Israelis on their territory, nor had he been lawfully extradited from his residence (in Argentina). Rather, the Israeli government authorized an operation to kidnap Eichmann from the streets of Buenos Aires and to secret him to Israel. This solved the problem that the Ethiopians had faced with absent Italian war criminals, but it engendered significant other problems,[31] many under international law.

First, the Argentines complained vociferously, arguing that the Israeli action was a blatant violation of its sovereignty. Israeli Prime Minister David Ben-Gurion announced Eichmann's capture by "the security services"[32] on 23 May 1960. The "security services" were thought to have been from Israel's Central Bureau of Intelligence and Security (Mossad). Immediately after the announcement, which was met by a standing ovation in the Israeli parliament, Argentina submitted a formal protest to Israel, demanded Eichmann's return and the punishment by Israel of those responsible. Interestingly from the perspective of international law, the Argentines addressed Israel's concerns about Eichmann's involvement in the Holocaust, contending that if Israel complied with its request Argentina could arrange for Eichmann's extradition "through means contemplated by international law." However, extradition for the crime of genocide would either have to be to Germany, where the crimes took place, or to an international court.[33]

Even the Israelis were clearly somewhat uncomfortable with the precedent that their actions may have set (which, in the words of the Argentines could, if repeated, upset the entire international order[34]), and proceeded to backtrack from Ben-Gurion's claims. The Israelis at first revoked Prime Minister Ben-Gurion's admission that state agents had seized Eichmann, alternatively contending in a 3 June 1960 *note verbale* to Buenos Aires that Eichmann had consented to his removal to Israel, and/or that the removal was not an official act of the state of Israel but rather an act of independent parties partisan to the cause of justice for Eichmann.[35] Argentina was unswayed and after being unable to receive redress via bilateral negotiations with Israel, Argentina requested the United Nations Security Council (UNSC) convene an urgent meeting to discuss the matter.

Throughout June 22 and 23 the UNSC debated the issue, in the end passing Security Council Resolution 138, a masterfully compromised position that respected both the importance of Argentina's claims and the unique situation that resulted from the enormity of Eichmann's crimes. The resolution concluded with the UNSC stating that it:

1 Declares that acts such as that under consideration which affect the sovereignty of a Member State and therefore cause international friction, may, if repeated, endanger international peace and security;
2 Requests the Government of Israel to make appropriate reparations in accordance with the Charter of the United Nations and the rules of international law.
3 Expresses the hope that the traditionally friendly relations between Argentina and Israel will be advanced.[36]

The resolution quickly removed the issue from the wider world's consciousness, and after a few months of strained relations, the Israelis and Argentines resumed their normal diplomatic relations (during the height of the disagreement Argentina had recalled its ambassador to Israel). Eichmann remained in Israel.

However, legal problems were more than the public international law problems of inter-state relations. Rather, for those wishing to prosecute Eichmann there were a host of other hurdles. First, though the Security Council did not explicitly state that Eichmann's capture was illegal, those who maintained that it was asked how any resulting trial could be legal. Argentina made a similar argument in its war of words with Israel, stating that it "could not allow a crime to be judged as a direct result of the violation of Argentina's rights [i.e. an illegality]."[37]

His capture aside, an additional difficulty was one of jurisdiction; under what basis could Israeli law and an Israeli court be said to have the right to prosecute Eichmann? After all, "Israel" as a juridical entity did not exist until May 1948, three years after the fall of the Third Reich. All of the crimes of the Holocaust took place before there was any Israeli law. And yet, the Israelis planned to undertake a domestic trial against Eichmann, in the Jerusalem District Court, under the auspices of an Israeli-law mandated three-judge panel, and run, more or less, under Israeli criminal procedures. The only clear concession to the international realm would be the presence of four translators simultaneously rendering the proceedings into Hebrew, French, English, and German.

The legal basis for the charges allayed against Eichmann—four counts regarded crimes against the Jewish people, eight concerned crimes against humanity, and one alleged war crimes—was also domestic and rested on the Israeli state's Nazi and Nazi Collaborators (Punishment) Law, one of the first pieces of legislation the state passed upon its formation.[38] The law provided an extensive basis for finding liability, evidently borrowing language and concepts from the statutes of the Nuremberg and Tokyo trials that preceded it,[39] while adding specific protections for crimes against the Jewish people. In relevant parts in stated:

Nazis and Nazi Collaborators—Punishment—Law—5710—1950[40]
1. (a) A person who has committed one of the following offences—
    (1) done, during the period of the Nazi regime, in an enemy country, an act constituting a crime against the Jewish people;
    (2) done, during the period of the Nazi regime, in an enemy country, an act constituting a crime against humanity;

(3) done, during the period of the Second World War, in an enemy country, an act constituting a war crime, is liable to the death penalty.

(b) In this section—"crime against the Jewish people" means any of the following acts, committed with intent to destroy the Jewish people in whole or in part:

(1) killing Jews;

(2) causing serious bodily or mental harm to Jews;

(3) placing Jews in living conditions calculated to bring about their physical destruction;

(4) imposing measures intended to prevent births among Jews;

(5) forcibly transferring Jewish children to another national or religious group;

(6) destroying or desecrating Jewish religious or cultural assets or values;

(7) inciting to hatred of Jews;

"crime against humanity" means any of the following acts:

murder, extermination, enslavement, starvation or deportation and other inhumane acts committed against any civilian population, and persecution on national, racial, religious or political grounds;

"war crime" means any of the following acts:

murder, ill-treatment or deportation to forced labour or for any other purpose, of civilian population of or in occupied territory; murder or ill-treatment of prisoners of war or persons on the seas; killing of hostages; plunder of public or private property; wanton destruction of cities, towns or villages; and devastation not justified by military necessity.

[...]

Membership in an enemy organisation.

3. (a) A person who, during the period of the Nazi regime, in an enemy country, was a member of, or held any post or exercised any function in, an enemy organisation is liable to imprisonment for a term not exceeding seven years.

(b) In this section, "enemy organisation" means—
  (1) a body of persons which, under article 9 of the Charter
  of the International Military Tribunal, annexed to the
  Four-Power Agreement of the 8th August, 1945, on the
  trial of the major war criminals, has been declared, by a
  judgment of that Tribunal, to be a criminal organisation; (2) any other body of persons which existed in an
  enemy country and the object or one of the objects of
  which was to carry out or assist in carrying out actions
  of an enemy administration directed against persecuted
  persons.
  […]

The Eichmann defense team made much of the fact that the law was not
only written after Eichmann's charged crimes took place, but in its own
language specifically referred to crimes that occurred before the state of
Israel was created. Section 16 of the law defines the Nazi period (during
which time crimes under its jurisdiction had to be committed) as concluding on 8 May 1945, almost exactly three years before the state's
declaration of independence. Eichmann's defense argued inter alia that
to prosecute Eichmann in such a fashion was contrary to international
law, a clear case of ex post facto law-making and enforcement, and a
violation of the *nullum crimen* principle; his appeal focused almost entirely
on this issue. However, in a famous passage from its judgment, the district
court (later affirmed by the Israeli Supreme Court) illustrated the Israeli
view regarding the role of international law in domestic courtrooms when
issues of international justice are at stake. Speaking of the Nazi and Nazi
Collaborators (Punishment) Law, the judges responded to critics of
both the legality of Eichmann's capture and of his trial, and said that:

> [t]he abhorrent crimes defined in this Law are not crimes under Israeli
> law alone. These crimes, which struck at the whole of mankind
> and shocked the conscience of nations, are grave offences against
> the laws of nations itself (*delicta juris gentium*). Therefore, so far
> from international law negating or limiting jurisdiction or countries
> with respect to such crimes, international law is, in the absence of
> an International Court, in need of the judicial and legislative
> organs of every country to give effect to its criminal interdictions
> and to bring the criminals to trial.[41]

Picking up on these concepts, some supporters of Israel went further,
explicitly invoking the piracy analogy (addressed earlier in this book);

acts of piracy, like the Nazi crimes, were international crimes and thus Israel had both jurisdiction and a mandate to try such crimes equal to that of any other state.[42] Such supporters could even cite to the Moscow Declaration of 1943 which held, in part, that the Nazi crimes did not take place in any "specific geographical locality."[43]

The *Eichmann* trial saw not just the internationalization of domestic law (via the international crimes Eichmann was accused of), but also the internationalization of domestic criminal process. As historian Stephen Landsman has noted, though Israeli procedures were purportedly in place throughout the trial, "Nuremberg had a dramatic influence on the Eichmann prosecution."[44] The interplay between the Nuremberg prosecutions and the *Eichmann* trial was present throughout the proceedings: proof originating at Nuremberg was offered to the Jerusalem court, statements and testimony that appeared at Nuremberg were directly offered into evidence in Jerusalem, and the prosecution even called a presiding judge from the Nuremberg trials, Michael Musmanno, to testify as to his conversation with Hermann Göring which had implicated Eichmann.

As Musmanno's testimony may suggest, the rules of evidence at the *Eichmann* trial were, as in Nuremberg, relaxed. Section 15 of the Nazis and Nazi Collaborators (Punishment) Law explicitly allows that "[i]n an action for an offence under this Law, the court may deviate from the rules of evidence if it is satisfied that this will promote the ascertainment of the truth and the just handling of the case." Evidence allowed in the *Eichmann* trial represented an even further departure from the normal "rules of evidence" than was seen even at Nuremberg.

On 11 December 1961 Eichmann was pronounced guilty and four days later was sentenced to death. Eichmann appealed to the Israeli Supreme Court, recycling some of his defense team's arguments regarding jurisdiction and the illegality of his capture. On 28 May 1962 his appeal was rejected, and he was put to death on 1 June.

Criticisms of the *Eichmann* case have been copious and multifaceted. Most famous among the critics, Hannah Arendt argued that the prosecutors had theatricalized the trial for political ends—memorializing the Holocaust and promoting Zionism.[45] Others have had related problems with bias. Landsman lists a large number of such concerns: The defense operated in a highly hostile public environment, from the moment of the announcement of Eichmann's capture through to the final verdict on appeal. Newspapers from across the political spectrum editorialized incessantly about the need to prosecute Eichmann, and Israel's president—the normally apolitical head of state—along with several other senior officials made damning and damaging remarks about the accused. Added to this environment were unfair processes which arguably denied the defense full legal protections. The rules of evidence were bent and relaxed to such a degree that many observers remarked that the trial became unfocused as judges allowed witnesses to tell their tales of Holocaust survival, in engrossing detail, even if their stories were irrelevant to the issue of Eichmann's guilt. The availability of witnesses for the defense was also limited with the attorney general stating that some of Eichmann's proposed witnesses, such as Erich von dem Bach-Zelewski and Edmund Veesenmayer, were also suspected Nazis and would be arrested if they attempted entry into Israel, even if only to participate in the trial.[46]

In a sense, the *Eichmann* trial (and subsequent trials of past abusers brought before a court of the abused—see, for instance, the Saddam Hussein trial discussed later) represented the opposite problem to that seen in the domestic trials after World War I. There it was argued that states bringing their own into the dock will be overly kind and deferential. However, bringing a former enemy into the dock, the courts will be unbendingly harsh. And indeed, Eichmann's primary defense counsel, Robert Servatius, summed up many of his concerns on this matter by referencing the unique nature of Israel as both the protector of the Jewish people and as made up in large part of Holocaust survivors. Servatius was concerned about prejudice on behalf of judges, prosecutors and others in the system because they or "near relatives of theirs were harmed by the acts brought forward in the charges."[47]

Israel followed the *Eichmann* trial several years later with another celebrated proceeding, that against John Demjanjuk, accused of being "Ivan the Terrible," a sadistic concentration camp guard. On 16 February 1987, John Demjanjuk appeared before the Israeli Supreme Court. One year earlier the retired Cleveland autoworker had had his US citizenship stripped and been extradited to Israel. To many observers the scene of Demjanjuk awaiting judgment before the court and in front of a nation of rapt viewers bore an uncanny resemblance to the *Eichmann* trial. Demjanjuk, however, despite being positively identified by nearly a dozen Holocaust survivors and being found guilty of committing extraordinarily savage acts of violence during the war, was released and returned to the United States, his American citizenship reinstated.[48]

The Israeli Supreme Court exonerated the defendant, despite the fact that the prosecution demonstrated that he was a Nazi death camp guard. The problem was that the state did not meet its burden of showing beyond a reasonable doubt that Demjanjuk was the *specific* Nazi death camp guard he was accused of being. There remained some doubt as to whether he was "Ivan the Terrible" who held murderous sway at Treblinka from 1942–43, or another guard who served with equal violence during a similar period at Sobibor, Majdanek, and Flossenberg. It was the problem that the British and the Americans had been concerned about at Nuremberg—the defendant was given "too much" process.[49]

France

The Nazi occupation of France and the post-war revelations of substantial levels of cooperation (if not complicity) on behalf of many French citizens in the Vichy government left France in an awkward position after the war. This, combined with the Cold War and concerns about damaging the still-nascent Fourth (and then Fifth) Republic led the state to hold off on war crimes trials for decades.

When France finally did act, in the late 1980s against Klaus Barbie, the resulting trial represented a classic mix of domestic and international law, and proved an affirmation not just of French rule of law, but also of the rectitude of the Nuremberg decisions 40 years earlier. As Nicholas Doman, an observer of the Barbie trial, and an assistant prosecutor at Nuremberg, noted "[w]ithout the application of international law ... the proceedings against [Barbie] would have been different."[50] "Different" is an understatement; without resort to international understandings, and an allowance by French courts to defer to international judgments, the trial may not have taken place at all.

Klaus Barbie was the head of the Gestapo in Lyon, and the brutality of his reign earned him the sobriquet "the Butcher of Lyon." The scope and savagery of his crimes were legion, and included torture, murder and deportation of Jews (and others) to face certain death at Auschwitz. Through various machinations Barbie managed to escape justice in the years after the war, moving with his family to South America in 1951. His absence did not stop the Permanent Tribunal of the Armed Forces of Lyon from trying him, in absentia, for war crimes and other delicts. He was tried and convicted twice, once in 1952 (sentenced to death for war crimes) and again in 1954. These cases would provide a challenge 30 years later when Barbie actually appeared before French justice.

After World War II, and in light of both the seeming rehabilitation of some Nazi officials to high positions in European states, and the existence of numerous others who escaped justice altogether by absconding to locales such as South America, a generation of "Nazi hunters" emerged to track down Nazis and expose them for the past crimes. Serge and Beate Klarsfeld, French Nazi hunters, had heard rumors about Barbie's residence in Peru as early as 1971. The Klarsfelds convinced the French government to pursue his extradition in Peru, compelling Barbie to escape to Bolivia (where he had befriended members of the junta running the country). Despite a personal admonishment from French president Georges Pompidou to the Bolivian leader, it was only upon the end of Bolivian military rule and the rise of the Hernán Siles Zuazo government in 1983 that Barbie was finally arrested and extradited. Barbie's trial in France would not begin until May 1987.

Barbie was called before a French court in Lyon under an indictment for crimes against humanity. The law he was charged under was a French regulation, Law No. 64–1326 enacted on 26 December 1964. This was also an internationalized domestic law, but it internationalized jurisdiction in a different manner than some other states. The law explicitly incorporated both the London Charter and the UN Resolution that affirmed the charter and the judgments of Nuremberg. As such, the French understandings of war crimes and crimes against humanity (the two charges Barbie faced) were identical to the understandings at Nuremberg.[51]

French law allows civil parties to join a criminal case, and numerous parties joined in against Barbie: survivors, spouses, children of victims. French law was even changed to specifically allow organizations to join the civil suit.[52]

Though the French trial faced several challenges, the initial hurdle that needed to be overcome regarded the question of statute of limitations. Under French law, war crimes carried with them a 10-year statute of limitations, thus putting Barbie's war crimes out of reach. However, under Law No. 64–1326, crimes against humanity, in line with Nuremberg's findings, were not subject to statutes of limitations. So, the prosecution had to show that Barbie's crimes were crimes against humanity, not war crimes. In this regard, the Barbie trial offered an important expansion of the notion of crimes against humanity. The French Cour de Cassation ruled that

> Inhumane acts and persecution which were perpetrated in a systematic way in the name of the state practicing a political system of ideological hegemony not only against persons belonging to a racial or religious community but also against the adversaries of this political system, whatever form their opposition takes, are crimes against humanity.[53]

A consequence of this finding was that Barbie's acts against almost all French people during the war—including the Jews and members of the

French Resistance (most famously against Jean Moulin)—were all cast as crimes against humanity.

The second difficulty was related to the trials conducted in the 1950s against an absent Barbie. Most countries, including France, have a rule against "double jeopardy," which holds that one can only be tried for a crime once. International tribunals have also usually incorporated such protections. Barbie argued that his 1987 trial was merely a replay of the two trials against him years earlier. However, the court avoided this charge and managed to "find" that the 1987 trial had different victims and encompassed slightly different crimes than did those under examination in the 1950's.

The Barbie trial was similar to Eichmann's in the degree it was sensationalized. Jacques Vergès served as Barbie's defense counsel; Vergès would come to be famous for defending so many accused war criminals and other international villains (terrorist Carlos the Jackal and Slobodan Milosevic to name two) that he became known as "Terror's Advocate."[54] Vergès took advantage of the intense spotlight not just to highlight the procedural and legal errors amassed against his client, but also to posit the sensationalist, yet irrelevant argument that Barbie's crimes, if they existed, were no worse than the crimes of European colonialists being committed throughout the world.

Vergès arguments were to no avail. On 4 July, Barbie was convicted of committing crimes against humanity and sentenced to life in prison. Barbie's appeal, which in part also rested on international law, when he claimed that the lower court failed to comply with Article 8 of the Nuremberg Charter (about mitigation for actions), was rejected. Barbie died of leukemia four years later while in prison.

The Barbie trial set the stage for further trials against other wartime actors, some of which extended into the post–Cold War era. Proceedings against Maurice Papon were perhaps the most emotionally charged of these trials due to Papon's post-war activities. Papon had managed to effectively excise his work for the Vichy government rising to heights in French post-war government, eventually serving as prefect of Paris police and in the government of President Valéry Giscard d'Estaing. Charles de Gaulle even awarded him the Legion of Honor. Evidence of his wrongdoing emerged in the 1980s, again thanks in part to the Nazi-hunting Klarsfelds. Throughout the 1980s and 1990s Papon filed several suits alleging defamation, losing them all. He was indicted and his trial commenced in October 1997. He was convicted in 1998 and sentenced to 10 years in prison. Inexplicably, the 88-year-old managed to elude police (after already being in custody) and fled to Switzerland under an assumed name. He was extradited by the Swiss in 1999 and took up residence in a Paris prison.[55]

A March 2002 law, however, would allow his release. Proposed by Bernard Kouchner, then minister of health (and subsequently foreign minister in the Sarkozy government) the law mandated the release of ill and elderly prisoners in order to receive medical care. Doctors testified that Papon was incapacitated and he was released from prison in September 2002. Papon died in 2007.

Canada

Canada's brief experience with war crimes trials reveals similar problems with "process." For much of its post–World War II existence, Canada chose not to address any questions of war crimes, even those that may have been committed by some who migrated to Canada after the war. The Canadians had started a process of war crimes shortly after World War II, but the United Kingdom had asked Ottawa to "dispose of the past as quickly as possible" and cease all such trials "in view of future political developments in Germany."[56] Again, the beginnings of the Cold War stymied attempts. Nothing would be done for 45 years.

In 1980 a German-born Canadian who had come to Canada after the war was extradited to West Germany for trial, accused of leading the liquidation of the Kovno ghetto in Lithuania. In the process of his extradition hearings information was revealed suggesting that there could be hundreds of Nazis who had escaped to Canada. In 1985 Prime Minister Brian Mulroney ordered a Commission of Inquiry on War Crimes which resulted a year later in the enactment of Criminal Code Section 7 (3.71). This law provided for a radical extension of Canadian criminal jurisdiction both geographically—reaching almost any war crime and crime against humanity committed globally, and temporally—reflecting that it was explicitly promulgated with past Nazi war crimes in mind.[57]

The new code provided that:

(3.71) Notwithstanding anything in this Act or any other Act, every person who, either before or after the coming into force of this subsection, commits an act or omission outside Canada that constitutes a war crime or a crime against humanity and that, if committed in Canada, would constitute an offence against the laws of Canada in force at the time of the act or omission shall be deemed to commit that act or omission in Canada at that time if,

(a) at the time of the act or omission,
    (i) that person is a Canadian citizen or is employed by Canada in a civilian or military capacity,

(ii) that person is a citizen of, or is employed in a civilian or military capacity by, a state that is engaged in an armed conflict against Canada, or

(iii) the victim of the act or omission is a Canadian citizen or a citizen of a state that is allied with Canada in an armed conflict; or

(b) at the time of the act or omission, Canada could, in conformity with international law, exercise jurisdiction over the person with respect to the act or omission on the basis of the person's presence in Canada and, subsequent to the time of the act or omission, the person is present in Canada.

This was yet another example of domestic law looking outward, toward international crimes, the goal of which was recognized by the Canadian Supreme Court when it was asked to rule on the issue:

> Parliament intended to extend the arm of Canada's criminal law in order to be in a position to prosecute these extraterritorial acts if the alleged perpetrators were discovered here.[58]

However, the law imposed difficult obstacles for prosecutors.

Canada mounted several cases under the new regulations, including against Michael Pawlowski (accused of crimes committed in Byelorussia), Stephen Reistetter (accused of misdeeds in Czechoslovakia) and Imre Finta (charged with crimes in Hungary). In the end it was Finta's case that proved the most combustible and became the hardest test for the new Canadian legislation.

Finta was the first person indicted under the new law in December 1987, and over the next several years his trial wound through the domestic justice system, beginning in November 1989 in a Toronto courtroom, being appealed to the Ontario Court of Appeal in 1992 and finally reaching the Canadian Supreme Court in 1993. Under the law Finta was to be tried, in the first instance, by a jury of 12, a process that immediately removed the trial from the sole province of the bench, and introduced other issues unseen in some of the prior war crimes trials. For instance, it required significant time to choose jurors, as few could be found that could afford to take the projected six months off work to attend the proceedings. Even once the proceedings started, the slow pace of trial resulted in jurors complaining to the court that "several ... were suffering severe economic hardship" due to the length of the case.[59]

In addition to the practical difficulties introduced by having non-professional jurors, the presence of the lay jury led the court of first instance to be far stricter with the rules of evidence than was seen at Nuremberg or in the Eichmann prosecution. Hearsay rules were comparatively strictly followed, and Finta's defense team ably attacked both procedural irregularities and the memories of some of the aging witnesses the state put forward. Further, the judge was arguably even deferential to the defense, on his own motion calling two witnesses who had not been requested by either side and allowing the defense, inter alia, to digress during closing arguments to the jury, to make an emotional rather than legal or factual plea, and to even suggest that the jury should ignore the "bad" war crimes law in order to exonerate Finta.[60]

The result was a jury acquittal. The appeals that followed focused not just on the behavior of the defense counsel, but also on some obtuse points of law raised by the new war crimes regulations. In the end, though, by the slimmest of margins, both the provincial appellate court and the Canadian Supreme Court upheld the jury's decision.

This was such a shock to the Canadian government, and the case had raised such passions on both sides of the issue, that Ottawa immediately exercised an about-face. Canada abandoned any efforts to prosecute war criminals and instead moved toward its old system of deporting, rather than prosecuting, any war criminals found in its midst.

An interesting postscript to the Finta case came in June 1997 when United States Secretary of State Madeleine Albright asked Canadian Foreign Minister Lloyd Axworthy if his government would be willing to request the extradition from Cambodia of Pol Pot to stand trial on a charge of genocide. Axworthy recognized that Canadian law would permit Canada to do so, but, perhaps still smarting from *Finta*, Ottawa turned Albright down.[61]

Australia

The Canadian experience mirrored that of other Commonwealth states. Australia was one of the 14 nations that participated in the Tokyo trials, and on its own conducted military trials of about 1,000 minor war criminals. Despite this early enthusiasm, for decades after the war Australia similarly chose not to pursue the issue, with prominent members of the government stating that prosecution was unnecessary and unwise. In 1961, Sir Garfield Barwick (who would become the chief justice of Australia three years later) even said that "while Australians felt an abhorrence for offenses against humanity, the nation should provide the opportunity for people to turn their backs on the past and to make a new life."[62]

However, in the 1980s, Australia followed Canada's lead and ordered an investigation into allegations that numerous Nazis had entered Australia after World War II.[63] Working from a script remarkably similar to that followed by the Canadians, in 1986 allegations of war crimes against an elderly man living in Adelaide, South Australia surfaced. The political firestorm that emerged led to the 1988 amendment of Australia's War Crimes Bill, which stated Parliament's concern "that a significant number of persons who committed serious war crimes in Europe during World War II may have entered Australia and become Australian citizens or residents."[64] The legislation allowed the prosecution of European war criminals in ordinary civil (rather than military) courts. A Special Investigations Unit of the Office of the Attorney General was established which quickly built up a roster of dozens of investigations against individuals.[65] Indictments were filed against an Adelaide resident, one Ivan Polyukovich, and two other individuals. A challenge to the validity of the war crimes legislation was lodged before the High Court of Australia in 1990, which upheld the validity of the law in 1991.[66] Despite this, in each case brought under the Act defendants were acquitted on various grounds ranging from insufficient evidence to the ill-health of the defendant.[67] In June 1992, likely mindful of the *Finta* firestorm brewing in Canada and realizing that the political and legal will to proceed with trials had dissipated, Australia disbanded the Special Investigations Unit—which had undertaken more than 850 investigations—and ceased prosecutions.[68]

West Germany

Apart from the *Eichmann* trial, some of the most watched Cold War proceedings were conducted in West Germany against alleged Nazis. To some, this was a replay of post–World War I efforts with German courts prosecuting German defendants. Similar results were to be expected. The judiciary had been heavily complicit in the Nazi regime—so much so that the occupying powers considered "closing all German courts for ten years and replacing them with a 'colonial' system, so that a new generation of judges could be educated in the meantime."[69]

Trials were conducted, at least initially, following orders of the occupation authorities. On 20 December 1945 the Allied Control Council for Germany promulgated Law No. 10 concerning "Punishment of Persons Guilty of War Crimes, Crimes against Peace and against Humanity." Trials began immediately, expanding in the 1950s, 1960s and beyond.[70] Though trials were held under the aegis of the occupation, they relied upon pre-war domestic German law: the Strafgesetzbuch (StG) was the primary basis for prosecutions, a law which dated from 1871.

The number of trials held, let alone the number of those convicted and sentenced, would prove disappointing. In all, between 1945 and 1995, less than 7,000 people were convicted, despite the investigation of nearly 110,000 people over that time.[71] Indeed, the Germans were slow to prosecute Nazis, and it was often only in response to extreme political pressures that trials were commenced. The Fischer-Schweder trial was just such an occasion. Pursuant to the occupation's de-Nazification orders, senior officials in the National Socialist government were stripped of their official rank and civil service status. Bernhard Fischer-Schweder was a brigadier general under Hitler, and in 1956 decided to sue the authorities for a resumption of his civil service status. He likely calculated that the risk of his doing so was minimal given the scant enthusiasm for Nazi trials. His case reached the media, and after some investigations it was revealed that he had served as the military police chief of Tilsit, Lithuania, a position in which he participated in mass executions of Jews. Fischer-Schweder was brought to trial, convicted, and incarcerated for 12 years.

In the wake of the Fischer-Schweder trial, the West German states came together in 1958 to form a Central Office for the Investigation of Nazi Crimes.[72] Though the office was encumbered by limitations on its operations—most notably it could not examine acts that had occurred on the military frontlines—and the office had no powers of detention, its efforts nonetheless brought results.[73] In 1959, the first year of its existence, the Central Office initiated over 400 investigations, including among them cases striking at the heart of Nazi criminality: cases addressing the concentration camps of Auschwitz, Belzec, Sobibor, Treblinka, and Chelmno were commenced.

A notable series of cases aided by these investigations were the Frankfurt-Auschwitz trials, or the second Auschwitz trials, a series of proceedings held in Frankfurt over two years, from 1963 to 1965.[74] It was by far the largest and most extensive of the postwar trials in Germany. Twenty-two defendants were charged, again under German domestic criminal law, for their roles in the Holocaust and in particular their work at the Auschwitz-Birkenau concentration camp (the largest of the Nazi concentration camps). The trial was notable not only for it implicitly following on from domestic proceedings in Poland from right after the war (the first Auschwitz trials held at Krakow), but also for the passions it raised amongst ordinary Germans. The *Eichmann* trial had taken place just two years earlier and Germans had watched the proceedings with rapt attention. This trial was subjected to (and was partly based on) the lingering interest amassed by the events in Jerusalem.

Much more so than the Fischer-Schweder trial, this prosecution attracted the full interest of the nation; there was enormous media attention with nearly 1,400 articles published throughout Germany about the trials between 1963 and 1965.[75] At least 20,000 German citizens visited the trials while in session, and one scholar has noted that the trials provided not just the basis for significant historical work, but they were so captivating that at least one major play was written about them.[76]

Despite this, there were criticisms of the trials. One common criticism was that the Auschwitz facility employed at least 6,000 staff, and yet only 22 were brought to trial. Moreover, it was only mid- and lower-level members of the camp hierarchy who were prosecuted. Some of the leaders had already been charged in Poland during the first Auschwitz trials which saw both Rudolf Höss (the first commandant of the camp) and Arthur Liebehenschel (who had served as commandant of both Auschwitz and Majdanek) convicted and executed. Josef Mengele had managed to escape to South America and was also unavailable. Only Richard Baer remained; he was the last commandant of Auschwitz and though arrested and arraigned, he would die before trial.

Ironically, some have argued that it was precisely because the trials were of lower level officials that the public became so captivated. The people on trial were "normal" Germans, and the details of their abuses (brought to life by testimony from 359 witnesses) combined with the media coverage thereof, introduced most Germans, for the first time, to the possibility that they were, or could have been, complicit.

Despite this, most historical analyses of the Frankfurt-Auschwitz trials conclude that they were not particularly helpful in bringing Germany and Germans to the point of recognition, let alone contrition and repentance. There was a "considerable degree of ambivalence in the public reaction to the Auschwitz Trial."[77]

Several shortcomings existed. First, because German law did not follow the French example of incorporating international law (and in particular the findings of Nuremberg),

> Holocaust perpetrators in German courts were not charged with Crimes Against Humanity. ... Rather, in German courts, the only charge which could be leveled at Nazi defendants was that of First Degree Murder.[78]

The defense furthered this theme with one lawyer declaring that the crimes committed were not a special kind of illegality, but simply "criminal offenses in the statutory sense."[79] As such, there was nothing in the trials that rendered the Holocaust unique in the eyes of the German legal system; it was a simple example of murder, albeit on a large scale. Complicity of the German state, and of the German people, in any such crimes was thus limited and even immunized through the trial. Second, even when convicted, the penalties were often statutorily minimal. Wilhelm Boger and Oswald Kaduk were among the six who received life sentences; the remainder were either released or received periods of incarceration of as little as three years. This led Polish commentators at the conclusion of the trials to calculate that in the German courts "the average sentence for a Nazi murderer works out at about 10 minutes per victim."[80]

Despite the various difficulties encountered with the trials, they are a noteworthy example of the slow encroachment of international process into domestic proceedings. The internationalization of the German statute of limitations is a key example of this. By the beginning of the 1960s the West Germans, even those enthusiastic about prosecutions, foresaw a problem based on their domestic law. Under domestic rules, statutes of limitation were onerous and strict. In particular, any serious crime—which had the potential for more than 10 years of incarceration— was limited to being prosecuted only for 20 years after its commission. Consequently, by the middle of the 1960s, there was a chance that all World War II trial activity would have to cease.

In February 1965, as the 20th anniversary of the end of the European war approached, the minister of justice told the Bundestag: "It cannot be ruled out that unknown crimes of significance or unknown perpetrators in important positions may yet become known after May 8, 1965,"[81] the date when the statute of limitations would run out on Nazi crimes committed during the Holocaust.

The German government came under a huge amount of international pressure to continue the Nazi trials. Spurred on at least in part by threats to its international image, on 10 March 1965, the Bundestag decided to extend the statute of limitations for murder by five years, to 1970 (allowing the Auschwitz trials to commence). When the statute again came up for debate in 1969, it was extended by 10 years to 1980, and in 1979 the statute for murder and genocide was completely eliminated,[82] bringing West German criminal procedure into line with international practice.

Argentina

A final set of Cold War prosecutions important to discuss had nothing to do with Nazi crimes of World War II. Instead they focused on events in South America and on the human rights abuses perpetrated by the military junta that ran Argentina from 1976 to 1983. During that period, a succession of leaders orchestrated a "dirty war" against supposed leftist agitators, resulting in thousands of "disappeared" citizens, torture, and scores of extrajudicial killings.

The military was compelled to relinquish power in 1983, hamstrung by both mounting revelations about their human rights violations and decreased public esteem following the disastrous war with Britain over the Falklands. The military opted to organize elections. Debates about whether trials would be conducted against those implicated in the Dirty War played a large role in the presidential campaign, with the two leading candidates having diverging views. Italo Luder, the Peronist candidate, argued against prosecutions, while the eventual winner Raúl Alfonsín promised to investigate abuses and bring to trial military chiefs and officers who committed the worst excesses. Alfonsín's election was predicated in large part on his commitment to the return of the rule of law,[83] and as a marker of that goal, his promise to try former regime leaders. True to his platform, immediately upon assuming power he decreed a presidential order to begin legal processes against the junta.[84]

The Argentine case is an important precedent because of the political similarities post-junta Argentina shares with many states in today's world attempting to judicially address past regime crimes. Unlike at Nuremberg, or even with any of the domestic trials discussed above, the end of the Argentine junta did not mark the end of the Argentine military. Argentina was not an occupied state, nor did the former military leaders depart the country. Rather, the primary abusers remained in the country and, importantly, ardently in opposition to any trials. Speaking to the regional precedent, as the *New York Times* described it, the 1985 trials "marked the first time a Latin American country had tried former military rulers while the armed forces were still intact."[85]

The political reality of a still powerful military forced Alfonsín to balance the competing notions of justice for victims and the re-establishment of rule of law with the real concerns that the military might decide to re-enter the public arena if it felt too threatened by the judicial process. Alfonsín could only rely on the support of the people's commitment to democracy, not force, to further his promise of trials.

In retrospect, Alfonsín's solutions were not perfect, but he did manage to construct a fragile *modus vivendi* between competing sectors of society. His first act was to creation the Commission on the Disappeared, a presidential body that was tasked to investigate the disappearances, widely viewed as the most horrifying of the junta's actions. The commission's report, *Nunca Mas* ("No More") was published within a year and the harrowing detail it provided on the junta's behaviors and the disposition of so many of those who had "disappeared" would prove to be one of the most important legacies of Alfonsín's trials.[86] The emotional weight of *Nunca Mas* was aided by the fact that Alfonsín had chosen a noted poet and novelist, Ernesto Sabato, to direct the commission. In the report's preface Sabato wrote hauntingly of the junta's victims:

> From the moment of their abduction, the victims lost all rights. Deprived of all communication with the outside world, held in unknown places, subjected to barbaric tortures, kept ignorant of their immediate or ultimate fate, they risked being either thrown into a river or the sea, weighted down with blocks of cement, or burned to ashes. They were not mere objects, however, and still possessed all the human attributes: they could feel pain, could remember a mother, child or spouse, could feel infinite shame at being raped in public.[87]

When the time for trials arrived, the state made numerous strategic choices. First, paying heed to concerns brewing in the military establishment, the state decided to set a limit to the length of trials and the scope of accountability. Second, Argentina did not recall Nuremberg or even explicitly implement any international law—indeed documents publicized after the fall of the junta revealed that a "Nuremberg situation in Argentina" was precisely what the military wished to avoid.[88] Rather, as Luis Moreno Ocampo, who became the first chief prosecutor at the International Criminal Court and was a prosecutor at the junta trials, put it, "we applied the law that prohibits homicide and murder, that is, the nation's penal code."[89]

The choice to rely on domestic law engendered several initial difficulties. First, the perpetrators of almost all of the abuses were in the military and conducted their crimes in the service of the military. Consequently, it was not civilian courts, but military courts that constitutionally had jurisdiction. And military courts were made up of military judges and it was difficult to believe that they would provide for robust justice for their soldier colleagues. In this Alfonsín was masterful, and while his initial order to arraign perpetrators made explicit that they were to be charged in military court,[90] the president arranged to provide military courts only with first instance jurisdiction, promulgating that there would be mandatory civilian review of military decisions or the automatic assumption of civilian jurisdiction if the military courts failed to act within six months.[91] As it turned out, the military courts refused to engage in any proceedings against the initial indictees (due to pressure from their comrades) and federal civilian courts assumed jurisdiction.[92]

However, even once the trials were removed from the military, federal courts were forced to address the self-amnesty law that the military leaders had passed prior to relinquishing power to elected leaders. The Argentine penal code and the national constitution both made a simple abrogation of the amnesty law ineffectual, necessitating resort to "innovative Constitutional arguments" regarding the validity of these laws.[93] Instead, Congress was called upon to declare the amnesty "null and void," a technical difference that made a practical difference, and opened the way for prosecution against those to whom amnesty had been granted.

The second difficulty came from the "due obedience to orders" defense that was explicitly incorporated in the Argentine Code of Military Justice. The code stated that

> When [a] crime was committed in [the] execution of [an] order ... , [the] superior who gave [the] order will be [the] sole responsible person, and [the] subordinate will only be considered [an] accomplice when he has exceeded ... that order.[94]

This defense by its very nature limited the potential number of defendants, a positive outcome for a government unsure of its ability to keep soldiers in their barracks. However, by its nature it also was over-encompassing, essentially shutting off prosecution of all but the most senior officials. This was not a positive interpretation either. The solution again required a technical, legal approach to the problem. Alfonsín recommended the passage of a law allowing "a revocable presumption that those who committed crimes under orders, and without decision-making capacity [i.e. were low-ranking] had mistakenly relied on the legitimacy of the orders received."[95]

The initial series of trials against nine former junta leaders, the Trial of the Juntas (*Juicio a las Juntas*) was held "amidst great public attention and emotion."[96] These first proceedings began on 22 April 1985 and concluded on 9 December 1985 when the Argentine National Chamber of Federal and Correctional Appeals convicted five military commanders for human rights abuses, acquitting four others of all charges.[97] More trials continued; in 1985 and 1986, "in all 481 military and police officers were indicted; 16 were tried ... 11 were convicted."[98]

However, after the first set of trials, with each subsequent proceedings anxiety within the military grew. Alfonsín was again forced to assess different equities and decided that the best way forward was to set an explicit, concrete deadline for indictments so that those who were under legal suspicion would know and those who were not could cease worrying that they may soon be. In December 1986 Alfonsín proposed the "full stop" law which gave the justice system 60 days to indict all military personnel involved in the Dirty War. Much as West Germany's statute of limitations rules was pilloried, the "full stop" law was vehemently criticized by both domestic and international human rights advocates as placing an artificial bar on necessary prosecutions.

Ironically, this limitation, which Congress passed overwhelmingly, led to a rejuvenation of the formerly sleepy process of prosecution. Within the two months, more than 450 soldiers were indicted, which led to the very response on behalf of the military about which Alfonsín had been concerned. At Easter in 1987 a group of soldiers launched "Operation Dignity" and refused to obey judicial orders. It was only in the face of a huge popular uprising in support of democracy that Alfonsín managed to secure the rebels' capitulation.

All was still not copacetic; further soldiers announced their lack of willingness to follow judicial orders, short of rebellion. The government quickly descended into a modicum of chaos in trying to figure out the next steps. The result was a further cabining of legal responsibility when Congress amended the Due Obedience law, changing the revocable presumption that a subordinate could not be held liable for following due orders, to an *irrevocable* presumption of subordinate immunity. Again this legislation encountered mass dissent both at home and abroad and though it succeeded in reigning in the military, it no doubt played a role in the quick dissolution of Alfonsín's government.

Carlos Menem assumed the presidency in 1989, and while he had campaigned as a critic of the Due Obedience amendments and other Alfonsín-authored limitations on prosecutions, within his first three months he issued "sweeping presidential pardons" releasing all of the major leaders convicted during the Alfonsín trials—Jorge Rafael Videla, Emilio Eduardo Massera, and Roberto Eduardo Viola were all released in order to, as Menem argued, "definitively close a sad and black period of national history."[99] Even more galling for supporters of trials was that not only did Menem refuse to include Congress in any pardon decision (as required by the Argentine constitution) but also that the acts of clemency included the mandated cessation of then ongoing trials against military officers accused of human rights violations.

Despite this arguably unfortunate postscript, the Argentine case remains a critical marker in modern attempts to account for violations of international humanitarian law by prior regimes. The Argentine case set the stage for the current proceedings in Chile against the Pinochet regime, and has been referred to in discussions of proceedings as varied as the Cambodian Extraordinary Chambers dealing with the crimes of the Khmer Rouge, the Sierra Leone Special Court addressing the violations of various leaders in the West African wars of the 1990s and early 2000s, and the Iraqi Special Tribunal established to provide justice for the excesses undertaken by the regime of Saddam Hussein. Subsequently, the Dirty War also provided Spain with its first test case of its own domestic universal jurisdiction law when in April 2005 the Spanish government convicted former Argentine naval officer Adolfo Scilingo for crimes against humanity related to his role in some of the junta's activities. And in today's Argentina, the trials are still being used as a new wave of desire to account for the junta's crimes is passing over the country. Prior to his leaving office President Nestor Kirchner, who himself was incarcerated by the junta, introduced two further repeals of the amnesty laws; their successful ratification removed the Alfonsín-negotiated bar on prosecutions, and proceedings began again in Argentina against those involved in abuses that took place as much as 30 years prior. Success came quickly: in October 2007, Christian von Wernich, a priest and one-time chaplain of the Buenos Aires provincial police force, was sentenced to life in prison.

5 Post–Cold War justice

The UN ad hoc tribunals, mixed courts, and the ICC

By the end of the Cold War the world had seen thousands of prosecutions for violations of international law, but other than the brief examples of Nuremberg and Tokyo, they were all domestic in nature. As the Berlin Wall fell, there was still scant movement toward the return of international judicial institutions, let alone the creation of a permanent, sitting international criminal court. Indeed, as Robert Cryer notes, by 1990 material on an international criminal court and even international justice itself was slowly being excised from standard legal textbooks. Consequently, it was not unreasonable for Ian Brownlie to pronounce in 1990 that "the likelihood of setting up an international criminal court is very remote."[1]

However, the world was moving, perhaps imperceptibly, in the direction of a new international era in justice. Unfortunately it would take thousands of further deaths and human rights violations, most famously in the Balkans and Rwanda, before international justice would see its full return.

The immediate wake of the Cold War saw several seemingly discrete and non-related events dovetail and come to coalesce around the idea for a return to "true" international justice. Although in the early 1990s violence in Rwanda and the former Yugoslavia were perhaps the most public of these factors, initial post–Cold War work towards international justice actually preceded carnage in the African Great Lakes and the Balkans.

First, several academics and observers of international justice, who had always played a central role in international law (and indeed under Article 36 of the International Court of Justice treaty actually serve as *sources* of international law) latched upon to a new internationalism in the wake of the Cold War. The rise of *Pax Americana* and the "end of history" opened new possibilities to return to the international notions of justice that had seemed to permeate, even if ephemerally, in the years after World War II.

Box 5.1   Timeline of commencement of Post–Cold War institutions/prosecutions

ICTY	1993
ICTR	1994
Special Panels in East Timor	2000
Kosovo International Judges and Prosecutors	2000
Extraordinary Chambers in Cambodia	2001 (Agreement with UN: 2003)
ICC	2002
Special Court for Sierra Leone	2002
Iraqi Special Tribunal	2003
Special Chambers of Belgrade District Court	2003
State Court of Bosnia and Herzegovina	2005
Special Tribunal for Lebanon	2007

In addition there have been various domestic movements toward addressing (if not prosecuting) international crimes in countries including Ethiopia, Chile, Spain, France, Britain, Liberia, Ghana and elsewhere.

Second, John Dugard notes that though the Cold War effectively limited the development of international justice, it did not completely limit the development of international law. That is, during the last decade of the Cold War, there was a marked

> increase in the [creation of a] number of international crimes in treaties outlawing hijacking, hostage-taking, torture, seizure of ships on the high seas and attacks on diplomats.[2]

Dugard also notes new transnational pressures that emerged in the late 1980s, including the rise "of powerful drug cartels capable of subverting the judicial systems of weak states."[3]

Interestingly, it was this last problem that proved the silent catalyst for the new era of international justice. In 1989, beset by a debilitating problem regarding illicit drugs shipment, Trinidad and Tobago asked the UN General Assembly to revive the idea for an international criminal court primarily in order to more effectively tackle the transnational drug trade.[4] The United Nations' International Legal Commission took to its task with alacrity, and it was out of the draft statute that the ILC completed, essentially regarding an "international drug court" (though its jurisdiction would have been broader) that the statute for the International Criminal Court would germinate. Ironically, and much to the chagrin of some, despite its critical role in forming the court, international drug crimes would not be within the ICC's jurisdiction.[5]

The Rwandan and Yugoslav violence, which erupted while the ILC was working on its draft, would prove the final stimulants to a return of international justice. The judicial responses devised for crimes committed in Rwanda and the former Yugoslavia would play critical roles in finalizing a standing international criminal court, but the world would have to wait; beset by unspeakable violence, the international community decided to act to form *ad hoc* tribunals.

The International Criminal Tribunal for the Former Yugoslavia; The International Criminal Tribunal for Rwanda

Though the courts the UN developed to address Rwanda and Yugoslavia are different in several ways, for reasons that will become clear it makes sense to address them in concert. Their legal basis comes from the UNSC and in particular its powers under Chapter VII of the UN Charter. This chapter of the charter, entitled "Action with Respect to Threats to the Peace, Breaches of the Peace, and Acts of Aggression," sets out the means by which the Security Council can act "to maintain or restore international peace and security."[6] Absent from the list of such actions is the creation of an international court. Regardless, when faced with the Yugoslav crisis, and after at least three Security Council resolutions had failed to end the conflict (and Security Council Resolution 780 which mandated a Commission of Experts to investigate violations of international humanitarian law in the Balkans revealed the scope of the brutality), the Security Council decided to act, creating the Hague-based International Criminal Tribunal for the Former Yugoslavia (ICTY) in 1993. Importantly, the court was created under Chapter VII which demanded legally cognizable cooperation from UN member states in its work. It was enforceable against all UN members, not just those who agreed to the resolution.

The resolution clearly set out the goals of the tribunal:

> *The United Nations Security Council*:
> Expressing … its grave alarm at continuing reports of widespread violations of international humanitarian law occurring within the territory of the former Yugoslavia, including reports of mass killings and the continuance of the practice of "ethnic cleansing,"

Determining that this situation constitutes a threat to international peace and security,

Determined to put an end to such crimes and to take effective measures to bring to justice the persons who are responsible for them,

Convinced that in the particular circumstances of the former Yugoslavia the establishment of an international tribunal would enable this aim to be achieved and would contribute to the restoration and maintenance of peace ...

Decides that an international tribunal shall be established for the prosecution of persons responsible for serious violations of international humanitarian law committed in the territory of the former Yugoslavia since 1991.[7]

Some states, notably China and Brazil, questioned the legal propriety of the Security Council's establishing a tribunal—as such a power was absent in Chapter VII. However, in the end the argument prevailed that Chapter VII powers conferred on the Security Council allowed it to forcibly remove threats to international peace and security, and this was a broad enough grant to allow for the erection of such courts. Clearly threats to peace and security were rife in the impacted regions. Though the resolution finally passed unanimously, the question of the legality of the court remained very much alive and was even challenged in early cases before the tribunals.[8]

Eighteen months after the Yugoslav court was formed, and with the Yugoslav precedent firmly in mind, the Security Council acted again, passing Resolution 955 and providing for a sister institution in the form of the International Criminal Tribunal for Rwanda (ICTR), headquartered in Arusha, Tanzania.

Unsurprisingly, the two UN courts are structured very similarly. Each is set up with the same tripartite structure (the Office of the Prosecutor, the Chambers [including a court "president"], and the Registry), and each is explicitly an "ad hoc," temporary institution. The two courts share an appellate court, and for most of their lives even had the same prosecutor, until the Security Council split the role in Resolution 1503 (passed in August 2003).

There are some differences, however, emanating from their statutes. Articles 2, 3, 4, and 5 of the ICTY statute respectively empower the court to try grave breaches of the Geneva conventions, violations of the laws and customs of war (including those occurring in non-international armed conflicts), genocide and crimes against humanity committed on the territory of former Yugoslavia since 1991. The ICTR statute provided the tribunal with jurisdiction over crimes of genocide, crimes against humanity, violations of "Common Article Three" (a clause present in the four Geneva conventions of 1949 which addresses the conduct of military forces and humanitarian concerns in non-international armed conflict) and of the 1977 Additional Protocol Two to the Geneva Conventions (which provides further protection to civilians in non-international armed conflicts).

The ICTY's temporal jurisdiction is unbounded going forward, until otherwise decided by the Security Council, and consequently the ICTY has prosecuted crimes that occurred after 1995 which marked the cessation of civil war hostilities. Notable in this regard are the charges against former Serbian leader Slobodan Milosevic stemming from his 1999 incursion into Kosovo. The ICTR, meanwhile, though arguably enjoying a wider scope of coverage than its Yugoslav cousin—bringing into its purview crimes committed by anyone on the territory of Rwanda, or by Rwandans in neighboring countries—is more temporally limited; it is only charged to deal with infractions that occurred in the 12-month period between 1 January 1994 and 31 December 1994.

Structurally, there is one final important similarity, again deriving from their Chapter VII mandates. Though the first paragraph of Article 9 of the ICTY statute provided concurrent jurisdiction with domestic Yugoslav courts in the prosecution of war crimes, paragraph 2 provides the tribunal with

> primacy over national courts. At any stage of the procedure, the International Tribunal may formally request national courts to defer to the competence of the International Tribunal.[9]

This primacy was legislated due to concerns about the ability of local courts in the Balkans to provide fair trials. Similar concerns regarding domestic justice in Rwanda led to Article 8 of the ICTR Statute providing for the same concurrence in jurisdiction and an equal ability for the ICTR to assert primacy over the domestic courts of Rwanda.

Similarities between the two tribunals extend even to the difficulties and tests they were faced with after they began their work.[10] Despite the fact that Chapter VII resolutions must be obeyed by all UN members, the courts faced uncooperative states—who, inter alia, refused prosecutors access to evidence, witnesses, and even to those indicted by the tribunals. The Croatian government of Franjo Tudjman proved almost entirely unwilling to allow ICTY officials access to anything in Croat possession. Even Western states, many of whom had intelligence resources present during the wars and consequently had amassed valuable evidence, proved to be of only intermittent assistance.

Similar lack of cooperation was seen in the ICTR, where, ironically one of the most frequent obstacles to assistance was the Rwandan government itself which developed a complicated relationship with the tribunal. For both tribunals the only avenue of redress if facing an uncooperative state has been a "referral" of the stubborn state to the UN Security Council.[11] Such referrals of uncooperative states have resulted in strongly worded rebukes from the UN urging cooperation, but little concrete action.[12]

In the ICTY context, cooperation has been so uncertain that the tribunal adopted its "Rule 61" procedures whereby, in public hearings, prosecutors can have their indictments publicly "reconfirmed," a tool designed to make it even clearer just how egregious certain violations were. One of the hopes was clearly the shaming of the international community into providing some sort of assistance.[13]

The second challenge faced was that of court and trial procedures. In line with the precedent established by the London Charter, the Security Council did not mandate any particular rules of evidence and procedure for the tribunals, leaving it to the elected judges to devise appropriate regulations. Over the decade of their existence they have developed broad sets of regulations that, despite being frequently amended and at times representing an uneasy blend of common and civil law, have served as a solid foundation for court operations. Though there are slight differences between ICTR and ICTY rules and practices, they essentially mirror each other.

Successes and failures of the ICTY and ICTR

The ICTY and ICTR have been expensive institutions; at their height of operations they together accounted for more than 10 percent of the UN's entire annual operational budget. This cost, combined with their relatively modest judicial output (after more than a decade of operation, they had together "completed" less than 70 cases), has led some to question whether the tribunals have been "worth it." And this has led the tribunals themselves to defend their costs, with the ICTY publicly arguing that its budget covers "activities that would not be undertaken by a court in a national system" (such as translation), and that any cost "pales in comparison to the true cost of the crimes."[14]

Other criticisms have also been raised. One central concern raised early by defense counsel alleges unequal rights for defendants. The offices of the prosecutors are necessarily well resourced in respect of the quality of their staff and their facilities. Most of the lawyers who represent defendants before international tribunals are not similarly well resourced and some have been fundamentally unprepared to serve clients or the court.[15] To some, this "inequality of arms" replays the situation in Nuremberg, and it was one of the reasons that critics of the Nuremberg process have branded it "victors' justice." The ICTY and ICTR have not ignored these criticisms, and both have undertaken various efforts to provide for more equal resources. Though the problem is enduring, further steps have been taken by post–ICTY/ICTR tribunals— such as the Special Tribunal for Lebanon (STL) (see below)—attempting to remedy this inequality. Despite this, we would suggest that, whether in international or domestic courts, there can never in reality be true "equality of arms." The real question is whether the defendant has adequate resources to ensure a fair trial.

A related critique has also emerged regarding the disposition of those convicted. There have often been inconsistencies in the punishments received by defendants, even among those convicted of similarly grave international crimes. Such inconsistencies have been present across the various bodies dispensing international justice and even within single courts. Sentences of like defendants have differed in significant (and in some observers' estimations unconscionable) ways, including in the time of incarceration received, in the conditions of their incarceration (e.g. with some defendants serving time in developed-country prisons, and others in poor-country facilities), and in defendants' rights to counsel, appeal, and parole. In this regard, an interesting part of the ICTY and ICTR sentencing jurisprudence has been the statutory reference to domestic practices. Article 24 of the ICTY Statute and Article 23 of the ICTR Statute provide that

> [t]he Trial Chambers shall have recourse to the general practice regarding prison sentences in the courts of Yugoslavia [or Rwanda].

Sentencing practice should consequently at least arguably be as consistent as that practiced in the former Yugoslavia or Rwanda; and thus one might expect sentences to differ between tribunals, but perhaps not within tribunals.

One of the reasons sentences have differed is controversial in its own right: plea bargaining. Though the first prosecutor of the ICTY and ICTR opted against using plea bargains, some subsequent prosecutors have been willing to do so. A plea bargain can have as its outcome a decreased penalty in exchange for agreeing to plead guilty and/or assist the tribunal in securing further prosecutions. The result, of course, is that some individuals receive seemingly lighter sentences than those who committed exactly (or nearly so) the same offense. The *Biljana Plavsic* case in the ICTY is a leading example of the outcome of plea bargaining, and of the dissent that it can raise in the populace, especially a populace unfamiliar with plea bargaining.[16] It must be remembered that plea bargains are regularly used in only a few common law countries.

Outside the operation of the courts, there has long been a concern that the tribunals "politicize justice," or more accurately, are a result of politicized justice. Indeed, it is noteworthy that no ad hoc tribunals were established to investigate war crimes alleged to have been committed by any of the five permanent members of the UNSC or those nations these powerful states might have wished to protect. Though this is true, it is also true that in the wake of the NATO bombing of Yugoslavia, the ICTY prosecutor did authorize an examination of NATO members' actions (which included three of the five permanent members) to determine if they might constitute crimes under the ICTY statute and whether there was sufficient evidence to justify an investigation by the Office of the Prosecutor. Controversially, it was concluded that there was not.

Finally, for as long as there have been courts, there has existed a debate about the relationship between peace, justice and wider goals. It is no different in the former Yugoslavia or in Rwanda. Clearly, in some situations a war crimes investigation and the issuing of indictments and arrest warrants might retard peace negotiations or otherwise endanger policy goals. Tribunals do not operate in a vacuum, and ICTY and ICTR actions have clearly had an impact on the situation on the ground in the Balkans and Rwanda; and the hybrid courts have similarly influenced (and been influenced by) the political environments of their home states. For instance, it has been much debated why the ICTY prosecutor issued a second indictment against Radovan Karadzic and Ratko Mladic during the week that the Dayton peace talks were being held. The prosecutor was accused by some of using the indictment to ensure that the ICTY was not used as a "bargaining chip" in the negotiations. Similar arguments were raised when the ICTY indicted Slobodan Milosevic during the NATO bombing over Kosovo and at a time when talks were being held with Milosevic aimed at stopping the war. Concerns have more recently been raised with regard to the issuing of indictments by the ICC against Ugandan leaders, and the July 2008 application for an arrest warrant issued by the ICC prosecutor against Sudanese President Omar Al-Bashir. In the Ugandan case, the principal mediator in the peace talks threatened to resign if such indictments were issued, and in the case of Al-Bashir, the African Union expressed its displeasure at the move and requested that the Security Council act to suspend the ICC proceedings.

Added to these concerns is the incompleteness of the tribunals' work; several senior figures from both the Balkans and Rwanda have yet to be captured and brought to trial. As of this writing, Ratko Mladic, the ICTY's primary fugitive, as well as some of the most notorious of ICTR's indictees—including Félicien Kabuga, Charles Sikubwabo and Aloys Ndimbati—remain free. Moreover, especially regarding the ICTY, some of the tribunals' marquee cases have failed to conclude positively. Key among them was the prosecution of former Yugoslav president Milosevic. He faced a mammoth 66-count indictment spread across the full scope of actions he commanded in Croatia, Bosnia and Herzegovina, and Kosovo.[17] His death in March 2006 after four years of trial and an estimated $200 million in expense, removed what many thought would be a litmus test for both the success of ad hoc tribunals in general, and for the potential of international justice writ large.[18]

Despite these difficulties, the tribunals have also had many successes, with their primary achievement being the broad-based furthering of the development and application of international criminal law. Some of the leading cases[19] to have aided this development include *Tadic* (among other things establishing the legality of the tribunals),[20] *Blaskic* (defining culpability under command responsibility),[21] *Akayesu* (finding rape to be a form of genocide),[22] *Musema* (extending command responsibility to civilian enterprises),[23] *Kambanda* (holding that one can be personally responsible for genocide),[24] and *Barayagwiza* (which was the first-ever verdict against members of the media for inciting genocide).[25] In addition to these cases, the tribunals have encouraged the growth of domestic war crimes legislation and prosecutions. Their presence and the publicity they have given to international humanitarian law has likely deterred some war crimes in subsequent military campaigns in Kosovo, Afghanistan, and Iraq, and encouraged the movement toward a permanent ICC. Further, through the dissemination of evidence— such as the June 2005 release of the graphic video of several murders of Muslims by Bosnian Serb forces at Srebrenica—they have impeded the ability of both deniers and perpetrators to hide behind the "unknown."

"Completion strategy" of the ICTY and ICTR

From their inceptions, the ad hoc tribunals were designed to be temporary institutions, and with the July 2004 release of their "completion" strategies,[26] both bodies began the process of winding up operations. Though it is rare for judicial systems to intentionally terminate their operations, there is a clear precedent in the Nuremberg and Tokyo trials which similarly closed. However, in the ICTY and ICTR case the goal is not to cease prosecutions—which was one of the goals of ending the post–World War II institutions—but rather to continue them, albeit on a domestic level. This has involved a delicate political and legal debate, and as such the tribunals are faced with a host of unique challenges in the process of completing their mandates.

For both bodies, "completion" comprises three stages: first, pro-secutors ceased issuing any new indictments after 31 December 2004, with the goal of completing all trials by 31 December 2008, and all appeals by 31 December 2010. Such strict timing has already engendered some discord, especially amongst those who wish to see major war criminals, who are as yet uncaptured, appear before the tribunals. The argument is that with a strict deadline, the indicted individuals will simply have to avoid capture until the end of 2008, at which point they would face no more risk of international justice. As a result, there has been talk of making these deadlines flexible and fluid; on one occasion Pierre Richard-Prosper, the former US ambassador-at-large for war crimes, even stated that the tribunal will "always" be open for Mladic and Karadzic.[27]

The second stage of completion requires the tribunals to winnow their caseloads and focus attention and resources on trying only the most senior-level military and political leaders charged with violations of law. This too has raised some controversy as identifying who "senior leaders" are has at times proven difficult. The third step follows from this identification and asks the tribunals to transfer cases involving mid- and low-level perpetrators to national courts for prosecution.

Though the ICTY and ICTR have similar completion strategies and deadlines, the two tribunals have diverged in practice. At the ICTY, the transfer of responsibility to local courts has been one of the most controversial components of its completion strategy, engendering debate both within the tribunal and outside it. Internally, the strategy has required amendments in the Rules of Evidence and Procedure, providing for the transfer of cases (Rule "11 *bis*"[28]) and ensuring that only the most senior perpetrators are kept on the tribunal's docket (Rule 28). The prosecutors balked at Rule 28, concerned about the limitations it posed on their investigatory autonomy. The transfer of cases is controversial for several procedural and practical reasons. Procedurally, in its writing—and operations thus far—it is not apparent what guides the decision to transfer. In particular, to what country are individuals to be transferred?

The importance of this question can not be over-estimated. Not only do there remain concerns about the ability of ethnic minorities to receive fair trials throughout the states of the former Yugoslavia, but also all Balkan states have constitutional prohibitions against extradition. If a defendant was arrested in Croatia, transferred to The Hague and then transferred to Bosnia, the extradition prohibition would be obviated, much to the displeasure of Croats throughout the Balkans. Second, due to concerns about judicial fairness and competence, new courts have been built throughout the Balkans specifically designed to handle war crimes trials. The scope of international involvement and oversight in these courts differs substantially, and remains in flux. The new courts vary from a body established in Belgrade, which is a "pure" domestic court (it is legally and physically a unit of the Belgrade District Court), to the new State Court of Bosnia and Herzegovina that is also a domestic court, but one which for its first five years will operate with international prosecutors, administrators and judges serving alongside local counterparts. It is a leading example of the mixed/hybrid courts discussed below. As of December 2007, 13 cases have been referred to national jurisdictions, with the vast majority going to the State Court of Bosnia and Herzegovina (Croatia has received only two defendants, Rahim Ademi and Mirko Norac, and Serbia only one, Vladimir Kovačević).[29] Interestingly, motions have been made to refer four further defendants to national jurisdictions, but the judges denied the request.[30]

The ICTR, meanwhile, faces numerous unique problems that have had an impact on its completion strategy. The key difference between it and the ICTY is based on the nature of the crimes over which the ICTR has jurisdiction. The slaughter of Tutsis and moderate Hutus during the genocide of 1994 was undertaken in a much more decentralized manner than were the crimes committed in the Balkans. Consequently, though there have been no definitive counts of perpetrators, and only 72 arrests have been made at the ICTR's instigation (and only 55 are currently detained in Arusha awaiting or undergoing trial),[31] there are tens of thousands of perpetrators. The magnitude of potential defendants, combined with Rwanda's ill resourced judicial infrastructure, has threatened to overwhelm the country's justice system. Despite this, very soon after the genocide was perpetrated, the country began vigorous prosecution against thousands of defendants. Though a similar process also occurred throughout the Balkans, the magnitude of the Rwandan domestic prosecution system has been unmatched. Approximately 6,500 individuals have been tried in Rwanda, and the government has another 80,000 people imprisoned, theoretically awaiting trial.[32] Meanwhile, the state has also paroled 30,000 others, many of whom have pledged to participate in a system of informal community dispute resolution, known as *gacaca*.[33]

In addition to the difficulties resulting from the types of crimes committed, the ICTR has suffered at times from lack of full governmental support. Again, the same problems have appeared in the ICTY context. As mentioned, Rwanda, which had one of the rotating seats on the Security Council during debates on the ICTR, actually voted against the tribunal's creation, even though Kigali had explicitly asked for the establishment of an international court. Consequently, the Rwandan government has welcomed the completion process; and in a sense, without the existence of multiple states, as in the former Yugoslavia which emerged after the wars as seven independent states, the process of transfer is procedurally somewhat easier. Despite the fact that many Rwandans continue to view their national court system with skepticism, the ICTR has also begun engaging in the transfer process under Rule 11 *bis*; the first group of 15 cases was presented to Rwandan authorities in February 2005. In order to make the transfer of these cases possible, the Rwandan parliament abolished the death sentence, the existence of which produced a longstanding gulf between Rwanda and the ICTR (whose most severe penalty is life incarceration). The ICTR required the waiver of the death penalty for any cases that would be transferred. Yet, even so, the first three applications by the Prosecutor for transfer of trials to the courts of Rwanda were denied by the ICTR due to concerns that domestic trials would be unfair.

The rise of the "hybrid" or "mixed" courts

In the decade between the establishment of the ICTR and ICTY and the formation of the International Criminal Court, the UN became aware that several other countries attempting to address past abuses could benefit from establishing similar tribunals. Managing these countries' needs proved challenging to the UN. The international community was eager to promote judicial tools for societal reconciliation and redress, and given that many post-conflict states lacked the judicial capacity to handle complex war crimes trials, the UN was cognizant that its assistance would be required in establishing any new tribunals. However, the financial and administrative burdens of the ICTY and ICTR made UN member states wary of setting up additional "subsidiary" courts.

Consequently, the UN began developing a compromise judicial model, creating tribunals similar to the ICTY/ICTR, but based in and largely owned by local states. Thus were born the "mixed" or "hybrid" courts, so named because their jurisdictions, administrations and compositions are partially locally derived and partially international. The hybrid courts have clear, domestic foundations but also have critical international components, inserted specifically to mitigate concerns about judicial capacity and trial fairness.

There are two, broad classes of such courts; the first, as in East Timor (the "Panels with Exclusive Jurisdiction Over Serious Criminal Offices"), Kosovo (the "International Judges and Prosecutors" [IJP] system whereby international personnel are introduced into the domestic justice system on an ad hoc basis), and Bosnia and Herzegovina (the "State Court of Bosnia and Herzegovina") arose in regions under the actual or effective control of international administrators (the UN directly, as in East Timor and Kosovo, or UN-approved authorities, as in Bosnia and Herzegovina). As such these courts share the "imposed" character of the ICTY and ICTR. Though local officials in each region may have welcomed their arrival and may have even been involved in their establishment, it was external pressure that implemented these hybrid court systems.

Regarding East Timor, which emerged from a quarter century of Indonesian occupation in 1999, the Security Council passed Resolution 1272 (passed under the Security Council's Chapter VII enforcement powers) requiring the UN Transitional Administration in East Timor (UNTAET) to bring to justice those who had been responsible for violence in the country.[34] UNTAET established "mixed panels"[35] of judges within the existing District Court and the Court of Appeals in East Timor's capital Dili.[36] Though the courts were "existing," the end of Indonesian occupation left a devastated East Timorese justice system, requiring substantial initial construction by the UN and other international agencies.[37] Each panel was composed of three judges, two international and one East Timorese; prosecution was charged to international lawyers, operating under the authority of the local general prosecutor. Though they recorded some modest successes during their 2000–2005 tenure, the "mixed panels" were hampered by reluctant Indonesian cooperation, a UN that intermittently distanced itself from its proceedings (as the UN did when the court issued a politically incendiary indictment against Indonesian General Wiranto), and persistent concerns regarding financial and administrative shortcomings.

Operating under the mandate of the 1999 Security Council Resolution 1244, the UN Interim Administration Mission in Kosovo (UNMIK) initially attempted to establish a separate "Kosovo War and Ethnic Crimes Court." Following recognition of the costs and logistical difficulties of doing so, UNMIK opted to inject international judges and prosecutors into the existing Kosovar judicial system. Introduced in 2000, the IJP system gave UNMIK the power—upon a request by prosecutor, accused or defense counsel—to appoint an international prosecutor, an international judge, or a panel of three international judges, to proceedings throughout the region.[38] Depending upon the case, international judges may either operate alongside domestic colleagues, or they may completely supplant them. Though there have been concerns regarding the limited size of the IJP program, it is widely recognized both that the international presence has been critical to the re-establishment of the rule of law in Kosovo, and that internationalizing components of the domestic system has been, at least in this case, preferable to creating a separate, international tribunal system.

In Bosnia and Herzegovina a third kind of "mixed" court has been established. Drawing its authority from Article V of Annex 10 to the 1995 Dayton Agreement (which ended the Bosnia/Croatian/Serbian part of the Yugoslav conflict), the new State Court officially opened in March 2005, and is linked directly to the completion strategy of the ICTY.[39] The court is explicitly designed to take on cases transferred to it from The Hague. As such, it is a manifestly domestic court, but one in which international judges, administrators and prosecutors work alongside locals. According to plan, the international presence is to deplete over the next five years, resulting in a fully domestic State Court. As of this writing, the appeals chamber of this new court has confirmed the first conviction and lengthy prison sentence handed down in the *Gojko Janković* case.[40] A decision by the appeals chamber in a second case is awaited.

A newer, related development in the world of "hybrid courts" has been directly spurred by the completion strategies of the Yugoslav and Rwandan tribunals detailed above. The strategies mandate that cases be transferred to "competent" courts in the home jurisdictions, a requirement that has led to the rise of unique, post ICTY/ICTR courts. Courts such as those in Croatia and Serbia are often specialized chambers of existing, domestic courts, but they have been internationalized in process and/or funding, if not personnel.

The second category of mixed courts, one established in 2002 in Sierra Leone (the "Special Court for Sierra Leone" [SCSL]) and the other, more recently beginning judicial operations, in Cambodia (the "Extraordinary Chambers for Cambodia" [ECCC]), and Lebanon (the Special Tribunal for Lebanon [STL]), were formed in response to requests from independent governments for international assistance in establishing tribunals to deal with, respectively, the human rights abuses and war crimes perpetrated during the Sierra Leone civil war of the 1990s, the mass killings orchestrated during Cambodia's Khmer Rouge regime of the late 1970s, and the murder of former Lebanese prime minister Rafiq Hariri on 14 February 2005. The independent status of the requesting states meant that the establishment of these hybrid courts proceeded from often contentious negotiations between states, the UN, concerned third-party governments, and NGOs. In fact, in some instances negotiations were so fraught that, at least regarding the Cambodian tribunal, the UN secretary-general publicly stated his skepticism whether the negotiated structure of the court could produce robust trials conducted to international standards. Despite this, in the Cambodian case the General Assembly finally approved the agreement.[41]

The negotiated tribunals have presented a host of difficulties, many of which were reflected in the tense nature of the discussions leading to their formation. Among the contentious issues included the questions of whether domestic or international law would control (though unsettled and still largely untested in all three of the courts, domestic law holds, but as in many of the domestic prosecutions mentioned earlier, "relevant" international law is usually said to be "incorporated" into domestic statutes as needed); the legal status of amnesties given to several perpetrators prior to the courts' establishments (the prosecutors are called upon to use their "discretion" in issuing indictments); and several unique problems associated with the particular nature of the crimes at issue. For instance, despite the scope of killings in Sierra Leone and Cambodia, "genocide" in the strict, legal sense, did not occur in either country as killings were not ordered on an ethnic basis. In Sierra Leone an added complexity is the fact that many of the worst abuses were perpetrated by children who had been forcibly conscripted into various factions and often compelled to commit crimes.

While the Sierra Leone court has completed most of its trials, it remains unclear how successful it has been at both securing justice for victims and mending the rifts created by the conflict. The deaths while in custody of Foday Sankoh and Samuel Hinga Norman, respectively the leader of the main rebel group and the leader of a primary government-backed armed group during the war, and two of the court's most important indictees, were severe blows. The capture of Charles Taylor, the former Liberian leader and the alleged catalyst in much of the Sierra Leone bloodshed, initially promised to resurrect the tribunal's fortunes. However, Taylor's trial, which was planned to start in April 2007, has been beset by delays. For reasons of security and administration the trial was moved to The Hague and into premises leased from the International Criminal Court. The dual-continent operations thrust on the SCSL have drastically reduced the efficiency of what was once hailed as the new, more streamlined model of international justice. However, far from working more efficiently than the other previous tribunals, a 2006 report issued by the UN indicated that "[b]ecause of numerous mistakes and cost-cutting, [the SCSL] has become comparatively more expensive and slower than the other tribunals."[42] Taylor's defense budget is thought to run as high as $70,000 per month.[43] In addition to the Taylor imbroglio, the tense relationship that developed between the SCSL and the Sierra Leone TRC (which operated alongside the court and had markedly different—and perhaps incompatible—goals), has posed significant hurdles.

The Cambodian court has made substantial progress, even though it remains hampered by insufficient funds and persistent criticisms of corruption and even "malpractice in hiring."[44] In September 2007 Pol Pot's "Brother No. 2," the regime's chief ideologue, Nuon Chea, was arrested, an apprehension which followed the July arrest and indictment of Guek Eav, the commandant of a brutal prison used by the Khmer Rouge and in which at least 14,000 people were killed.[45] Trials are scheduled to begin in 2008, and it appears that some proceedings shall be launched.

The STL was established in May 2007 and, other than establishing its seat in Leidschendam (a town on the outskirts of The Hague) and continuing investigations, has yet to begin operations.

International Criminal Court

Though it was doing so in the shadows of the UN ad hoc and hybrid courts, throughout the 1990s the process of creating a permanent international criminal court progressed. Indeed, in some ways the difficulties encountered by the ad hocs and hybrids made the establishment of the court seem all the more urgent. Amongst other benefits, such a court would reduce the confusions produced by competitor ad hoc and mixed court models of tribunal operations, providing for a stable, uniform model of international criminal justice.

As mentioned, the 1998 Rome Conference and the treaty that led to the formation of the International Criminal Court (ICC) was the culmination of a process that began in 1989 when the General Assembly asked the International Law Commission (ILC) to address the establishment of an international criminal court. In 1993 the General Assembly followed up on this request and asked the ILC to write a draft statute for such a court; one year later the Assembly established an ad hoc committee to review the major issues arising out of the draft. Annual Preparatory Committee meetings followed, laying the foundation for the Rome Conference in 1998. The United Nations Diplomatic Conference of Plenipotentiaries on the Establishment of an International Criminal Court took place in Rome from 15 June to 17 July 1998. 160 states, 33 inter-governmental organizations, and 236 NGOs participated in the deliberations. The conference concluded with the adoption of the Rome Statute of the International Criminal Court[46] by a vote of 120 in favor, 7 against, and 21 abstentions. The United States and China publicly indicated that they voted against the statute, but other permanent members of the Security Council—France, the United Kingdom and the Russian Federation—supported it.

The treaty, which codified much of the international humanitarian law that had been developed at the ICTY and ICTR, was opened for ratification in July 1998 and came into force on 1 July 2002, following ratification by its 60th state party. The ratification process was far more rapid than even the most optimistic supporters of the ICC had anticipated. The treaty borrows much from the ICTY and ICTR, with similarities in its basic structure and, as the ad hoc tribunals continue to wind up, a substantial number of personnel, with senior tribunal lawyers and other officials finding employment at the ICC.

The primary administrative body for the court is the Assembly of States Parties (ASP), made up of all member states. It meets annually and each state has one vote. Amongst other tasks, the ASP elects the court's judges, its prosecutor and deputy prosecutor, all of whom have nine-year terms. While selection of the prosecutor and deputy prosecutor is limited primarily by the requirement that they be of different nationalities, judicial selection is much more constrained. Judicial selection is governed by Article 36(8) of the Rome Statute, with the choice of judges statutorily informed by the ASP taking into account the "principal legal systems" of the world, equitable geographic representation and, for the first time in a statute of any international court, a fair representation of male and female judges.

Though the ICC is not a constituent body of the UN, the treaty provides for the establishment of a legal relationship between the two. Not only does the Rome Statute empower the UN, through the Security Council, to refer matters to the court and even to ask the ICC to defer investigation or prosecution, but also its Article 2 posits that the court and the UN will have a broad-based working partnership. The details of this partnership were elaborated in the ICC–UN Agreement, affirmed in September 2004.[47] The underlying principle of this agreement is "mutual respect" between the two organizations with both parties pledging to closely cooperate so as to increase the effectiveness of the ICC and to limit any duplication of work. The agreement asks the UN, if requested, to provide the ICC with information or documents and to facilitate the provisions of testimony by UN officials or agencies. The ICC, meanwhile, has the power to suggest certain items for the General Assembly or Security Council agenda.

The Rome Statute gives the ICC jurisdiction over four types of crime: genocide, crimes against humanity, war crimes, and crimes of aggression. The first three crimes are defined in exhaustive detail by the treaty in Articles 5–8. The definition of the crime of aggression proved too contentious and thus though it remains in the statute, it remains undefined. The ASP has deferred further consideration of this issue until 2009. Though various states parties have regularly convened to further the discussions (and an official Special Working Group on the Crime of Aggression has been established and has met several times[48]), the debate over the term (let alone over its very inclusion in the statute) has become even more heated owing in part to the United States' misadventures in the "war of terror". As Benjamin Ferencz famously noted in 1992, it has been far easier to commit aggression than to define it.[49] Unfortunately, the advent of the ICC and even the inclusion of aggression in the crimes under its jurisdiction has not dulled Ferencz's pithy observation.

The court's jurisdiction is constrained both in the means by which the ICC can begin a case and the necessary characteristics for a crime to be included in its jurisdiction. Under Article 13, the ICC can open an investigation if a matter is referred to it by the Security Council or by states parties. There is also an opportunity for the prosecutor to begin a prosecution on his or her own initiative, though this has yet to occur. The ICC can exercise its jurisdiction only if the crime is alleged to have been committed in the territory of a member state, the alleged perpetrator is a national of a member state, or if a non-member state formally accepts the court's jurisdiction.

As of July 2008, the ICC has four "situations" before it.[50] Three of them have been referred to the court by states parties: in January 2004, Uganda referred crimes allegedly committed by the Lord's Resistance Army in Northern Uganda for investigation, in April 2004, the Democratic Republic of the Congo asked for an examination of crimes in the Ituri region, and in January 2005, the Central African Republic requested investigation into alleged crimes committed throughout its territory. The prosecutor has thus far decided to proceed with investigations in Uganda, the Democratic Republic of the Congo and the Central African Republic. The UN Security Council referred the court's fourth situation, regarding the situation in Darfur, Sudan, to the ICC in March 2005. At the time of writing, pre-trial chambers have been satisfied that the prosecutor has gathered sufficient evidence to justify the issue of warrants of arrest in the situations concerning Uganda, the Democratic Republic of the Congo and Darfur.

While as of July 2008, the first indictee in the Central African Republic situation has been detained by the ICC—former Congolese vice-president Jean-Pierre Bemba—it is the Congo situation that has gained the most traction toward trial. Three individuals are in the court's detention facilities awaiting proceedings—militia leader Thomas Lubanga, former

Congolese general Germain Katanga, and former Congolese colonel Mathieu Ngudjolo Chui. On 2 July 2008, the trial chamber ordered Lubanga released, an order that followed the court's finding that the prosecutor had failed to provide the defendant with exculpatory evidence. Coming on the tenth anniversary of the Rome Treaty, the ruling was bittersweet. On the one hand, it delayed the start of the court's first trial. Yet, on the other hand, it offered some measure of comfort that the ICC plans to take defendants' rights seriously. As of this writing Lubanga remains detained, pending an appeal of the trial chamber's order.[51]

Other aspects of the ICC also bring with them measures of promise and peril. For instance, the ICC's growing caseload bodes well, but it is also a potential problem. All of the court's cases, thus far, have been from Africa, leading some to surmise that the institution will provide "international justice" only for those countries too weak to resist it. Indeed, without expanding to other corners of the world, the ICC does risk being branded, at best, as a selective prosecutor, and at worst, as a purveyor of racially conscious justice.

It is in the wider issue of the relationship between the ICC and member and non-member states that the new court will likely be most challenged. Without a police force of its own, the ICC, like the ICTY and ICTR, requires the cooperation of states in fulfilling its duties, ranging from the collecting of evidence, to the arresting of those against whom warrants have been issued, to the housing of those convicted and serving sentences. The dynamics of the relationships between the ICC and states remains in flux, with the first real tests of the principle of complementarity—which underlies the Rome Statute in Article 18 and calls for the ICC to only become involved in prosecutions if a state fails to appropriately investigate its own alleged perpetrators—yet to come. Additionally, the lack of support rendered to the endeavor by the United States, which has resulted in its signing of dozens of mutual bilateral immunity agreements with states by which the United States and the co-signatory pledge not to surrender their nationals (civilian or military) to the court, is troubling. Although the United States has brokered more than 100 of these "Article 98 agreements"—named for the article in the Rome Statute under which they are purportedly allowed—they have yet to definitively impact the workings of the court, and it remains unclear how much they will alter its operations.

It is the US opposition to the ICC that presents the most serious concern to its officials and supporters. Without US political and economic support, the ad hoc tribunals, in all likelihood, would not have been able to operate successfully. For instance, American threats to deny financial assistance to Croatia and Serbia directly led to their surrender of important alleged war criminals to the ICTY. The June 2001 transfer of Milosevic to the ICTY by the government of Serbian prime minister Zoran Djindjic came in the face of the threatened denial of aid worth more than $1 billion from the Clinton administration.

The US opposition to the ICC appears to be based upon fears, especially in its armed forces, that a runaway prosecutor or biased judges will launch politically motivated and unjustifiable trials (and subsequent convictions) of American military personnel or political leaders. This seems an unlikely eventuality and one which is seemingly addressed by the several safeguards built into the Rome Treaty. The first such safeguard is the requirement that judges on the ICC must receive the affirmative vote of two thirds of all of the states parties, ensuring a broad level of support of states for those serving on the ICC bench. The second safeguard is the principle of complementarity referred to earlier. According to the treaty itself, the United States could thwart an investigation by the ICC by launching its own bona fide investigation. The third safeguard is the requirement that the prosecutor requires the permission of a pre-trial chamber in order to proceed with an investigation or cause an arrest warrant to issue. This can be a serious hurdle, as a nation whose citizen is sought to be investigated has standing to oppose the motion of the prosecutor. Moreover, the decision of the pre-trial chamber to investigate a given citizen may be appealed to the appeals chamber of the ICC.

It is a matter for regret that these safeguards were not sufficient to persuade the United States to join its traditional allies in ratifying the Rome Treaty. It is hoped that if the ICC succeeds in its mission and its operations are handled professionally and with integrity, that the United States will take a leadership role in the ASP.

6 Post-ICC prosecutions

New domestic proceedings and international proceedings beyond ICC justice

Prompted in part by the prominence of the ad hoc and special tribunals, and the ICC, let alone the international rise of human rights as a politically potent global force, individual states have also continued domestic prosecutions for international crimes. In so doing, they have embarked on one of two courses. First, some states have altered their domestic criminal codes so as to allow for prosecution of international crimes that have no clear connection to the state. Such assertions of "universal" jurisdiction, while arguably somewhat depressed ever since Belgium was forced to tone down its assertions of jurisdiction and the British House of Lords effectively refused such an assertion regarding the detainment of former Chilean dictator Augusto Pinochet, have nonetheless markedly changed the delivery of international justice.

The second route many states have taken has involved the belated prosecution of mass crimes perpetrated by prior regimes. The most famous of such prosecutions has been the ongoing Iraqi Special Tribunal, but similar courts/investigations have occurred in states such as Ethiopia (the Dergue trials), Chile, and France (notably the trial of Vichy collaborator Maurice Papon as mentioned above).

This chapter will briefly detail these two phenomena (by way of an analysis of the multifaceted Pinochet situation and the Iraqi and Lebanese special tribunals), each of which has had, and promises to continue to have, determinative influences on the make up of, and provision of, international justice.

The Pinochet situation

Augusto Pinochet was the Chilean president from 1974 until 1990, and head of a cruel junta from 1973 to 1981. Reports authored after the return of democracy in 1990 revealed that nearly 3,000 people were murdered by the junta during Pinochet's rule and as many as 30,000 were tortured during that period. Much like in Argentina, prior to their relinquishment of power, the military rulers granted themselves amnesty for any crimes committed during this period. However, unlike in Argentina, the Chilean government chose to respect this grant. Pinochet himself even stayed active on the political stage for years after his regime, serving as a "Senator for Life" in the government.

In the 1990s, again thanks in no small part to the end of the Cold War (which provided the backdrop and putative justification for much of the Pinochet regime's activities), interest rose, initially outside Chile, to prosecute members of his regime. For almost the entire 1990s, the Chilean government expressed no interest in pursuing trials, and indeed would complain once moves outside Chile gained momentum to do so. Consequently, so long as Pinochet remained in Chile, he was safe from prosecution. However, once he left the country, he became vulnerable. It was this vulnerability which proponents of his prosecution exploited when the former president was detained in England in October 1998. The events surrounding his capture, arrest, and eventual return to Chile speak to several aspects of modern, domestic international justice, most notably the basis of jurisdiction under which domestic courts can prosecute international crimes.

In a sense there was little actually "international" about the legal machinations surrounding Pinochet's arrest; indeed, it is perhaps more accurate to call the events multinational (in that they involved several states) rather than international. As Naomi Roht-Arriaza noted, the discussions and arguments made by proponents and opponents of Pinochet's arrest grounded their debate in international concepts (like "universal jurisdiction") but in reality relied explicitly on domestic statutory constructs.[1] However, the Pinochet case provides a clear example of how the line between domestic law and international law, at least in the criminal realm, is becoming ever more difficult to discern.

Pinochet was arrested in London by English authorities on the basis of an international arrest warrant filed by a Spanish judge. That warrant was in turn based on the domestic criminal code of Spain, Article 23.4 of the Spanish Judicial Law, which "allows prosecution of non-Spanish citizens for some crimes committed outside Spain." The international component of this domestic law arose in the list of these crimes, including as it does "genocide, terrorism, and other crimes under international law contained in treaties ratified in Spain."[2] Interestingly, however, the Spanish warrant charged Pinochet with nearly 100 counts of torture of *Spanish* citizens and the assassination of a *Spanish* diplomat. The jurisdictional basis was consequently not necessarily "universal jurisdiction"—which is for many controversial—

but rather could have arisen under the far less controversial "protective" or "nationality" principles.[3]

Despite this, in the immediate wake of Pinochet's detention, it seemed that domestic law would take a back seat to the international concepts that emerged out of his arrest. The warrant requested Pinochet's extradition to Spain, and thus the case wound its way through the English courts based primarily on the question of the legal propriety of extraditing Pinochet to Madrid. The former leader's primary claim was that he was immune to charges allayed by the Spanish judge, based on his status as a former head of state. The case rose to the House of Lords, functioning as the United Kingdom's highest court, and the Lords forcefully rejected Pinochet's immunity. Michael Ratner notes that all seven of the Law Lords issued opinions specifically addressing international legal issues: "customary international law, the immunities of heads of state and former heads of state, fundamental norms of human rights and universal jurisdiction."[4] Though the majority agreed on the correct disposition, they diverged on the rationale. Some argued that head of state immunity referred solely to "acts of state" and that torture, which is illegal, could never be such an act of state. Others even suggested that there may not be such a thing as "former head of state immunity" either in customary international law or domestic law.

Simultaneous judicial actions also occurred in Spain where the appeals chamber of the Audencia Nacional affirmed Spanish jurisdiction over the case. The court found both that domestic, Chilean grants of amnesty could not bind Spanish courts, and that jurisdiction was proper under Spanish criminal law because of the crimes alleged, namely genocide.[5]

The only question that remained for the Lords was the scope of the international crimes under which they could exercise their jurisdiction in order to authorize the extradition. And in this, the Lords again turned to domestic UK law, and in particular the implementing legislation that Parliament had passed after ratifying the 1984 Torture Convention. In this, the Lords held that it was only for the crimes the indictment alleged Pinochet committed *after* the passage of the implementing legislation that it could ground jurisdiction. This was,

> despite the fact that torture was considered an international crime long before 1988. It was the incorporation of the Torture Convention into UK law that gave the court jurisdiction, not [any] underlying customary [legal] norm.[6]

It was not the universal jurisdiction enjoyed by the crime of torture, but the strictly legal incorporation of that crime into UK law that concerned the Law Lords. Regardless of the legal rationale, the result was that the extradition could proceed.

Chile was again a notable dissenter from these proceedings. Santiago complained about Pinochet's treatment and even withdrew its ambassador to Spain in protest.[7]

The only issue left for the purposes of extradition concerned Pinochet's alleged poor health. For several months at the beginning of 2000, legal wrangling between human rights organizations, the courts, and the British Home Office (which has the final say in extradition matters) argued about whether Pinochet's health was bad enough to warrant a refusal to extradite.[8] In March 2000 the Home Secretary issued his ruling, siding with Pinochet; the former president was free to return to Chile.

However, by the time he returned to Chile, the domestic political environment had changed. In May 2000 the Chilean Court of Appeal voted to lift Pinochet's immunity regarding at least one instance of abuse (the "Caravan of Death" case), and the Supreme Court affirmed. Pinochet was indicted in December 2000 for his role in the matter, but again Pinochet's health would intervene. He was ruled "demented" in July 2002, a ruling that was overturned in May 2004, allowing the resumption of proceedings. In 2004, the Supreme Court also expanded the scope of Pinochet's lost immunity, allowing further indictments to be lodged against him. He was again detained in December 2004 and placed under house arrest. Various legal machinations ensued, Pinochet's immunity being partially restored for some cases, while its illegitimacy being maintained for others. In September 2006, in what would be the final bout in this immunity struggles the Supreme Court appeared to fully strip his immunity. Pinochet would be dead three months later, prior to being convicted of any of these crimes.

Though Pinochet "escaped" justice, the process against members of his regime continues. And consequently even though it is unfortunate that Pinochet did not face justice, the legal events surrounding his capture and debates about immunity in Chile laid the foundation for the current prosecutions against those who participated in abuses in the name of the Pinochet regime.

The Iraqi Special Tribunal (IST)

Though the IST and the Pinochet prosecutions have had the same basic goal—making a prior regime accountable for its abuses—the models are vastly different. The Pinochet case, while litigated in Europe, implicitly relied on international law, even if domestic law was the determinative factor. In Iraq, as will be seen below, the IST is an explicitly Iraqi institution, and there is only passing (but potentially determinative) reference to explicit international law. However, given the scope of crimes under its jurisdiction, and the clear international delicts committed by the Saddam Hussein regime, the IST is an important way station in understanding the more recent attempts to come to grips with crimes of an international scope committed by former regimes.

In December 2003, the Iraqi Governing Council (the provisional Iraqi government that operated while the US-backed Coalition Provisional Authority [CPA] ruled the country) promulgated the creation of the IST.[9] Under CPA Order No. 48, the Administrator (L. Paul Bremer III) stated that:

> The Governing Council is hereby authorized to establish an Iraqi Special Tribunal to try Iraqi nationals or residents of Iraq accused of genocide, crimes against humanity, war crimes or violations of certain Iraqi laws.[10]

Though the order was unclear regarding the scope of international crimes (rather than domestic crimes that included international violations) over which the IST would have jurisdiction, it did explicitly cite to one international document: Security Council Resolution 1483, a Chapter VII, legally binding resolution which called for "accountability for the crimes and atrocities committed by the previous Iraqi regime," and demanded that "Member States ... deny safe haven to those members of the previous Iraqi regime who are alleged to be responsible for crimes and atrocities and to support actions to bring them to justice."[11] Thus ironically, if domestic law was to be used, it would be based in part on a mandate provided by international law.

To some the IST is yet another example of the confusion instigated by a CPA overwhelmed by the task at hand. Indeed, it would be hard to claim that the IST was the product of reasoned and balanced decision making. It seemed that there was never any doubt that the final fate of Saddam Hussein's government would be decided by judicial means. There was very little debate and analysis surrounding this decision, even though fringe elements of the invading coalition had considered alternatives to trials; they were never given the opportunity to impact the creation of the Iraqi Special Tribunal.[12]

Despite this, the IST is a fascinating hybrid, and given the direct and disproportionate role of American influence in establishing the institution, its statute and operations shed some light on the Bush administration's views about international justice and how best to dispense it. It must be acknowledged that even if the Bush administration had not expressed its disregard for the ICC, it would have been impossible for the Saddam Hussein crimes to be litigated before that body, as the regime's crimes under indictment occurred prior to the ICC's establishment. Thus, if there were to be trials, a different system would need to be relied upon. Instead of standing up the Iraqi judicial system, the CPA ventured toward a stand-alone "special" tribunal that had some interesting characteristics and has in consequence had some interesting (if not unfortunate) outcomes.

The structure of the IST appears to mimic that of the ICTY and ICTR, though the IST separates various parts of the structure in a different manner. The judicial chambers are separated into trial, appeals and tribunal judicial investigative units (the latter paying heed to the continental, civil law tradition allowing judges an active, investigatory role), while the statute also provides for a "Prosecutions Department" and a registry, the name of which was Americanized to the "Administrations Department" (Article 3).

Judicial selection is strictly controlled, first under the CPA (with its powers delegated to the Governing Council) and then under any "successor governments." There is no tiered structure for selection, with the only broad, substantive qualifications, again mirroring those in the UN ad hoc tribunals, that "judges shall be persons of high moral character, impartiality, and integrity" (Article 5), and cannot have been a member of the leadership Ba'ath Party (no one in the tribunal can be) (Article 33). The melding of Iraqi law into the tribunal is first made in this regard, as the statute states that the "terms and conditions of service [for judges] shall be those of the judges of the Iraqi judicial system as set out in the Law Number 160 of 1979 (Judicial Organization Law)." An additional and sadly necessary codicil to these "terms and conditions" was the qualifier placed in Article 5 allowing for "matters of compensation" to differ from those established in Law Number 160 "in light of the increased risks associated with the position."

The IST's jurisdiction is expansive. Article 10 provides for its temporal coverage to extend from the first time Saddam achieved any real power (short of the presidency), until his final removal from office. Thus the court can investigate all events from 17 July 1968 (when Saddam was a prime mover behind the bloodless coup orchestrated by Ahmad Hassan Al-Bakr, his predecessor as Iraqi president), until 1 May 2003, by which time the US-led invasion had secured Baghdad. Geographically, no doubt paying heed to Saddam's extraterritorial crimes committed in Kuwait and Iran, jurisdiction extends to those crimes perpetrated "in

Iraq or elsewhere." In short, the IST is unique in the annals of such tribunals in that it literally puts a dictator's entire reign on trial.[13]

Despite this, the statute's Article 10 provides a unique limitation on jurisdiction that some would claim is a direct function of American authorship. The IST only has jurisdiction "over any Iraqi national or resident of Iraq," thus removing the potential for any member of the occupying forces to stand trial. While the Nuremberg and the Tokyo trials limited jurisdiction to those "acting in the interests of the European axis countries" and "Far Eastern war criminals" respectively, and de facto limited their jurisdiction to specific nationalities (German and Japanese respectively), no other similar tribunal, and certainly no other modern tribunal, has so explicitly cabined its personal jurisdiction. The ICTY, for instance, has exercised jurisdiction over "persons responsible for serious violations" with no reference to their residence or citizenship. The ICTR has had jurisdiction over only Rwandan citizens who committed crimes in neighboring states, but over anyone who committed crimes inside Rwanda. And, the Special Court for Sierra Leone has had no jurisdiction over peacekeepers and "related personnel" who fought in the country, but again, as is evident by its indictment of both Sierra Leoneans and non-Sierra Leoneans (such as Liberia's Charles Taylor), there is no citizenship or residency limitation.

Regarding the crimes over which the IST has jurisdiction, clear shades of both the ICTY and ICTR and even the ICC are present. Article 11 includes the crime of genocide, which "for the purposes of this Statute [is defined] in accordance with the Convention on the Prevention and Punishment of the Crime of Genocide, dated December 9, 1948, as ratified by Iraq on January 20, 1959." "Crimes against humanity" are covered in Article 12 which, short of including the "crime of apartheid," directly transposes the list of component crimes in Article 7 of the Rome Statute for the ICC. Finally, Article 13 includes "war crimes," similarly following the ICC's lead in its Article 8, and defines such crimes as "Grave breaches of the Geneva Conventions of 12 August 1949." Further, as needed, in interpreting these provisions, the IST statute provides for the judges to "resort to the relevant decisions of international courts or tribunals as persuasive authority for their decisions" (Article 17b).

However, the role of purely international law, or even international law incorporated into domestic law, was significantly cabined by Article 14, which adds Iraqi laws into the criminal jurisdiction of the tribunal.

Article 14: Violations of stipulated iraqi laws
The Tribunal shall have the power to prosecute persons who have committed the following crimes under Iraqi law:

(a) For those outside the judiciary, the attempt to manipulate the judiciary or involvement in the functions of the judiciary, in violation, inter alia, of the Iraqi interim constitution of 1970, as amended;

(b) The wastage of national resources and the squandering of public assets and funds, pursuant to, inter alia, Article 2(g) of Law Number 7 of 1958, as amended; and

(c) The abuse of position and the pursuit of policies that may lead to the threat of war or the use of the armed forces of Iraq against an Arab country, in accordance with Article 1 of Law Number 7 of 1958, as amended.

This article clearly pays homage to the fact that the IST was legally designed to be an Iraqi institution. Similar respect for Iraqi traditions is provided in Article 17(a).

Article 17: General Principles of Criminal Law

(a) Subject to the provisions of this Statute and the rules made there under, the general principles of criminal law applicable in connection with the prosecution and trial of any accused person shall be those contained:

(i) in Iraqi criminal law as at July 17, 1968 (as embodied in the Baghdadi Criminal Code of 1919) for those offenses committed between July 17, 1968 and December 14, 1969;

(i) in Law Number 111 of 1969 (the Iraqi Criminal Code), as it was as of December 15, 1969, without regard to any amendments made thereafter, for those offenses committed between December 15, 1969 and May 1, 2003; and

(i) and in Law Number 23 of 1971 (the Iraqi Criminal Procedure Law).

An additional unique component in the IST, and perhaps no clearer a talisman of the United States' involvement in the IST's establishment, comes in the realm of punishments. Article 24 allows that the "penalties that shall be imposed by the Tribunal shall be those prescribed by Iraqi law (especially Law Number 111 of 1969 of the Iraqi Criminal Code)." One of these penalties is death, the exclusion of which from potential penalties has been the hallmark of all of the post–Cold War tribunals. Indeed, the exclusion of the death penalty played a role in forcing the moving of the ICTR from Rwanda to Tanzania, as Rwanda insisted that death be an option for any court operating on its soil. And, the absence of the penalty in the ICTR has also been blamed for subsequent reduced enthusiasm on behalf the Rwandan government regarding trials. As mentioned earlier, in order to enable the ICTR to transfer trials to Rwanda, the Rwandan government has abolished the death penalty.

The legal structure of the IST is clearly mixed, though it would be a mistake to call this a "mixed" or "hybrid" tribunal along the lines of the Special Court in Sierra Leone. It is an Iraqi institution; however, its Iraqi character is arguably dampened by one final element critical to understanding the IST: the statutory presence of non-Iraqis providing oversight to many of the IST's key positions. Such a provision is made in Article 7(n) which discusses the functions of the investigative judges.

Article 7
The Chief Tribunal Investigative Judge shall be required to appoint non-Iraqi nationals to act in advisory capacities or as observers to the Tribunal Investigative Judges. The role of the non-Iraqi nationals and observers shall be to provide assistance to the Tribunal Investigative Judges with respect to the investigations and prosecution of cases covered by the this Statute (whether in an international context or otherwise), and to monitor the protection by the Tribunal Investigative Judges of general due process of law standards.

Article 8 imposes a similar requirement for prosecutors. Naturally the role and control of these "advisors" and "observers" has been contentious. When the IST was integrated into domestic law by the independent Iraqi government in 2005, the presence of non-Iraqi advisors ceased being mandatory.

How has it operated? Though the IST is still functioning and thus a final assessment is premature, some initial observations are warranted. The first one suggests that despite its international-cum-American overlay, the IST has become an Iraqi court, at least in aspects of its procedure. The Saddam Hussein trial, the marquee proceeding against the former president that concluded in November 2006, provides some evidence for this. As discussed, the potential scope of crimes over which the IST has jurisdiction could have made a trial against Hussein logistically unwieldy if not impossible. Comparing the Milosevic case at the ICTY is instructive. There, prosecutors amassed a 66-count indictment, based on a much narrower time frame (only crimes committed since 1991), and arguably a fewer set of crimes; yet the prosecutors were unable to get through the case in four years. Interestingly, the American advisors to the IST wished, perhaps for reasons of political gain, to amass a similarly hefty indictment against Saddam and wanted to prosecute the entirety of the case at once. The Iraqis balked and decided to split the cases, resulting in an initial prosecution for Saddam's activities against the residents of the town of Dujail in 1982, many of whom were tortured after a failed assassination attempt. The unfortunate side of this decision was that this was Saddam's only trial; he was convicted of his Dujail misdeeds, and even as further cases were developed, he was executed on 30 December 2006. Despite the elements of Iraqi control indicative in the Saddam trial, other aspects indicate a more direct American role; for instance the initial director of the IST was the inexperienced Salem Chalabi, a relative of Ahmed Chalabi, an Iraqi dissident and a favorite of those forces in Washington who had agitated for the invasion.

Further, despite the fact that some Iraqis have expressed pride in the fact that the court is at least in Iraq (if not fully Iraqi), there remain serious doubts as to the fairness of Saddam's trial. Yet, in light of procedural and legal inequalities in some other multinational judicial institutions some have even questioned whether Saddam's trial, or that of others before the IST is any less fair than those prosecuted before other, international institutions.[14] Others question the benefit or harm the entire IST (which has continued to operate) has on Iraq itself. Judges and lawyers have been killed and threatened and it would be difficult to claim that the trials have aided reconciliation. However, given the multifaceted nature of the difficulties in Iraq it might be equally difficult to conclude that the IST has made reconciliation more difficult; an optimist might even claim that it has aided, or will soon, in some way, the ability of Iraqis to look ahead.[15]

A new wrinkle in international justice: the Special Tribunal for Lebanon

Further evidence of the continued dynamism of international criminal law and the institutions erected to address it came in 2007 with the formation of the Special Tribunal for Lebanon. The tribunal is a manifestation of the expanding bounds of what crimes rightly belong in "international" law. It is no longer war crimes or even "mass" crimes like genocide that receive such attention. Rather, international criminal law is being increasingly used for "smaller" crimes, and even those focused on individual harms. Elements of this were seen prior to 2007. For instance, as mentioned, the UN's international tribunals in East Timor (the "Special Panels") had jurisdiction over simple murder as defined by the East Timorese criminal code (i.e. "murder" outside of its commission in conjunction with a war crime or larger infraction). However, the Lebanese tribunal represents an even more extreme version of this expanded jurisdiction; it was directly established to prosecute a crime that was almost universally agreed to be beyond the purview of international criminal justice.

Rafiq Hariri,[16] the two-time prime minister of Lebanon, was assassinated in Beirut on 14 February 2005. Twenty-one members of his entourage were also killed. Hariri had been an ardent critic of the de facto Syrian occupation of Lebanon and had often urged Damascus to withdraw its forces. Given Lebanon's history of politically motivated killings, suspicion for the murders immediately fell on Syria and pro-Syrian forces in the country. In an unprecedented move, UN secretary-general Kofi Annan dispatched an investigator, Irish deputy police commissioner Peter Fitzgerald, to provide an initial assessment of the killings and report back to the UN. This move was unprecedented because of the nature of the crime under investigation; there were no claims of violations of international humanitarian law (which catalyzed the various commissions that investigated the Yugoslav and Rwandan conflicts prior to the establishment of the ad hoc courts). Rather, even if the assassination would have far ranging impacts (which it did) Secretary-General Annan used the force of his international bully pulpit and the resources of the UN to order Fitzgerald to investigate the murder of a private individual. The Fitzgerald Report[17] provided some initial observations regarding the crime, but concluded that more investigation was needed. This prompted the Security Council to adopt Resolution 1595 on 7 April 2005.[18] The resolution authorized a comprehensive investigation of the murder. To that end, the Security Council ordered the establishment of

> an International Independent Investigation Commission based in Lebanon to assist the Lebanese authorities in their investigation of all aspects of the terrorist attack which took place on 14 February 2005 in Beirut that killed former Lebanese Prime Minister Rafiq Hariri and others, including to help identify its perpetrators, sponsors, organizers and accomplices.[19]

The commission was headed by a German judge, Detlev Mehlis, and in October 2005 provided the Security Council a 223-paragraph report detailing the assassination and, for the first time, directly implicating Syrian and pro-Syrian elements in the Lebanese government in the assassination. A further round of investigations was ordered by the Security Council under Resolution 1636[20] and a further report was presented 10 December 2005.[21]

Even before the release of the second report, there was action toward enforcing Mehlis' findings. In Lebanon, authorities arrested Mahmoud

Abdel-Ali, who was identified in the report, and placed travel restrictions on 11 others thought involved. At the UN, the United States and the United Kingdom both stated their confidence that the Security Council would agree to some sort of action against Syria. And Saad Hariri, Rafiq's son, called for the establishment of an international body to address the crime. The younger Hariri asked the UN and the wider international community

> to support the international commission into the assassination of Mr. Hariri to bring out the full truth and bring the perpetrators to justice in an international court.[22]

Hariri's remarks were supported by Walid Jumblatt, the leader of the Lebanese Druze minority, who was less passionate, but nonetheless stated that "[i]f necessary, we will [also] support an international tribunal."[23] These requests were formalized by the prime minister of Lebanon, Fouad Siniora, in a 13 December 2005 letter sent to the secretary-general in which he asked for an international court to address the assassination. In so doing, Siniora crafted an interesting neologism to describe what sort of judicial body he would like. Siniora stated that he

> would hereby like to convey to you the request of the Lebanese Government, as per its decision at its meeting on 12 December 2005, to ask the Security Council: —To establish a *tribunal of an international character* to convene in or outside Lebanon, to try all those who are found responsible for the terrorist crime perpetrated against Prime Minister Hariri.[24]

It remains unclear what a "tribunal of an international character" actually means, but the term has maintained through subsequent correspondence and Security Council actions. Consequently, when the Security Council consented to being involved in forming a court to cover the Hariri murder it authorized the secretary-general to begin negotiations with the government of Lebanon "aimed at establishing a tribunal of an international character based on the highest international standards of criminal justice."[25] While negotiations continued the UN re-extended the investigatory efforts; Mehlis was replaced at the beginning of 2006 by Belgian prosecutor (and then deputy prosecutor of the ICC) Serge Brammertz,[26] and his mandate was altered to both allow for the collection of evidence suitable for presentation at trial and to investigate 14 other suspicious assassinations.

In November 2006 the UN delivered to Lebanon its proposal for a court, and once Beirut accepted it the Security Council approved the proposal on 31 May 2007. Security Council Resolution 1757, like the resolutions approving the ICTY and ICTR, was passed under the Council's Chapter VII authority. The Resolution stated that the Security Council

> *Decides*, acting under Chapter VII of the Charter of the United Nations, ... on the establishment of a Special Tribunal for Lebanon [which] shall enter into force on 10 June 2007. ... [27]

The Special Tribunal for Lebanon is a fascinating organization and one that both expands the notion of "international justice"—or, more to the point, expands the notion of when international institutions ought to be formed to pursue justice—while incorporating much of the learning of the ad hoc tribunals and even of the still nascent ICC. The differences between all of these judicial institutions are enlightening, but they share one key background feature: they have all been products of specific political forces in addition to judicial ones. The Special Tribunal for Lebanon makes the political context even more evident. The Security Council's Resolution 1757 came after the Second Lebanon–Israel war and with the pro-Western Prime Minister Siniora struggling for survival. Supporting him became an important project for both US president George W. Bush and French president Jacques Chirac, the two leaders who pushed the tribunal through the Security Council (massaging the concerns of some permanent members like China who were concerned that the tribunal was a step too far in interfering in the internal matters of a member state).

The tribunal's statute is a mix of unique components and tried and tested clauses from the ICTY, ICTR, ICC, and the hybrid/mixed courts. Interestingly the statute does not stand alone, and the agreement between the government of Lebanon and the UN (to which the statute is appended) is a central part of the statute itself and sets out some of the procedural aspects of the tribunal (such as funding). A brief overview of some of the special tribunal's components (present in both the statute and the agreement)—and from where inspiration for their inclusion likely sprang—follows:[28]

Article 1: Establishment of the Tribunal
The Special Tribunal shall have jurisdiction over persons responsible for the attack on 14 February 2005 resulting in the death of former Lebanese Prime Minister Rafiq Hariri and in the death or injury of other persons. If the tribunal finds that other attacks that

occurred in Lebanon between 1 October 2004 and 12 December 2005, or any later date decided by the Parties and with the consent of the Security Council, are connected in accordance with the principles of criminal justice and are of a nature and gravity similar to the attack of 14 February 2005, it shall also have jurisdiction over persons responsible for such attacks. This connection includes but is not limited to a combination of the following elements: criminal intent (motive), the purpose behind the attacks, the nature of the victims targeted, the pattern of the attacks ... and the perpetrators.

Article 1 sets out the temporal and subject matter jurisdiction of the special tribunal; it is striking how different Article 1 is from its analogs in the statutes of either the ICTY or the ICTR. First, unlike in those tribunals which dealt writ large with "violations" and "grave breaches" this statute mentions a specific criminal instance as being the core of the tribunal's jurisdiction. It seems to limit jurisdiction by this specific act. The statute then follows the ICTY and ICTR in limiting its temporal jurisdiction. However, any limitations on jurisdiction are quickly rendered moot by the clause that not only potentially expands the temporal jurisdiction infinitely (if the parties [the UN and Lebanon] and the Security Council agree), but also expands the subject matter jurisdiction to include any other attack committed since 1 October 2004 if there is some potentially nebulous link between that attack and the Hariri murder.

Article 2: Applicable Criminal Law
The following shall be applicable to the prosecution and punishment of the crimes referred to in article 1 ...
(a)   The provisions of the Lebanese Criminal Code relating to the prosecution and punishment of acts of terrorism, crimes and offenses against life and personal integrity, illicit associations and failure to report crimes and offenses. ...

Regarding the law that will be used, the Lebanese tribunal follows the Argentine or the Iraqi Special Tribunal models and steers away from relying on explicit international law. The reason for this may well result not just from the fact that it was the United States that had a critical role in pushing forward the tribunal, but also from the more prosaic fact that the crime of political assassination or simple murder has not been previously prosecuted in international law. However, international law could have been implicated: the International Convention for the Suppression of Terrorist Bombings[29] requires parties to criminalize, under their domestic laws, certain types of criminal offenses, and also requires parties to extradite or submit for prosecution persons accused of committing or aiding in the commission of such offenses. However, neither Syria nor Lebanon are parties to this convention.

Alternatively, the tribunal could have relied on a host of customary international law commitments (regarding the impermissibility of terrorism in general). Yet, given the arguable novelty in doing so, the tribunal's creators likely felt it would be easier and perhaps more acceptable to the Lebanese people if domestic code was the explicit referent rather than international.

Note also that even if it is Lebanese law that will be followed, there is one critical exception: Article 16 of the special tribunal statute allows it to ignore prior grants of amnesty by Lebanese courts, holding that such an "amnesty already granted ... shall not be a bar to prosecution."

Article 7: Composition of the Special Tribunal and Appointment of Judges

1   The Special Tribunal shall consist of the following organs: the Chambers, the Prosecutor, the Registry and the Defense Office ...

An intriguing aspect of the tribunal structure is its departure from the tripartite system of the ICTY and ICTR (in Articles 11 and 10 in their respective statutes) and its introduction of a quadpartite structure which includes the chambers, prosecutor, and registry (as in the ICTY and ICTR) *and* defense.[30] As noted, there have been some shortcomings in the ad hoc tribunals regarding adequacy of defense support, in some cases exacerbated by the positioning of the defense function statutorily outside the central structure of the institution. By making defense a central, foundational pillar of the tribunal's structure, concerns about inequality of arms between defense and prosecution could perhaps be alleviated.

... 3   The Chambers shall be composed of no fewer than eleven judges and no more than fourteen such judges, who shall serve as follows:

(a) A single international judge shall serve as a Pre-Trial judge;

(b) Three judges shall serve in the Trial Chamber, of whom one shall be a Lebanese judge and two shall be international judges;

[...]

(d) Five judges shall serve in the Appeals Chamber, of whom two shall be Lebanese judges and three shall be international judges; and

(e) Two alternate judges, of whom one shall be Lebanese and one shall be an international judge.

In establishing the judicial body the special tribunal clearly pays due regard to the hybrid/mixed models of courts, bringing in both Lebanese and international jurists. The international judges serve as the majority at all stages of the proceedings, a system similar to that in place at the Special Court for Sierra Leone (Article 12 of the Statute of the Special Court for Sierra Leone) and was in place in the East Timor "Special Panels." Similarly the statute calls for an international chief prosecutor, assisted by a Lebanese deputy, also a like structure to that of many of the hybrids.

Article 11: The Prosecutor
[...]
3. The Prosecutor shall be appointed, as set forth in Article 3 of [the] Agreement [between Lebanon and the United Nations]: [The Secretary-General shall appoint the Prosecutor, upon the recommendation of a selection panel he has established after indicating his intentions to the Security Council. The selection panel shall be composed of two judges, currently sitting on or retired from an international tribunal, and the representative of the Secretary-General.]

This layered system by which the prosecutor is to be selected is similar to that of the Special Court for Sierra Leone but different from the election system in the ad hoc tribunals and the ICC. In the case of the ICTY and ICTR, the Security Council itself has elected the prosecutor on the nomination of the secretary-general. In the case of the ICC, the prosecutor is elected by the Assembly of States Parties. A similar process has been in place for the selection of judges to these tribunals. This at times hugely politicized the process; for instance judicial selections in 2001 for "the ICTY were noted for their extreme politicization, marked by the 'amount of money spent on campaigning, as well as [the fact that] political considerations were reportedly much greater factors in the outcome of the elections than the qualifications of the candidates.'"[31]

Incorporating a selection panel of "sitting ... or retired" judges will, if they are adequately insulated from political pressures, reduce the potential for politicization. Given the sensitivity around the Lebanese tribunal, such a reduced politicization will be critical to the tribunal's success.

Article 4: Concurrent Jurisdiction
The Special Tribunal and the national courts of Lebanon shall have concurrent jurisdiction. Within its jurisdiction, the Tribunal shall have primacy over the national courts of Lebanon.

This Article mirrors Articles 8 and 9 from the ICTR and ICTY statutes respectively. One could argue that this marks a retreat from the complementarity model in the ICC; however, the key difference in this regard (which is also different from the ICTR and ICTY) is that it was the government of Lebanon that explicitly requested the tribunal and in its agreement with the UN subsequently consented to the special tribunal's primacy.

Article 5 (Agreement): Financing of the Special Tribunal
(a) Fifty-one per cent of the expenses of the Tribunal shall be borne by voluntary contributions from States;
(b) Forty-nine per cent of the expenses of the Tribunal shall be borne by the Government of Lebanon.

This article reflects the international community's desire to avoid the expenses of the tribunal being paid for by the UN. This move from UN funding to state funding is an important post-ICTY/ICTR change in the financing of international judicial institutions.

Article 8 (Agreement): Seat of the Special Tribunal
1. The Special Tribunal shall have its seat outside Lebanon. The location of the seat shall be determined having due regard to considerations of justice and fairness as well as security and administrative efficiency, including the rights of victims and access to witnesses.

As with the *ad hoc* tribunals, there exists a concern that locating the special tribunal in Lebanon could be deleterious to both Lebanese security and the ability of the tribunal to engage in its work. Consequently, the agreement provides for the tribunal's seat to be outside Lebanon. However, the agreement does recognize some of the concerns expressed with the distance between the ad hoc tribunals and the countries of their focus. The article requires that in establishing its seat the institution must give consideration not just to its own operations, but also to the "rights of the victims and access to witnesses." As noted above, the tribunal has chosen the Dutch city Leidschendam for its seat.

Article 17: Rights of Victims
Where the potential interests of the victims are affected, the Special Tribunal shall permit their views and concerns to be presented and considered at stages of the proceedings determined to be appropriate ... in a manner that is not prejudicial to ... the rights of the accused. ...

[...]

Article 25: Compensation to Victims
The Special Tribunal may identify victims who have suffered harm as a result of the commission of crimes by an accused convicted by the Tribunal.
[...]
Based on the decision of the Special Tribunal and pursuant to ... relevant national legislation, a victim ... may bring an action in a national court ... to obtain compensation.
[...]
For the purposes of a claim ... the judgment of the Special Tribunal shall be final and binding as to the criminal responsibility of the convicted person.

Critics of the ICTY and ICTR often note the absence of an acknowledgment of victims in the work of the courts. Indeed, from a statutory/institutional basis, it has only been the physical protection of witnesses that is provided, with the potential for "in camera proceedings and the protection of [a] victim's identity."[32] It was an innovation of the Rome Statute of the ICC that brought victims more to the fore, and its Article 75 and 79 make explicit mention of victims rights to reparation (Article 75) and even establishes a trust fund to that end (Article 79). The Special Tribunal for Lebanon arguably goes even further by making clear provision and reference to the rights of victims, and even speaks to the possibility of private rights of action on behalf of victims, who could base their claims on the decisions of the tribunal.

Article 22: Trials in Absentia
1. The Special Tribunal shall conduct trial proceedings in the absence of the accused, if he or she:
    (a) Has expressly ... waived his or her right to be present;
    (b) Has not been handed over to the Tribunal by the State authorities concerned;

(c) Has absconded or otherwise cannot be found and all reasonable steps have been taken to secure his or her appearance before the Tribunal and to inform him or her of the charges confirmed. ...

This article both recalls aspects of the Nuremberg/Tokyo model, while respecting the Lebanese domestic criminal system. Absentia trials, which were allowed at Nuremberg and Tokyo, have not been permitted in the ICTY and ICTR, nor in the Special Court of Sierra Leone. They are, however, present in the special tribunal, while according to Cecile Aptel (who headed the legal advisory unit of the Mehlis Commission) they, along with the role of the judges in conducting the hearings, and the participation of victims in proceedings "reflect the intention of the drafters to draw up a more efficient international criminal procedure."[33]

Article 26: Appellate Proceedings
1. The Appeals Chamber shall hear appeals from persons convicted by the Trial Chamber or from the Prosecutor on the following grounds:
    (a) An error on a question of law invalidating the decision;
    (b) An error of fact that occasioned a miscarriage of justice.
2. The Appeals Chamber may affirm, reverse or revise the decisions taken by the Trial Chamber.

Article 26 continues the allowance of appeals in international justice. As noted, appeals were absent from Nuremberg and Tokyo, but appeared at the ICTY and ICTR and have maintained in all tribunals since. Though there have some debates regarding the logic of appeals systems in international justice[34], Article 26 maintains the now likely irreversible trend of providing for such appeals.

Article 28: Rules of Procedure and Evidence
... The judges ... shall ... adopt Rules of Procedure and Evidence for the conduct of the pre-trial, trial and appellate proceedings, the admission of evidence, the participation of victims, the protection of victims and witnesses and other appropriate matters and may amend them, as appropriate.

This article mimics the provisions first provided at Nuremberg for the judges appointed to the tribunal to establish their own rules of procedure and evidence. This suggests that evidentiary rules will, once again, likely be broadly interpreted. The only difference between this article and similar provisions in the statutes of prior institutions is the degree of explicitness provided in the article regarding the scope of the rules of procedure and evidence (e.g. including the protection and participation of victims).

> *Article 29*: Enforcement of Sentences
> ... Imprisonment shall be served in a State designated by the President of the Special Tribunal from a list of States that have indicated their willingness to accept persons convicted by the Tribunal.

Finally, Article 29 again illustrates the fact that the international system has neither a police force nor a prison system. Consequently international courts are reliant on state cooperation both to secure the presence of defendants and then to handle the physical disposition of convicts once proceedings conclude. This latter requirement for the ICTY and ICTR has involved establishing cooperation agreements between the courts and a number of potential host states that have agreed to house those convicted in any trials. The Lebanese tribunal appears to be establishing a similar system.

7 Conclusion
The future of "international" justice—active at home and abroad

This book began with the notion that "international justice" is a complex, intricate concept, perhaps uniquely unamenable to easy definition. Consequently, it should not be surprising that institutions and methods employed to pursue international justice have themselves been varied and multifaceted. Though some trends and broad coalescence can be seen, any close examination of the diversity of institutions constructed for this purpose must conclude that in as much as there is a "system" of international justice that system remains in flux.

This continuation of uncertainty as to what comprises international justice, let alone international judicial institutions, has been frustrating for many. At each stop on the journey of institutional design some have sought closure and a conclusion that the international community had uncovered the "right" way to dispense justice. After Nuremberg and the Tokyo trials some hoped for an institutionalization of these processes; once the ICTY and ICTR were formed it was thought by some that the mass, international tribunal would be the way forward, while the subsequent rise of the hybrids and mixed courts, let alone increasingly robust domestic prosecutions, have further muddied the waters. For a time, the ICC seemed to be the enduring model, and indeed the permanent international criminal court has a better chance than many at becoming the model of choice if only because it is "permanent" rather than ad hoc or temporary. Yet, even here, we have arguably moved beyond the ICC, to post-ICC institutions that take into account more law as worthy of international institutions (like the Lebanese Special Tribunal), and even the development of mass domestic tribunals (such as the Iraqi Special Tribunal) that are evidently based on international bodies, and even have some international referents, but are institutionally and operationally distinct from either the ICC model, or even those of the internationally backed "mixed" or hybrid courts.

The greatest clarity that we can provide in this conclusion is not to suggest an "answer" as to what is the "best" option for dispensing international justice. Each of the institutions described in this book has much to recommend it and much to fear from it. Each that has been in operation has recorded notable successes along with failures. Each has provided some modicum of "justice" to some people, but each has also been accused of flagrant disregard of justice and even the dispensation of manifest injustice. What the cataloging of the various institutions and processes reveals is a menu of sorts that has emerged from which institutional designers have picked the ingredients to develop their specific "solutions" to addressing international crimes.

While a micro-examination of the institutions reveals a potentially dizzying array of variables that differ from one court to the next, a wider view reveals several of the macro-choices, many of them inter-related, that have proven to be guiding and even determinative forces for institutions and thus the sources of bona fide distinctions between them. It is our assessment that the critical differences among tribunals—those existing today and those surely to be created tomorrow to address unforeseen calamities and brutalities—can be found by looking to these differences. How have institutional designers answered particular questions? Note that all of these questions broadly revolve around the issue of how international and how domestic each aspect of an institution will be.

Questions for institutional designers

Will there be an "institution" at all?

International justice need not be dispensed by an institution dedicated to its provision. As seen in Israel, Argentina, Chile, and elsewhere, the dispensation of international justice does not need a purpose-built structure, but rather can rely on existing domestic legal and judicial institutions. Consequently, the first question that needs to be asked is whether a new institution, or a different institution apart from existing bodies, is even needed for the pursuit of international justice.

What law should be employed?

A second initial, critical question concerns the nature of the law used in any institution. There are two related questions in this regard. First, and most centrally, how much "international" law is to be relied on? Institutions have adopted several positions on the spectrum between no international law and complete reliance on it. The ICTY and ICTR seem to be completely internationalized institutions, though even they, through statutory reference to practices conducted in Yugoslavia and Rwanda (in sentencing for instance)[1] and case law which has at times explicitly referenced national legislation,[2] leave the door open for resort to domestic legal process. Meanwhile the proceedings against Pinochet or the Argentine junta were apparently the opposite, with the former having little reliance on international law and the latter arguably having none. The French prosecution of Klaus Barbie occupies the center ground as it was French law that was used in the trial, but a law that explicitly adopted international precedent regarding international crimes.[3]

The choice, it seems, is not solely based upon the availability of international law to cover the crimes over which the institution has jurisdiction. This is likely one of the key reasons that the Special Tribunal for Lebanon has opted to follow Lebanese,[4] rather than international codes. Rather, a key issue, and one that appears in so many variables, concerns ownership and buy-in on behalf of the countries in whose name justice is being dispensed. Some states have expressed ambivalence over its citizens being subject to international law, citing many of the criticisms mentioned in Chapter 2—a democratic deficit, an inequality in application, etc. Other states are much more eager to refer to and respect international law, and even potentially to have their citizens held liable under it.

Though determining whether international or domestic law will be the foundation for the justice is critical, from a practical perspective what the cataloging of institutions reveals is that it may be increasingly a distinction without a difference. Domestic law, in many instances, is becoming internationalized. This is happening at the margins—for instance, in the gradual elimination of a statute of limitations for war crimes in the German penal system, thus bringing it in line with international law—and more centrally in the full adoption of the ICC treaty and all its constituent crimes into domestic law on behalf of states parties to the court. We would refer again, in this context, to the abolition by Rwanda of the death sentence, which served to bring Kigali in line with international legal practice.

A good example of the simultaneous psychological importance of the debate between tribunals' use of international and domestic law, and the minimal impact such a choice may have on the ground, can perhaps be seen outside the bounds of international humanitarian law and in the realm of broader, inter-state international public law. In this regard the judicial events surrounding the security barrier/wall built by Israel between itself and Palestinian territories on the West Bank is instructive. In that case, during the summer of 2004, another international institution, the International Court of Justice, ruled on the legal propriety of the placement of the structure. The ICJ held that international law was violated by the barrier. Within a few days of the ICJ's ruling, the Israeli Supreme Court ruled on the case as well (based on a domestic case brought before it). The Israeli Supreme Court agreed with the ICJ, and even cited some of the same international precedents. However, it couched its decision in domestic Israeli law. Tellingly, the Israeli government explicitly denounced the ICJ decision while accepting its own Supreme Court's determinations. Ironically, and on the ground, the result was the de facto furthering of international law and legal conclusions via domestic instruments.[5]

The second question regarding the type of law to employ that has at least implicitly occupied institutional designers asks whether the institution should be concerned about criminal liability or civil liability. No institution of international justice has yet fully embraced solely a civil system, in which cases would be brought by those aggrieved, rather than by a "sovereign." However, the trend seems to be present to rely increasingly on civil components for institutions. This is directly related to the part victims play in proceedings. The Special Tribunal for Lebanon, along with the ICC, have gone the furthest in bringing civil aspects of trial—through providing clear victim rights and roles—into the criminal courtroom.

In the special tribunal and the ICC, victims are statutorily provided the potential for compensation, not unlike that they would receive if they launched a civil case on their own. This trend may well continue and indeed there could be international tribunals that attempt to address international crimes through solely, or at least initially, civil measures.

In addition to receiving some scholarly support,[6] there is some precedent for folding a civil case in with a criminal proceeding. The process of including victims in criminal cases accords with many domestic systems, such as in France and Spain, where individuals can join with the state in launching prosecutions. This happened in both the Barbie and Pinochet cases described earlier. Additionally, there is a movement in some states in which mass crimes have been committed to first prosecute criminals for their civil delicts (enriching themselves unjustly or abusing their office) before addressing their criminal conduct. The frequent near identity between those who commit mass crimes and those who profit from such crimes makes this an attractive and logical option. Given that he was sitting in a Belgrade jail charged with abuse of office at time of his extradition to The Hague, this is perhaps the model that the Serbian government was embarking on with Milosevic. In light of the riches he amassed, there have been some calls for this judicial ordering regarding the trial of Liberia's former president Charles Taylor.

Where will the court be located?

Early precedent on this question was somewhat misleading and may be uninstructive for the situations in which current and likely future proceedings will be held. What was noteworthy about the location of the Nuremberg and Tokyo trials was that they took place in the home country of the defendants. Yet, defeat of Nazi Germany and the Japanese empire and the consequent full demilitarization and occupation of the states gave these tribunals unfettered access to both witnesses and evidence, let alone security in their operations. The same cannot be said for today's tribunals. With the exception of the Iraqi Special Tribunal, no recent tribunal or attempt to procure international justice, has been undertaken in a country after an invasion. Indeed, even in the case of the IST, the continued inability of the "occupying" force to establish its full hegemony over the country makes the situation radically different from that which the Allies faced in post–World War II Germany and Japan.

With a potentially hostile and/or unstable situation in the country where either defendants are from or where abuses took place, institutions must be very careful in deciding where to base themselves. There are evidently competing equities, with the balance being between local ownership and the ability for witnesses and victims to see and feel justice being done, and the actual, pragmatic ability of any institution to succeed in its mandate. Most institutions have decided to decamp and set up operations elsewhere, sometimes thousands of miles away from the scene. However, in other instances, trials at home were attempted or at least desired; the Argentine junta trials, the East Timorese Special Panels, the Khmer Rouge Tribunal, and the Special Court for Sierra Leone, have all been based in-country. However, in the Sierra Leone case, the flexibility the institution exhibited by deciding to maintain its Freetown base while prosecuting its most important defendant in The Hague, was a testament to fears of instability. It was also in large part such fears that compelled the UN secretary-general to recommend that the ICTR be based in Tanzania, despite the robust arguments on behalf of the Rwandan government to house the court in Kigali.[7]

Who are the judges? Who are the prosecutors? Who are the staff?

A cynical way of asking this question, which concerns the makeup of the staff of any institution or proceedings, is "do we trust the locals to fairly seek justice?" In many cases, that question has been answered in the negative, resulting in the wholesale absence of nationalities from the body of institutions attempting to provide them with justice. The Nuremberg and Tokyo precedent has again been engrained; there, with the meek attempts at domestic prosecutions after World War I fresh in their mind, the proceedings only included Germans and Japanese in the dock, and nowhere else in the tribunals. The ICTY and ICTR picked up on this trend and were explicitly internationalized, with few, if any, potentially aggrieved party involved in either tribunal. However, the IST, and more recent mixed and hybrid courts in East Timor, Cambodia, and Sierra Leone have included local judges, prosecutors, and administrators alongside international counterparts. It seems that the trend toward including potentially aggrieved parties is, absent the ICC, well developed, with future tribunals likely relying on procedural protections along with the presence of international staff, to protect against miscarriages of justice caused by potential national biases. It is noteworthy that the ICC in this regard seems to be an anachronism; the nature of a standing court is that its personnel is also "standing" and thus the judges who will hear its cases will in all likelihood not be from the country of the accused, or the accuser.

What are the penalties?

This question relates both to the disposition of convicts, as well as the potential scope of any penalties. The more "international" an institution, the more likely that non-domestic players will be involved in housing convicts and actually dispensing penalties. Thus, in the ICTY and ICTR there are a host of states that have agreed to accept those convicted by the institutions.[8] However, in other cases, such as in East Timor[9] and likely to be the case in Cambodia,[10] it has been viewed sufficient for any convicts to be housed in local facilities. This determination is also related to ownership of the institution and its outcome; the fact that some convicted war criminals, in the ICTY for instance, are housed in prisons outside the former war zone has engendered discord in the Balkans, with thoughts that they are being treated too kindly or at least far more gingerly than they would be if incarcerated in a Balkan facility.

The second aspect of penalties relates to their severity. At one extreme there exists the question which has dogged the UN ad hoc courts regarding sentencing consistency and how to ensure that like defendants are similarly punished. How does one balance that desire with the administrative necessities that lead to plea bargaining and other tools that may "justifiably" alter sentences? At the other extreme is the question of the death penalty. Both the Nuremberg and the Tokyo trials had the death penalty and carried it out. Similarly, some of the domestic prosecutions for international crimes, notably the *Eichmann* case in Israel, also resulted in the sentence of execution. However, modern institutions have, with the exception of the IST, shied away from the death penalty. The Rwandan abolition of the death penalty was directly related to the UN's refusal to countenance the death penalty; the ICTR explicitly conditioned the transfer of any of its trial to Rwanda on that country's waiving the death penalty in respect of any such cases.[11] It remains to be seen how such a move will impact the perception of justice within the country.

What is the balance between different parties in the proceedings?

International justice, both the institutions formed to pursue it and the domestic attempts to provide it, has often been criticized for upsetting the balance between parties that exists in most domestic judicial systems. The key balance is the "equality of arms" that ought to exist between defendants and prosecutors; such equality is thought critical to a fair trial and to ensuring that a defendant's rights will be protected. However, in many cases it has seemed that such an assurance has been lacking. In the *Eichmann* case observers noted the distinctly unequal treatment received by the defendant, hampering his ability to mount an effective defense.[12] The extreme relaxation of rules of evidence, which occurred at Nuremberg and has continued in almost every instance of international justice since, has also often disadvantaged the defense. In the ICTY and ICTR, defense counsel have regularly complained about unequal access to evidence and other resources.[13] Recent reports indicate that defense counsel working on the ICC's first case have similarly "encountered several administrative and procedural challenges" leading to "a considerable lack in equality of arms" between the defense and the prosecution.[14] The Special Tribunal for Lebanon appears to try to right the balance between defense and prosecution by including the defense within its core structure. However, it is unclear how this balance will play out.

The second balance is that between the proceedings and victims. Historically, international justice has been criticized for neglecting the victim. Some may argue that victims have only a limited role in the dispensation of justice and their presence may unfairly sway a decision maker. Such was one of the rationales for "neglecting" the victim—i.e. leaving him or her statutorily unmentioned and/or procedurally disempowered—in several of the international institutions discussed in this book.[15] However, again more recently, institutions like the Special Tribunal for Lebanon[16] and the ICC[17] have brought victims directly into the process. The question has thus become not whether victims belong in the process, but how victim-centered justice should become— with the recognition that "victims' justice"[18] may be as problematic as "victors' justice." The extremes are evident, and it could be argued that some domestic proceedings, notably *Eichmann*, were prime examples of this.[19] While the *Eichmann* case, and indeed the entire circumstances surrounding his capture and trial were uniquely ripe for victims to take center stage,[20] it is nonetheless difficult, even in far less charged atmospheres, to achieve a satisfying balance between the rights of the defendant and the administrative burden on the court that an excessively victim-focused process may entail, with the rights of the victims.

Achieving justice: the goal remains, as do the challenges

In addition to these five questions, any discussion of the future of international justice must return to its foundational question: how best to ensure accountability and deter repetition of horrific crimes? In that regard, any future prognosis must recognize that courts—and indeed the law—are only one tool of many in achieving such a goal. Indeed, the menu of how best to deal with such crimes has become enriched and multifaceted. For instance, the truth and reconciliation commission model used in South Africa and Liberia (among other countries) employs an entirely different set of institutions designed to further "justice," but usually in the absence of prosecutions.[21] Still other states, and in particular some communities and clan groups, advocate a mix of the shaming of perpetrators combined with real forgiveness and reintegration, also without prosecution.

Unfortunately, as the Darfur tragedy continues, and many other instances of similar acts go on with considerably less media attention, there are only two clear certainties. First, the need for some sort of international justice, whether dispensed locally or internationally, is not receding. And, second, with the current trends toward an ever-greater diversity in how states and other entities wish to deal with such crimes, it seems that there will unlikely be a single method or institution formed that is capable of addressing international judicial needs in all their diversity and number. The International Criminal Court will likely play a leading role, but there will be many other actors. And there will undoubtedly be players who will continue to question the very worth, let alone validity, of internationalized justice.

Yet, leaving aside critics of the international judicial enterprise itself, with the increasing number of venues for trial or otherwise holding perpetrators to account, the challenge for the world community will be to harness the global consensus on the necessity for responding to such crimes, while ensuring that the interwoven set of organizations erected does not allow perpetrators to slip through the net created by over-lapping and inconsistent jurisdiction, goals, and enforcement. It would be an unfortunate irony if the world's enthusiasm for ending impunity were to in itself create the means for criminals to avoid justice.

Notes

Foreword

1 See David P. Forsythe and Barbara Ann J. Rieffer-Flanagan, *The International Committee of the Red Cross: a neutral humanitarian actor* (London: Routledge, 2007).
2 See Julie A. Mertus, *The United Nations and Human Rights* (London: Routledge, 2005); and Bertrand G. Ramcharan, *Contemporary Human Rights Ideas* (London: Routledge, 2008).
3 Quoted in William Korey, *NGOs and the Universal Declaration of Human Rights: "A Curious Grapevine"* (New York: St. Martin's Press, 1998), 9.
4 See Edward Newman, *A Crisis of Global Institutions? Multilateralism and international security* (London: Routledge, 2007).
5 See Richard Goldstone, "International Criminal Court and Ad Hoc Tribunals," in *The Oxford Handbook on the United Nations*, ed. Thomas G. Weiss and Sam Daws (Oxford: Oxford University Press, 2007), 463–78.

Introduction

1 IHL is part of the much broader construct "international criminal law" which includes international and transnational crimes such as drugs and human trafficking. This book, and the institutions it describes, is limited to discussing the smaller sub-part of international criminal law that makes up IHL—war crimes, genocide, and crimes against humanity.
2 Rome Statute of the International Criminal Court, (UN document A/CONF.183/9), 17 July 1998.
3 Philippe Sands, "After Pinochet: the role of national courts," in *From Nuremberg to The Hague,* ed. Philippe Sands (Cambridge: Cambridge University Press, 2003), 68. See *Regina v. Bow Street Metropolitan Stipendiary Magistrate, ex parte* Pinochet Ugarte, [1998] 3 W.L.R. 1456 (H.L.), *reprinted in* 37 I.L.M. 1302 (1998); *Regina v. Bow Street Metropolitan Stipendiary Magistrate, ex parte* Pinochet Ugarte, [1999] 2 W.L.R. 272 (H. L.), *reprinted in* 38 I.L.M. 430 (1999); *Regina v. Bow Street Metropolitan Stipendiary Magistrate, ex parte* Pinochet Ugarte, [1999] 2 W.L.R. 827 (H.L.).
4 See generally Eric A. Posner and Adrian Vermeule, "Transitional Justice as Ordinary Justice," *Harvard Law Review* 117, no. 3 (2004): 762; Martha

Minow, *Between Vengeance and Forgiveness: facing history after genocide and mass violence* (Boston, Mass.: Beacon Press, 1998).

5 See e.g. Desmond Tutu, *No Future Without Forgiveness* (New York: Doubleday, 1999).

6 Priscilla B. Hayner, *Unspeakable Truths: facing the challenge of truth commissions* (London: Routledge, 2002).

7 Office of the United Nations High Commissioner for Human Rights, *Rule of Law Tools for Post Conflict States: truth commissions* (New York: United Nations, 2006).

8 See e.g. Jose E. Alvarez, "Rush to Closure: lessons of the Tadic judgment," *Michigan Law Review* 96, no. 7 (1998): 2101; John F. Murphy, "Civil Liability for the Commission of International Crimes as an Alternative to Criminal Prosecution," *Harvard Human Rights Journal* 12 (spring 1999): 3.

9 See e.g. Richard Overy, "The Nuremberg Trials: international law in the making," in *From Nuremberg to The Hague*, ed. Philippe Sands (Cambridge: Cambridge University Press, 2003), 15.

10 Rome Statute of the International Criminal Court, (UN document A/CONF.183/9), 17 July 1998, arts. 5–8.

11 United Nations Transition Authority in East Timor (UNTAET), "On the establishment of panels with exclusive jurisdiction over serious criminal offences," Regulation No. 2000/15, (UNTAET/REG/2000/15), 6 June 2000, section 3.

12 United Nations Security Council Resolution 1757, 31 May 2007 (S/Res/1757 (2007)).

13 *Treaty of Peace Between the Allied and Associated Powers and Germany*, 28 June 1919, 225 Consol. T.S. 188, arts. 227–30; *Treaty of Peace Between the Allied and Associated Powers and Turkey*, 10 August 1920 (never adopted).

14 *Papers Relating to the Foreign Relations of the United States, 1915, Supplement*, Washington, D.C.: US Government Printing Office, 1928: 981; cited in Antonio Cassese, *International Criminal Law* (Oxford: Oxford University Press, 2003).

15 Peter Maguire, *Law and War: an American story* (New York: Columbia University Press, 2001), 238.

16 United Nations General Assembly, Resolution 260 B (III), 9 December 1948.

17 United Nations Security Council Resolution 827, S/Res/827 (1993), 25 May 1993.

18 United Nations Security Council Resolution 955, S/Res/955 (1994), 8 November 1994.

19 Patricia M. Wald, "To Establish Incredible Events by Credible Evidence: the use of affidavit testimony in Yugoslavia War Crimes Tribunal proceedings," *Harvard International Law Journal* 42, no. 2 (2001): 536.

20 Rome Statute of the International Criminal Court (UN document A/CONF.183/9), 17 July 1998, art. 1; Mahnoush H. Arsanjani, "The Rome Statute of the International Criminal Court," *American Journal of International Law* 93, no. 1 (1999): 22–43.

1 International humanitarian law: a short review

1 Antonio Cassese, *International Criminal Law* (Oxford: Oxford University Press, 2003), 16.

2 Georg Schwarzenberger, "The Judgment of Nuremberg," *The Tulane Law Review* 21, no. 3 (1947): 329.

3 Schwarzenberger, "The Judgment of Nuremberg," 329; see also Timothy L. H. McCormack, "From Sun Tzu to the Sixth Committee: the evolution of an international criminal law regime," in *The Law of War Crimes: national and international approaches*, ed. Timothy L. H. McCormack and Gerry J. Simpson (The Hague, The Netherlands: Kluwer, 1997), 31.

4 It was regularly the violation of divine will which served as the basis for finding liability in early prosecutions. As discussed below, in 1474 Peter von Hagenbach was charged with "trampl[ing] under foot the laws of God and man."

5 See e.g. Eugene Kontorovich, "The Piracy Analogy: modern Universal Jurisdiction's hollow foundation," *Harvard International Law Journal* 45, no. 1 (2004): 183; Princeton University Program in Law and Public Affairs, *The Princeton Principles on Universal Jurisdiction* (2001), 23. Online. www.princeton.edu/~lapa/unive_jur.pdf (accessed 14 November 2007).

6 *Barcelona Traction, Light and Power Company Case, Belgium v. Spain*, ICJ Rep 1970 (1998): 33.

7 Note that it is this book's concern with analyzing institutions that create individual liability, rather than state liability, that explains the absence of the International Court of Justice from its pages.

8 Eduardo Greppi, "The Evolution of Individual Criminal Responsibility Under International Law," *International Review of the Red Cross* 835 (1999): 531.

9 Ibid.; Georg Schwarzenberger, *International Law as Applied by International Courts and Tribunals, vol. II: the law of armed conflict* (London: Stevens, 1968), 464.

10 Greppi, "The Evolution of Individual Criminal Responsibility Under International Law," 531.

11 Henry Wheaton, *International Law* (Cambridge, Mass.: Harvard University Press, 1836), 18.

12 Note that this discussion concerns solely the legally appropriate nature of battle once wars begin, not the legal rationale for going to war. The difference is that between causus belli (a legal rationale for starting hostilities) and causus in bello (the laws of war once battle commences).

13 See e.g. G. I. A. D. Draper, Michael A. Meyer, and Hilaire McCoubrey, *Reflections on Law and Armed Conflicts* (Boston, Mass.: Kluwer Law International, 1998), 28.

14 Greppi, "The Evolution of Individual Criminal Responsibility Under International Law," 531.

15 George J. Andreopoulos, Mark R. Shulman, and Michael Eliot Howard, *The Laws of War: constraints on warfare in the western world* (New Haven, Conn.: Yale University Press, 1994), 41, fn. 6.

16 Norman G. Cooper, "Gustavus Adolphus and Military Justice," *Military Law Review* 92 (Spring 1981): 129; W. Winthrop, *Military Law and Precedents* (2nd ed. 1896 and official government reprint 1920) (Buffalo, N. Y.: W. S. Hein Co., 2000).

17 James Snedeck, *A Brief History of Courts Martial* (Annapolis, Md.: United States Naval Institute, 1954), 9.

18 Rupert Furneaux, *The First War Correspondent: William Howard Russell of the Times* (London: Cassell and Company, 1994), 93.

19 C. P. Stacey, "Russell's Dispatches from the Crimea (Review)," *American Historical Review* 73, no. 2 (1967): 481.
20 Henry Dunant, *A Memory of Solferino* (Washington, D.C.: The American National Red Cross, 1939).
21 Richard Shelly Hartigan, ed., *Lieber's Code and the Law of War* (Chicago: Precedent, 1983).
22 James Wilford Garner, *International Law and the World War* (New York: Longman, Green and Co., 1920), 3.
23 Conditions for the Amelioration of the Condition of the Wounded in Armies in the Field, Aug. 22, 1864. (Known variously as the "Geneva Convention of 1864" and the "Red Cross Treaty of 1864").
24 Nicolas Borsinger, ed., *125th anniversary of the 1868 Declaration of St. Petersburg: international symposium on the law of war 1–2 December 1993: Summary of proceedings* (Geneva, Switzerland: International Committee of the Red Cross, 1994).
25 James Brown Scott, ed., *Resolutions of the Institute of International Law Dealing with the Law of Nations* (New York: Oxford University Press, 1916).
26 Yves Sandoz, C. Swinarski, and B. Zimmermann, eds., *International Committee of the Red Cross Commentary on the Additional Protocols of 8 June 1977 to the Geneva Conventions of 12 August 1949* (Geneva, Switzerland: International Committee of the Red Cross, 1977).
27 Professor Franz von Liszt of the University of Berlin was one of Germany's greatest "publicists" on this matter. For an example of his work in this area, see "How Germany Builds Up International Law in War," published in the *Frankfurter Zeitung* in November 1916; summarized in English in the *New York Times*, 19 November 1916.
28 *The Bryce Report: report of the committee on alleged German outrages.* Online. www.yale.edu/lawweb/avalon/brycere.htm (accessed 14 January 2008).
29 Johannes Bell, ed., *Volkerrecht im Weltkrieg: Das Werk des Dritten Untersuchungssausschusses.* 2: 185–86 (1927) in *The Wehrmacht War Crimes Bureau*, Alfred de Zayas (Lincoln: University of Nebraska Press, 1989), 5.
30 *German White Book Concerning the Responsibility of the Authors of the War* (Division of International Law, Carnegie Endowment for International Peace, trans., 1924).
31 *Treaty of Peace Between the Allied and Associated Powers and Germany*, 28 June 1919, 225 Consol. T.S. 188, arts. 227–30 (emphasis added).
32 *Papers Relating to the Foreign Relations of the United States*, 1915, Supplement (Washington, D.C.: US Government Printing Office, 1928), 981.
33 William Schabas, *Genocide in International Law* (Cambridge: Cambridge University Press, 2000), 17.
34 *Treaty of Peace Between the Allied and Associated Powers and Turkey*, 10 August 1920 (never adopted).
35 *Treaty of Peace with Turkey Signed at Lausanne*, 24 July 1923.
36 Despite this, there was logic behind the "military" appellation that perhaps reveals how *sui generis* the tribunals' conveners wished the courts to be. As Schwarzenberger notes, Nuremberg's chief prosecutor, Justice Robert Jackson, said that "[o]ne of the reasons this [Tribunal] was constituted as a military tribunal, instead of an ordinary Court of Law, was to avoid the precedent-creating effect of what is done here on our own law and the precedent

control which would exist if this were an ordinary judicial body." Georg Schwarzenberger, "The Judgment of Nuremberg," *The Tulane Law Review* 21, no. 3 (1947): 333, fn. 14, 337–38. See also Mr Justice Jackson, Speech at the Close of the Case against the Individual Defendants (London, 1946), 4.

37 ICJ Statute, Article 38.

38 Conditions for the Amelioration of the Condition of the Wounded in Armies in the Field, 22 August 1864.

39 ICJ Statute, Article 38.

40 Shabtai Rosenne, *Practice and Methods of International Law* (New York: Oceana Publications, 1984), 55; Antonio Cassese, "A Follow-Up: forcible humanitarian countermeasures and opinio necessitatis," *European Journal of International Law* 10, no. 4 (1999): 797.

41 Convention on the Laws of War: Laws and Customs of War on Land (the Fourth Hague Convention); 18 October 1907, preamble.

42 Rosenne, *Practice and Methods of International Law*, 55.

43 Theodor Meron, "The Geneva Conventions as Customary Law," *American Journal of International Law* 81, no. 2 (1987): 367.

44 Jean-Marie Henckaerts, "Study on Customary International Humanitarian Law: a contribution to the understanding and respect for the rule of law in armed conflict," *International Review of the Red Cross* 87 (2005): 175.

45 *Prosecutor v. Tadic*, Case No. IT-94-1, Decision on the Defence Motion for Interlocutory Appeal on Jurisdiction, P 98, 117 (2 October 1995). Online. www.un.org/icty/tadic/appeal/decision-e/51002.htm (accessed 2 December 2007).

46 Adding to this confusion is the fact that several states which have chosen not to sign or ratify the Additional Protocol, including the United States and Israel, have nonetheless stated their belief that the protocol reflects customary international law.

47 M. Cherif Bassiouni, *International Crimes: digest/index of international instruments 1815–1985* (Dobbs Ferry, N.Y.: Oceana Publications, 1986).

48 Jeffrey S. Morton, *The International Law Commission of the United* Nations (Columbia, S.C.: University of South Carolina Press, 2000), 20.

49 United Nations General Assembly, Resolution 174 (III), "Establishment of an International Law Commission," 17 November 1947, para. 1.

50 United Nations General Assembly, Resolution 260 B (III), 9 December 1948.

51 Morton, *The International Law Commission of the United Nations*, 38.

52 Draft Code of Crimes against the Peace and Security of Mankind, International Law Commission, 1996. Online. http://untreaty.un.org/ilc/texts/instruments/english/draft%20articles/7_4_1996.pdf (accessed 26 November 2007).

53 We recognize that parts of the international tribunal described in Article 230 of the unratified Treaty of Sèvres were constructed on Malta; however, the convenors quickly disbanded any attempt at prosecution. Nuremberg remains the first, truly consumated tribunal that emanated from an internationally authored statute.

54 Charter of the International Military Tribunal, art. 6.

55 The definition of the crime of aggression was explicitly left for elaboration nine years after the Rome Treaty came into operation. Thus, such a definition is due to be appended to the statute in 2009.

56 Georg Schwarzenberger, "The Problem of an International Criminal Law," *Current Legal Problems* 3 (1950): 295. See Christopher L. Blakesley, "Report

of the International Law Association," *Denver Journal of International Law and Policy* 25, no. 2 (1997): 234.

57 Sherri L. Burr, "From Noriega to Pinochet: is there an international moral and legal right to kidnap individuals accused of gross human rights violations?" *Denver Journal of International Law and Policy* 29, no. 2 (2003): 105.

58 For a criticism of this view see Aaron Fichtelberg, "Democratic Legitimacy and the International Criminal Court," *Journal of International Criminal Justice* 4, no. 4 (2006): 765.

59 W. Overy, "The Nuremberg Trials: international law in the making," in *From Nuremberg to The Hague*, ed. Philippe Sands (Cambridge: Cambridge University Press, 2005), 14–15.

60 *Prosecutor v. Barayagwiza*, Case No. ICTR-99-52-A (28 November 2007). Online. http://69.94.11.53/FRENCH/cases/Nahimana/decisions/071128.pdf (accessed 2 December 2007).

61 Anupam Chander, "Globalization and Distrust," *Yale Law Journal* 114, no. 6 (2005): 1193.

62 John F. Murphy, "Civil Liability for the Commission of International Crimes as an Alternative to Criminal Prosecution," *Harvard Human Rights Journal* 12 (spring 1999): 3.

2 The pre-dawn of international justice: through World War I

1 L. C. Green, "International Crimes and the Legal Process," *International and Comparative Law Quarterly* 29, no. 4 (1980): 572.
2 Ibid.
3 Convention on the Prevention and Punishment of the Crime of Genocide, U.N.T.S. no. 1021, vol. 78 (1951), arts. 5, 6.
4 M. Cherif Bassiouni and Peter Manikas, *The Law of the International Criminal Tribunal for the Former Yugoslavia* (New York: Transnational Publishers, 1996), 78.
5 Georg Schwarzenberger, "The Judgment of Nuremberg," *The Tulane Law Review* 21, no. 3 (1947): 330.
6 Eduardo Greppi, "The Evolution of Individual Criminal Responsibility Under International Law," *International Review of the Red Cross* 835 (1999): 531.
7 Gary J. Bass, *Stay the Hand of Vengeance* (Princeton, N.J.: Princeton University Press, 2000), 38.
8 See generally, Peter McGuire, *Law and War: an American story* (New York: Columbia University Press, 2001), 47–69.
9 "By Court-Martial," *Washington Post* (16 April 1902), 1; "More Courts-Martial in the Philippines," *New York Times* (16 April 1902), 1.
10 Letter from Secretary of War Elihu Root to Senator Henry Cabot Lodge, 17 February 1902. Senate Document no. 205, part i, 42. In Moorfield Storey and Julian Codman, *Secretary Root's Record: "Marked Severities" in Philippine Warfare: an analysis of the law and facts bearing on the action and utterances of President Roosevelt and Secretary Root* (Boston, Mass.: Geo. H. Ellis Co., 1902).
11 See generally, Nick Bleszynski, *Shoot Straight, You Bastards: the truth behind the killing of "Breaker Morant"* (New York: Random House, 2002).
12 "Lloyd George Plan to Punish ex-Kaiser," *New York Times* (7 December 1918). Online. http://query.nytimes.com/mem/archive-free/pdf?_r=1&res=9E04

E0DC1238EE32A25754C0A9649D946996D6CF&oref=slogin (accessed 14 November 2007).

13 George Gordon Battle, "The Trials Before the Leipsic [*sic.*] Supreme Court of Germans Accused of War Crimes," *Virginia Law Review* 8, no. 1 (1921): 1–2.

14 Ibid.

15 Larry Zuckerman, *The Rape of Belgium: the untold story of World War I* (New York: New York University Press, 2004): 215.

16 Bass, *Stay the Hand of Vengeance*, 72.

17 *Treaty of Peace Between the Allied and Associated Powers and Germany*, 28 June 1919, 225 Consol. T.S. 188.

18 Bruce Landrum, "The Globalization of Justice: the Rome Statute of the International Criminal Court," *Army Lawyer* 2002 (2002): 3. Note that nearly 1,700 other trials of more minor figures for wartime wrongs were undertaken in Leipzig between 1921 and 1927.

19 Battle, "The Trials Before the Leipsic Supreme Court," 8.

20 Bass, *Stay the Hand of Vengeance*, 86.

21 Vahakn N. Dadrian, "Genocide as a Problem of National and International Law: the World War I Armenian case and its contemporary legal ramifications," *Yale Journal of International Law* 14, no. 2 (1989): 223.

22 Henry Morgenthau Jr., quoted in Bass, *Stay the Hand of Vengeance*, 117.

23 Bass, *Stay the Hand of Vengeance*, 113.

24 Ibid.

25 Ibid., 123.

26 Ultimately the British agreed to a prisoner exchange between British soldiers captured by Mustafa Kemal Ataturk's nationalists and the remaining Turkish prisoners awaiting trial, in spite of many of these Turkish prisoners being held on suspicion of atrocities against Armenians.

27 *Treaty of Peace with Turkey*, signed at Lausanne, 24 July 1923, 28 L.N.T.S. 11; Timothy L. H. McCormack, "Conceptualizing Violence: Present and Future Developments in International Law: Panel II: problems confronting international law and policy on war crimes and crimes against humanity," *Albany Law Review* 60, no. 3 (1997): 704.

28 Vartkes Yeghiayan, *The Armenian Genocide and the Trials of the Young Turks* (La Verne, Calif.: American Armenian International College Press, 1990), xxvi.

29 Yoram Dinstein, *The Defence of "Obedience to Superior Orders" in International Law* (Leyden, The Netherlands: Sythoff, 1965), 11.

30 Bass, *Stay the Hand of Vengeance*, 58.

3 International justice following World War II: Nuremberg and Tokyo

1 Harold Fruchtbaum, "Investigating the Acts of Desperate Men: UN history entrenched in the United Nations War Crimes Commission of 1943," *UN Chronicle* (1994).

2 Richard Sorabij and David Rodin, *The Ethics of War* (Aldershot: Ashgate, 2006), 55.

3 Foreign Secretary Anthony Eden, PRO, PREM 4/100/10, minutes by the foreign secretary, 22 June 1942, 2–3.

4 W. Overy, "The Nuremberg Trials: international law in the making," in *From Nuremberg to The Hague*, ed. Philippe Sands (Cambridge: Cambridge University Press, 2005), 5.

5 See e.g. Geoffrey Robertson, *The Tyrannicide Brief: the story of the man who sent Charles I to the scaffold* (London: Pantheon, 2006), 188, 362.

6 See e.g. Bin Cheng, *General Principles of Law as Applied by International Courts and Tribunals* (Cambridge: Cambridge University Press, 2006), chapter 12.

7 In *Prosecutor v. Tadic*, Case IT-94-1-AR72, the appellate chamber of the International Criminal Tribunal for the former Yugoslavia (ICTY) found that the tribunal had the power to determine the propriety of its own jurisdiction (the power of "competence de la competence") and thus its finding that the tribunal was justly formed could stand.

8 International Court of Justice, *Case Concerning the Arrest Warrant of 11 April 2000 (Democratic Republic of the Congo v. Belgium)*, 14 February 2002.

9 See e.g. Kyle R. Jacobson, "Doing Business with the Devil: the challenges of prosecuting corporate officials whose business transactions facilitate war crimes and crimes against humanity," *Air Force Law Review* 56 (winter 2005): 167–232.

10 Iraqi Special Tribunal, *HRW and ICTJ Translation of Dujail Trial Chamber Judgment*: 179. Online. Available www.ictj.org/static/MENA/Iraq/DujailJudgment.eng.pdf (accessed 11 November 2007).

11 Overy, "The Nuremberg Trials: international law in the making," 7.

12 See Evan J. Wallach, "The Procedural and Evidentiary Rules of the Post World War II War Crimes Trials: did they provide an outline for international legal procedure?" *Columbia Journal of Transnational Law* 37, no. 3 (1999): 851.

13 See generally ibid.

14 Overy, "The Nuremberg Trials: international law in the making," 8.

15 Kellogg-Briand Pact, 27 August 1928, preamble—art. 1, 1928 U.S.T. LEXIS 6, 1.

16 Non-Aggression Pact, 23 August 1939, Germany–USSR.

17 This has fueled many criticisms of the Nuremberg trials, including that the accused were unfairly tried ex post facto and that existing international laws in 1945 did not provide for criminal sanction if they were violated. Karl A. Hochkammer, "The Yugoslav War Crimes Tribunal: the compatibility of peace, politics, and international law," *Vanderbilt Journal of Transnational Law* 28, no. 1 (1995): 142–43.

18 John F. Kennedy, *Profiles in Courage* (New York: Harper and Row, 1964), 190.

19 The charge of "crimes against humanity" was not levied at the Dachau trials. The charge at Dachau was limited to a conspiracy theory, with defendants indicted for participating in a common design to violate the laws and usages of war, according to the Geneva Convention of 1929 and the Hague Convention of 1907. Joshua Greene, *Justice at Dachau: the trials of an American prosecutor* (New York: Broadway Books, 2003), 42.

20 See Rep. John Dingell, "Commutation of Sentences of German War Criminals," *Congressional Record*, 7 March 1951.

21 Kennedy, *Profiles in Courage*, 191.

22 Ibid. Online. www.jfkmontreal.com/profiles_in_courage.htm (accessed 14 November 2007).

23 George A. Finch, "Book Review," *Harvard Law Review* 63, no. 3 (1950): 560.

24 J. Northey, "Book Review: *History of the United Nations War Crimes Commission and the Development of the Laws of War*," *University of Toronto Law Journal* 8, no. 2 (1949–50): 449.

25 Potsdam Declaration, para. 10 (emphasis added). Foreign Relations of the United States: The Conference of Berlin, 2 vols. (Washington, D.C.: Government Printing Office, 1960), II, 1475–476.

26 John Dower, *Embracing Defeat* (New York: W. W. Norton, 1999), chapter 15.

27 Ibid.: 325–26; Herbert Bix, *Hirohito and the Making of Modern Japan* (New York: Perennial, 2001), chapter 15.

28 Dower, *Embracing Defeat*, 451–53.

29 Stanley Falk, "Perceptive Analysis of Japan's Failures in 'Big Science,'" *Army* 56 (2006): 2. World War II in the Pacific: Japanese Unit 731, Biological Warfare Unit. Online. www.ww2pacific.com/unit731.html (accessed 14 November 2007).

30 Bix, *Hirohito and the Making of Modern Japan*, 595.

31 Norimitsu Onishi, "Decades after War Trials, Japan Still Honors a Dissenting Judge," *New York Times* (31 August 2007), 4.

32 See *Dissenting Opinion of the Member from India on Judgment*, IMTFE.

33 Onishi, "Decades after War Trials, Japan Still Honors a Dissenting Judge," 4.

4 The Cold War and the rise of domestic international justice

1 Such was the threat leveled against United States Supreme Court justice Anthony Kennedy in the wake of his citation to various foreign precedents in his opinion in *Roper v. Simmons*, 543 U.S. 551 (2005). Some members of Congress actually called for his impeachment. See e.g. "Supreme Court Ruling Reiterates Importance of Reaffirmation of American Independence Resolution," *US Federal News* (2 March 2005).

2 Adam M. Smith, "Making Itself at Home: Understanding Foreign Law in Domestic Jurisprudence: the Indian case," *Berkeley Journal of International Law* 24, no. 1 (2006): 219–20.

3 Ibid.

4 L. C. Green, "International Crimes and the Legal Process," *The International and Comparative Law Quarterly* 29, no. 4 (1980): 571.

5 See e.g. the *International Institute for the Unification of Private Law* (UNIDROIT), Study LXXVIII – Doc. 26 (February 2006), page 1, fn. 1. Online. www.unidroit.org/english/publications/proceedings/2006/study/78/s-78-26-e.pdf (accessed 11 November 2007).

6 Ibid.; Lori Damrosch, Louis Henkin, Richard Pugh, Oscar Schachter, and Hans Smit, *International Law* (St. Paul, Minn.: West Group, 2001): 160; Oscar Schachter, "The Charter and the Constitution," *Vanderbilt Law Review* 4, no. 3 (1951): 643.

7 Justice Michael Kirby, "The Growing Rapprochement Between International and National Law," *Visions of Legal Order in the 21st Century*. Undated speech. Online. www.hcourt.gov.au/speeches/kirbyj/kirbyj_weeram.htm (accessed 14 November 2007).

8 Alien Tort Claims Act, 28 U.S.C. §1350.

9 *Filartiga v. Pena-Irala*, 630 F.2d 876, 890 (2d Cir. 1980).

10 See e.g. Stewart Jay, "The Statute of the Law of Nations in Early American Law," *Vanderbilt Law Review* 42, no. 3 (1989): 823; William Oke Manning, *Commentaries on the Law of Nations* (Cambridge: Macmillan, 1875), 3.

11 *International Crime Control Act of 1998*, White House, Office of the Press Secretary, "Purpose" (12 May 1998). Archive available online at http://usinfo.state.gov/is/Archive_Index/INTERNATIONAL_CRIME_CONTROL_ACT_OF_1998.html (accessed 11 November 2007).

12 Smith, "Making Itself at Home: Understanding Foreign Law in Domestic Jurisprudence: the Indian case," 219.

13 *In re Yamashita*, 327 US 1, pp. 39–40 (1946) (Murphy, J., dissenting).

14 *Talisman*, 244 F. Supp. 2d at 296. Cited in Alex Canizares, "Interpreting International Criminal Tribunal Decisions Under the Alien Tort Claims Act," unpublished paper (George Washington University School of Law, 2004), 3.

15 *Prosecutor v. Anto Furundzija*, Case No. IT-95-17, Judgment, 2 June 1998.

16 Antonio Cassese, *International Criminal Law* (Oxford: Oxford University Press, 2003), 31.

17 Harold Fruchtbaum, "Investigating the Acts of Desperate Men: UN history entrenched in the United Nations War Crimes Commission of 1943," *UN Chronicle* (1994).

18 Ibid.

19 See, United Nations War Crimes Commission, *Trials of War Criminals* (New York: United Nations, 1947).

20 *Shigenori Kuroda v. Rafael Jalandoni and others*, Second Division [G.R. No. L-2662 26 March 1949]. Online. www.icrc.org/ihl-nat.nsf/39a82e2ca42b5297412 5673e00508144/7ebbe54f61055d6ac12570a500266fd7/$FILE/Kuroda%20-%20Case%20law%20-%20Philippines%20-%20EN.pdf (accessed 5 December 2007).

21 *United States of America v. Wilhelm List et al. (Case VII)*, 8 July 1947–10 February 1948.

22 Kenneth A. Howard, "Command Responsibility for War Crimes," *Journal of Public Law* 21 (1972): 16; Anne Mahle, "The Yamishita Standard," *Justice and the Generals*, PBS-Around the World. Online. www.pbs.org/wnet/justice/world_issues_yam.html (accessed 14 November 2007).

23 Gay McDougall, *MacDougall Report: final report on systematic rape, sexual slavery and slavery-like practices* (New York: United Nations, 1998), 33.

24 Daniel Barenblatt, *A Plague upon Humanity* (New York: HarperCollins, 2004), 220–21.

25 George A. Finch, "Book Review," *Harvard Law Review* 63, no. 3 (1950): 559–60.

26 *In Re Yamashita*, 327 US 1, 24, fn. 10.

27 Ibid.

28 Generally, ibid.

29 See generally, Stuart E. Hendin, "Command Responsibility and Superior Orders in the Twentieth Century: a century of evolution," *Murdoch University Electronic Journal of Law* 10 (2003). Online. www.murdoch.edu.au/elaw/issues/v10n1/hendin101_text.html (accessed 11 November 2007).

30 See e.g. Richard Parkhurst, "Italian Facist War Crimes in Ethopia," *Northeast African Studies* 6, no. 1–2 (1999): 128; Richard Parkhurst, "Ethiopia and the Evolution of International Morality," *The Addis Tribune*. Unknown date. Online. www.addistribune.com/. Archives/2000/09/29–09-00/Hist.htm; www.ethiopianreporter.com/modules.php?name=News&file=article&sid=15254 (accessed 11 November 2007).

31 See generally, L. C. Green, "Legal issues of the Eichmann trial," *Tulane Law Review* 37, no. 4 (1962–63): 641.
32 Stephen Landsman, *Crimes of the Holocaust: the law confronts hard cases* (Philadelphia: University of Pennsylvania Press, 2005), 56.
33 American Jewish Committee, *American Jewish Yearbook* (Philadelphia, Pa.: American Jewish Committee, 1961), 200.
34 Official Argentine complaint to the United Nations Security Council, reprinted in the *American Jewish Yearbook*, 201.
35 *United Nations Treaty Practice*, Article 36, at paras. 16–30. Online. http://untreaty.un.org/cod/repertory/art36/english/rep_supp3_vol2-art36_e.pdf (accessed 11 November 2007); *American Jewish Yearbook*, 199.
36 United Nations Security Council, Resolution of 23 June 1960 (138), S/4349.
37 Security Council, "Argentine Complaint Against the State of Israel," *International Organization* 14, no. 4 (1960): 576.
38 Landsman, *Crimes of the Holocaust*, 61.
39 Thomas Mertens, "The Eichmann Trial: Hannah Arendt's view on the Jerusalem court's competence," *German Law Journal* 6, no. 2 (2005): 414.
40 Nazi and Nazi Collaborators Punishment Law 5710–1950. Israeli Ministry of Foreign Affairs. Online. www.mfa.gov.il/mfa/go.asp?MFAH07tv0 (accessed 11 November 2007)
41 *The Attorney General v. Adolf Eichmanni, Criminal Case* 40/61: para. 12, page 26.
42 *American Jewish Yearbook*, 205.
43 "Declaration of the Four Nations on General Security" (Moscow Declaration), 1943.
44 Landsman, *Crimes of the Holocaust*, 61.
45 Hannah Arendt, *Eichmann in Jerusalem: the banality of evil* (New York: Penguin, 1994).
46 Landsman, *Crimes of the Holocaust*, 65.
47 Ibid., 67.
48 This was not the end of the Demjanjuk saga. He remained without American citizenship until 1998 when a US district court found that his citizenship could be restored; in 1999 he was again made the subject of a federal investigation for having been an active Nazi during World War II and thus having concealed this fact on his 1951 immigration application; in 2002 the same judge that ordered his citizenship reinstated found that the case against him was proven and an appellate court upheld this determination, concluding that Demjanjuk could again be stripped of his citizenship. In 2005, he was put before an immigration judge who ordered his deportation to Ukraine, a finding confirmed by an appellate immigration judge in 2006. He remains in the USA (with no state willing to accept him) as a "stateless alien" (as he is no longer an American citizen).
49 The Nizkor Project, "The Demjanjuk Case: factual and legal details." Online. www.nizkor.org/hweb/people/d/demjanjuk-john/israeli-data/ (accessed 15 November 2007).
50 Nicholas R. Doman, "Aftermath of Nuremberg: the trial of Klaus Barbie," *University of Colorado Law Review* 60, no. 3 (1989): 468.
51 Ibid.
52 Ibid., 458.
53 Judgment of December 20, 1985, Cass. Crim., in ibid. pp. 459, fn. 21.

54 Daphne Merkin, "Speak No Evil," *New York Times Magazine* (21 October 2007). Online. www.nytimes.com/2007/10/21/magazine/21wwln-lede-t.html?_r=1&n=Top/Reference/Times%20Topics/People/V/Verg&oref=slogin#232; s,%20Jacques (accessed 5 December 2007).
55 See generally, Richard Joseph Golsan, ed., *The Papon Affair* (London: Routledge, 2000).
56 David Matas and Susan Charendoff, *Justice Delayed: Nazi war criminals* (Toronto: Summerhill Press, 1987), 68.
57 David Matas, "Prosecution in Canada for Crimes against Humanity," *New York Law School Journal of International and Comparative Law* 11, no. 3 (1990): 348.
58 Supreme Court of Canada (*R. v. Finta* [1994] 1 S.C.R. 701), 15.
59 Landsman, *Crimes of the Holocaust*, 224.
60 *Finta Trial Transcript*, 10 May 1990, cited in ibid., 217.
61 Landsman, *Crimes of the Holocaust*, 239.
62 Gillian Triggs, "Australia's War Crimes Trials: a moral necessity or legal minefield?" *Melbourne University Law Review* 16, no. 2 (1987): 382.
63 See generally, M. Aarons, *War Criminals Welcome: Australia, a sanctuary for fugitive war criminals since 1945* (Melbourne, VIC: A&C Black, 2001).
64 Preamble to the War Crimes Amendment Act 1988 (Commonwealth of Australia), no. 3 of 1989.
65 Jonathan Steinberg, "Reflections on Intergenerational Justice," in Alice Henkin, ed., *The Legacy of Abuse: confronting the past, facing the future* (Washington, D.C.: The Aspen Institute, 2002), 72.
66 *Polyukovich v. The Commonwealth* [1991] HCA 32; (1991) 172 CLR 501.
67 David Bevan, *A Case to Answer: the story of Australia's first European war crimes prosecution* (Adelaide, SA: Wakefield Press, 1994): xli–xlii.
68 Simon Wiesenthal Center, *Nazi War Criminals Prosecution: annual status report—April 2001*, 18 April 2001.
69 Ingo Mueller, *Hitler's Justice: the courts of the Third Reich* (Cambridge, Mass.: Harvard University Press, 1991), 201.
70 Interestingly when (West) Germany re-established its system of military justice in 1954, it explicitly excluded military courts. The entire competence of adjudication rests in civilian courts. Friedhelm Krueger-Sprengel, "The German Military Legal System," *Military Law Review* 57 (1972): 17–18.
71 Kerstin Freudiger, *Die juristische Aufarbeitung von NS-Verbrechen* 26 (2002); reviewed in English in Phoebe Kornfeld, "Book Review: Kerstin Freudiger's *Die juristische Aufarbeitung von NS-Verbrechen* (Nazi Crimes Before the Courts)," *German Law Journal* 3, no. 12 (2002). Online. www.germanlawjournal.com/print.php?id=218 (accessed 14 November 2007).
72 See generally: Adalbert Rückerl, ed., *NS-PROSEZZE—Nach 25 Jahren Strafverfolgung: Möglichkeiten—Grenzen—Ergebnisse* (National Socialism Trials: After 25 Years of Prosecution: Possibilities—Limits—Results) (Karlsruhe, West Germany: C. F. Müller, 1971). Fritz Weinschenk, "The Murderers Among Them: German justice and the Nazis," *Hofstra Law and Policy Symposium* 3 (1999): 143.
73 See generally, Jadwiga Gorzkowska and Elżbieta Żakowska, *Nazi Criminals Before West German Courts* (Warsaw, Poland: Zachodnia Agencja Prasowa, 1965).

74 See generally, Rebecca Wittman, *Beyond Justice: the Auschwitz Trial* (Cambridge, Mass.: Harvard University Press, 2005).
75 Devin O. Pendas, "The Frankfurt Auschwitz Trial and the German Press, 1963–65," *Yale Journal of Law and the Humanities* 12, no. 2 (2000): 397.
76 Devin O. Pendas, *The "Boger Syndrome": torture vs. genocide in the Frankfurt Auschwitz trial, 1963–65*. Online. http://internationalstudies.uchicago.edu/torture/abstracts/devionpendas.htm (accessed 11 November 2007).
77 Pendas, "The Frankfurt Auschwitz Trial and the German Press," 397.
78 Pendas, *The "Boger Syndrome."*
79 Pendas, "The Frankfurt Auschwitz Trial and the German Press," 416.
80 Gorzkowska and Żakowska, *Nazi Criminals Before West German Courts*, 35.
81 Weinschenk, "The Murderers Among Them: German justice and the Nazis," 146.
82 See generally, Robert A. Monson, "The West German Statute of Limitations on Murder: a political, legal, and historical exposition," *American Journal of Comparative Law* 30, no. 4 (1982): 605.
83 Mark Osiel, "The Making of Human Rights Policy in Argentina: the impact of ideas and interests on a legal conflict," *Journal of Latin American Studies* 18 (1986): 135; Alejandro M. Garro, "Nine Years of Transition to Democracy in Argentina: partial failure or qualified success?" *Columbia Journal of Transnational Law* 31, no. 1 (1993–94): 10.
84 Argentine presidential order to proceed against the military juntas, Decree 158 of December 1983.
85 Shirley Christian, "Argentina Frees Ex-Junta Leaders," *New York Times*, 30 December 1990. Online. http://query.nytimes.com/gst/fullpage.html?res=9C0CE 7D9163EF933A05751C1A966958260 (accessed 11 November 2007).
86 *Comision Nacional Sobre La Desparicion de Personas, Nunca Mas* (1984), cited in Carlos S. Nino, "The Duty to Punish Past Abuses of Human Rights Put Into Context: the case of Argentina," *Yale Law Journal* 100, no. 8 (1990–91): 2623, fn. 15.
87 *Nunca Mas*, prologue.
88 Luis Moreno Ocampo, "The Nuremberg Parallel in Argentina," *New York Law School Journal of International and Comparative Law* 11, no. 3 (1990): 357.
89 Ibid.
90 Emilio Fermin Mignone, Cynthia L. Estlund, and Samuel Issacharoff, "Dictatorship on Trial: prosecution of human rights violations in Argentina," *Yale Journal of International Law* 10, no. 1 (1984–85): 125
91 Law No. 23049, 20 February 1984, [XLIV-A] A.D.L.A. 8 (1984).
92 Garro, "Nine Years of Transition to Democracy in Argentina: Partial Failure or Qualified Success?" 14.
93 Ibid., 13.
94 Cod. Justicia Militar art. 514 (Ediciones Librerin del Jurista, 1985). Cited in Carlos S. Nino, "The Duty to Punish Past Abuses of Human Rights Put Into Context": 2625, fn. 28.
95 Ibid., 2626.
96 Ibid.
97 Evan W. Gray, "Human Rights: Conviction of Former Argentine Military Commanders for Human Rights Abuses Committed by Subordinates," *Harvard International Law Journal* 27, no. 2 (1986): 688.

98 Luis Moreno Ocampo, "Beyond Punishment: justice in the wake of massive crimes in Argentina," *Journal of International Affairs* 52, no. 2 (1999): 1.

99 Shirley Christian, "Argentina Frees Ex-Junta Leaders," *New York Times* (30 December 1990). Online. http://query.nytimes.com/gst/fullpage.html? res=9C0CE7D9163EF933A05751C1A966958260&scp=1&sq=Argentina+ Frees+Ex-Junta+Leaders (accessed 14 January 2008).

5 Post-Cold War justice: the UN ad hoc tribunals, mixed courts, and the ICC

1 Ian Brownlie, *Principles of Public International Law* (Oxford: Clarendon Press, 4th ed., 1990), 563–64, cited in Robert Cryer, *Prosecuting International Crimes* (Cambridge: Cambridge University Press, 2005), 51.

2 John Dugard, "Obstacles in the Way of an International Criminal Court," *Cambridge Law Journal* 56, no. 2 (1997): 330.

3 Ibid.

4 Letter from the Permanent Representative of Trinidad and Tobago to the United Nations Addressed to the Secretary-General, 21 August 1998, UN Doc A/44/195 (1989); see also, Andreas Schloenhardt, "Transnational Organised Crime and the International Criminal Court: developments and debates," *University of Queensland Law Journal* 24, no. 1 (2005): 93.

5 See, e.g. George S. Yacoubin, "The Most International of International Crimes: toward the incorporation of drug trafficking into the subject matter jurisdiction of the International Criminal Court," *bePress Legal Series*, paper 1846 (2006). Online. http://law.bepress.com/cgi/viewcontent.cgi?article= 8812&context=expresso (accessed 11 November 2007).

6 United Nations Charter, Chapter VII, art. 39.

7 United Nations Security Council Resolution 827, (25 May 1993) ("Statute of the International Tribunal for the Prosecution of Persons Responsible for Serious Violations of International Humanitarian Law in the Territory of the Former Yugoslavia"); unanimously adopted 25 May 1993. Note that Security Council Resolution 808 of 22 February 1993 called for the imminent establishment of the tribunal, although it indicated neither how such a tribunal would be established nor on what legal basis.

8 *Prosecutor v. Tadic*, Case IT-94-1-AR72. *Prosecutor v. Kanyabashi*, Case ICTR-96-15-T.

9 Statute of the ICTY, Article 9, para. 2.

10 This section is based on Chapter 26 "International Criminal Court and Ad Hoc Tribunals" by Richard J. Goldstone, pp. 463–478 from *Oxford Handbook of the United Nations*, edited by Weiss, Thomas G. and Daws, Sam (2007). By permission of Oxford University Press.

11 *Prosecutor v. Blaskic*, Case No. IT-95-14 (29 October 1997) (Judgment on the Request of the Republic of Croatia for Review of the Decision of Trial Chamber II of 18 July 1997). The court held that "the ICTY cannot issue binding orders to specific officials of a state when acting in their official capacity, since it is for the state itself to determine which officials are responsible for the requested documents." Sean D. Murphy, "Progress and Jurisprudence of the International Criminal Tribunal for the Former Yugoslavia," *American Journal of International Law* 93, no. 1 (1999): 82. Murphy notes, however, that the ICTY does have the power to subpoena individuals acting in their "personal" capacities, but "[of]

course, whether national authorities will compel a reluctant witness to comply with the ICTY's order may depend on that state's municipal law." See also Jacob Katz Cogan, "The Problem of Obtaining Evidence for International Criminal Courts," *Human Rights Quarterly* 22, no. 2 (2002): 404.

12 See, for example, United Nations Security Council Resolution 1534 (26 March 2004) (calling "on Bosnia and Herzegovina, and on the Republika Srpska within Bosnia and Herzegovina, to intensify cooperation with and render all necessary assistance to the ICTY.")

13 See generally, Mark Thieroff and Edward A. Amley, Jr., "Proceeding to Justice and Accountability in the Balkans: the International Criminal Tribunal for the Former Yugoslavia and Rule 61," *Yale Journal of International Law* 23, no. 1 (1998): 231.

14 Annex: Cost of Justice, ICTY: At a Glance. Online. www.un.org/icty/glance-e/index.htm (accessed 11 November 2007).

15 Anthony D'Amato, "Defending a Person Charged with Genocide," *Chicago Journal of International Law* 1, no. 2 (2000): 468–69.

16 See e.g. Marlise Simons, "Bosnian Ex-Leader Sentenced To 11 Years for Her War Role," *New York Times* (8 March 2003). Online. http://query.nytimes.com/gst/fullpage.html?res=9C01E5DA133CF93BA15751C0A9659C8B63 (accessed 11 November 2007).

17 Indictment, *Prosecutor v. Milosevic*, et al., Case No. IT-99-37.

18 Adam M. Smith, "Balkan Legal: trying war crimes locally," *New Republic* (1 May 2006): 14.

19 All ICTY cases, indictments, etc., are available at: www.icty.org; all ICTR cases, indictments, etc., are available at www.ictr.org.

20 *Prosecutor v. Tadic*, Case No. IT-94-1-AR72.

21 *Prosecutor v. Blaskic*, Case No IT-95-14.

22 *Prosecutor v. Akayesu*, Case No. ICTR-96-4-T.

23 *Prosecutor v. Museum*, Case No. ICTR-96-13-A.

24 *Prosecutor v. Kambanda*, Case No. ICTR-97-23-DP.

25 *Prosecutor v. Barayagwiza*, Case No. ICTR-97-19-I.

26 Security Council Resolution 1534 (26 March 2004).

27 Karadzic was arrested in Serbia on July 21, 2008 and extradited to The Hague.

28 Rule 11 *bis* of this Tribunal's Rules allows referral for trial to be ordered to the authorities of (1) a state where the crime was committed, or (2) a state where the accused was arrested, or (3) a state which has jurisdiction and which is willing and adequately prepared to accept the case.

29 ICTY At a Glance.

30 Ibid.

31 ICTR Detainees—Status on 13 July 2007. Online. http://69.94.11.53/default.htm (accessed 11 November 2007).

32 Mark A. Drumbl, "Law and Atrocity: settling accounts in Rwanda," *Ohio Northern Law Review* 31, no. 1 (2005): 44.

33 Aneta Wierzynska, "Consolidating Democracy Through Transitional Justice: Rwanda's Gacaca courts," *New York University Law Review* 79, no. 5 (2004): 1934.

34 The formation of the tribunal was further recommended by a 2000 report of the UN Office of the High Commissioner for Human Rights. See *Report of the International Commission of Enquiry on East Timor to the Secretary General* (New York: United Nations, 2000).

35 These panels are not to be confused with Indonesia's own trials concerning abuses perpetrated during the time of East Timor's independence. The now-concluded "Jakarta Trials" were wholly domestic, Indonesian proceedings.

36 United Nations Transition Authority in East Timor (UNTAET), "On the Establishment of Panels with Exclusive Jurisdiction over Serious Criminal Offences," UNTAET Regulation No. 2000/15, 6 June 2000.

37 See generally, Hansjoerg Strohmeyer, "Policing the Peace: post-conflict judicial system reconstruction in East Timor," *University of NSW Law Journal* 24, no. 1 (2001).

38 United Nations Interim Administration Mission in Kosovo (UNMIK), "On the Appointment and Removal from Office of International Judges and International Prosecutors," UNMIK Regulation No. 2000/64, 12 January 2001.

39 See: Statement by the President of the Security Council, (UN document S/PRST/2002/21), 2002.

40 *Bosnia and Herzegovina v. Janković Gojko*, X-KR-05/161, 23 October 2007. Online. www.sudbih.gov.ba/?opcija=predmeti&id=19&jezik=e (accessed 25 November 2007).

41 General Assembly, "Approval of Draft Agreement, A/57/806, Annex" 13 May 2003, 85th plenary session.

42 Marlise Simons, "Liberian Ex-Leader's War Crimes Trial is Stalled," *New York Times* (27 August 2007). Online. www.nytimes.com/2007/08/27/world/africa/27taylor.html?_r=1&oref=slogin (accessed 11 November 2007).

43 Ibid.

44 Clifford Levy, "World Briefing, Cambodia: UN Finds Flaws in Tribunal," *New York Times* (3 October 2007). Online. http://query.nytimes.com/gst/full page.html?res=9804E6DE1239F930A35753C1A9619C8B63 (accessed 11 November 2007).

45 Seth Mydans, "Khmer Rouge Figure is First Charged in Atrocities," *New York Times* (1 August 2007). Online. www.nytimes.com/2007/08/01/world/asia/01cambodia.html (accessed 11 November 2007).

46 Rome Statute of the International Criminal Court, (UN document A/CONF.183/9), 17 July 1998.

47 United Nations General Assembly, "Cooperation between the United Nations and the International Criminal Court," GAOR, 2004, 58th session (A/Res/58/318).

48 See e.g. www.icc-cpi.int/asp/aspaggression.html (accessed 11 November 2007).

49 Benjamin Ferencz, "An International Criminal Code and Court: where they stand and where they're going," *Columbia Journal of Transnational Law* 30, no. 2 (1992): 375.

50 Up-to-date information about the ICC's current investigations, cases and other activities can be found at its website: www.icc-cpi.int

51 Richard J. Goldstone, cited in "Trial Chamber's decision to stay proceedings in Lubanga case is clear indication of the ICC's commitment to uphold fair trial rights, says IBA," The International Bar Association, 18 June 2008. Online. http://www.ibanet.org/iba/article.cfm?article=174 (accessed 16 August 2008); "Trial Chamber I ordered the release of Thomas Lubanga Dyilo – Implementation of the decision is pending," The International Criminal Court, 2 July 2008. Online. http://www.icc-cpi.int/press/pressreleases/394.html (accessed 16 August 2008).

6 Post-ICC prosecutions: new domestic proceedings and international proceedings beyond ICC justice

1 Naomi Roht-Arriaza, "The Pinochet Precedent and Universal Jurisdiction," *New England Law Review* 35, no. 2 (2000): 313.
2 See Ley Organica del Poder Judicial, art. 23(4) (1985); cited in Naomi Roht-Arriaza, "The Pinochet Precedent and Universal Jurisdiction," 312.
3 There are five traditional bases of jurisdiction: Territoriality (jurisdiction over crimes that took place in the state itself); Nationality (jurisdiction over crimes committed by nationals of the state); Passive Personality (jurisdiction over crimes of which a national is a victim); Protective (jurisdiction over crimes when the security of the state is at issue); and Universal. See Hari Osofsky, "Domesticating International Criminal Law: bringing human rights violators to justice," *Yale Law Journal* 107, no. 1 (1997): 192–93.
4 Michael Ratner, *The Lords' Decision in Pinochet III: A Legal Analysis.* Online. www.humanrightsnow.org/articles/pinochet%20ratner%20to%20reed. htm (accessed 11 November 2007). See *Regina v. Bow Street Metropolitan Stipendiary Magistrate, ex parte* Pinochet Ugarte, [1998] 3 W.L.R. 1456 (H.L.), *reprinted in* 37 I.L.M. 1302 (1998); *Regina v. Bow Street Metropolitan Stipendiary Magistrate, ex parte* Pinochet Ugarte, [1999] 2 W. L.R. 272 (H.L.), *reprinted in* 38 I.L.M. 430 (1999); *Regina v. Bow Street Metropolitan Stipendiary Magistrate, ex parte* Pinochet Ugarte, [1999] 2 W. L.R. 827 (H.L.).
5 Anto de la Salade lo Penal de la Audiencia Nacional confirmando la jurisdiccion de Espana para conocer de los crimenes de genocidio y terrorismo comtedidos durante la dictadura chilena, 5 November 1998, Rollo de Apelacion 173/98.
6 Naomi Roht-Arriaza, "The Pinochet Precedent and Universal Jurisdiction," 313.
7 "Talks Set to Ease Pinochet rift," British Broadcasting Corporation, 20 June 2000. Online. http://news.bbc.co.uk/1/hi/world/americas/798114.stm (accessed 11 November 2007).
8 For a complete timeline of the Pinochet case in England, and then in Chile, see http://news.amnesty.org/pages/pinochet_timeline (accessed 11 November 2007).
9 For a more detailed history and analysis of the IST, see, Adam M. Smith, "Transitional Justice in Iraq: The Iraqi Special Tribunal and the future of a nation," *International Affairs Review* 14, no. 1 (2005): 5.
10 Coalition Provisional Authority Order Number 48, Delegation of Authority Regarding an Iraqi Special Tribunal, CPA/ORD/9 Dec 2003/48. www.cpa-iraq.org/regulations/20031210_CPAORD_48_IST_and_Appendix_A.pdf (accessed 11 November 2007).
11 United Nations Security Council Resolution 1483, 2003, S/Res/1483 cited in Coalition Provisional Authority Order Number 48, Delegation of Authority Regarding an Iraqi Special Tribunal, CPA/ORD/9 Dec 2003/48.
12 See: Working Group on Transitional Justice in Iraq and Iraqi Jurists' Association, "Transitional Justice in post-Saddam Iraq: the road to re-establishing rule of law and restoring civil society: a blueprint: report of the Working Group on Transitional Justice in Iraq, and Iraqi Jurists'

Association" (2003). Online. https://www. jagcnet.army.mil/JAGCNETInternet /Homepages/AC/CLAMO-Public.nsf/0/ 85256a1c006ac77385256d2b0054e3b2/ Body/M2/Transitional%20Justice%20Report.doc?OpenElement (accessed 11 November 2007).

13 Adam M. Smith, "Transitional Justice in Iraq," 13.

14 E.g. Kingsley Chiedu Moghalu, "Saddam Hussein's Trial Meets the 'Fairness' Test," *Ethics and International Affairs* 20, no. 4 (2006): 517.

15 See generally, Dave Johns, "Defining Justice Victors' Justice," *FrontlineWorld* (PBS). Online. www.pbs.org/frontlineworld/stories/iraq501/defining_victors. html (accessed 11 November 2007).

16 Note that in both official documents and the press Hariri's name is alternatively transliterated as "Rafik" and "Rafiq."

17 *Report of the Fact-finding Mission to Lebanon inquiring into the causes, circumstances and consequences of the assassination of former Prime Minister Rafiq Hariri, S/2005/203 (24 March 2005)* ("FitzGerald Report").

18 United Nations Security Council Resolution 1595, 7 April 2005.

19 *Report of the International Independent Investigation Commission established pursuant to Security Council Resolution (2005), S/2005/662 (20 October 2005), 1595* ("Mehlis Report").

20 United Nations Security Council Resolution 1636 (2005), S/Res/1636 (2005).

21 *Second Report of the International Independent Investigation Commission Established Pursuant to Security Council Resolutions 1595 and 1636* (10 December 2005) ("The Second Mehlis Report").

22 Hassan Fattah, "Son of Slain Lebanese Seeks a Special Tribunal," *New York Times* (24 October 2005). Online. http://query.nytimes.com/gst/fullpage.html?res =9C01E1DD103FF937A15753C1A9639C8B63 (accessed 11 November 2007).

23 Ibid.

24 Letter from Lebanese Prime Minister to the United Nations Secretary-General, December 13, 2005, S/2005/783.

25 United Nations Security Council Resolution 1664, 29 March 2006 (S/Res/ 1664 (2006)).

26 In January 2008, Brammertz was appointed to succeed Carla del Ponte as chief prosecutor of the ICTY.

27 United Nations Security Council Resolution 1757, 31 May 2007 (S/Res/ 1757 (2007)).

28 See also, generally, Cecile Aptel, "Some Innovations in the Statute of the Special Tribunal for Lebanon," *Journal of International Criminal Justice* 5, no. 5 (2007): 1107–124.

29 International Convention for the Suppression of Terrorist Bombings, adopted by the General Assembly of the United Nations on 15 December 1997.

30 The Rome Statute also speaks of a four-part structure, but it does so by splitting the chambers into two ("The Presidency," and "An Appeals Division, a Trial Division, and a Pre-Trial Division") rather than explicitly incorporate a defense function as an organ of the court. See Rome Statute of the International Criminal Court, Article 34.

31 Adam M. Smith, "'Judicial Nationalism' in International Law: national identity and judicial autonomy at the ICJ," *Texas International Law Journal* 40, no. 2 (2004–5): 204, fn. 40.

32 Statute of the International Criminal Tribunal for the former Yugoslavia, art. 22.
33 Cecile Aptel, "Some Innovations in the Statute of the Special Tribunal for Lebanon," 1107–124.
34 See e.g. Mark Fleming, "Appellate Review in the International Criminal Tribunals," *Texas International Law Journal* 37, no. 1 (2002): 111.

7 Conclusion: the future of "international" justice—active at home and abroad

1 Statute of the International Criminal Tribunal for the former-Yugoslavia, art. 24; Statute of the International Criminal Tribunal for Rwanda, art. 23.
2 *Prosecutor v. Anto Furundzija,* Case No. IT-95-17, Judgment, 2 June 1998.
3 Nicholas R. Doman, "Aftermath of Nuremberg: the trial of Klaus Barbie," *University of Colorado Law Review* 60, no. 3 (1989): 468.
4 United Nations Security Council Resolution 1757, 31 May 2007 (S/Res/ 1757 (2007)), Statute of the Special Tribunal for Lebanon, art. 2.
5 Adam M. Smith, "Good Fences Make Good Neighbors? The "Wall Decision" and the troubling rise of the ICJ as a human rights court," *Harvard Human Rights Journal* 18 (spring 2005): 251.
6 See e.g. Jose E. Alvarez, "Rush to Closure: lessons of the Tadic judgment," *Michigan Law Review* 96, no. 7 (1998): 2101; John F. Murphy, "Civil Liability for the Commission of International Crimes as an Alternative to Criminal Prosecution," *Harvard Human Rights Journal* 12 (spring 1999): 3.
7 Report of the Secretary General Pursuant to Paragraph 5 of Security Council Resolution 955 (1994) 13 February 1995, S/1995/134.
8 See, e.g. Agreements on the Enforcement of Sentences, ICTY. Online. www. un.org/icty/legaldoc-e/index.htm (accessed 14 November 2007).
9 United Nations Transitional Administration in East Timor, On the Establishment of Panels with Exclusive Jurisdiction over Serious Criminal Offenses, Regulation No. 2000/15, Section 10.
10 Law on the Establishment of Extraordinary Chambers in the Courts of Cambodia for the Prosecution of Crimes Committed during the Period of Democratic Kampuchea, Chapter XI.
11 Reuters, "World Briefing: Rwanda: UN Welcomes Death Penalty Ban," *New York Times* (28 July 2007).
12 Stephen Landsman, *Crimes of the Holocaust: the law confronts hard cases* (Philadelphia: University of Pennsylvania Press, 2005), 56–109.
13 Anthony D'Amato, "Defending a Person Charged with Genocide," *Chicago Journal of International Law* 1, no. 2 (2000): 468–69.
14 International Bar Association, *IBA Monitoring Report: International Criminal Court,* November 2007, p. 33. Online. www.ibanet.org/images/ downloads/11_Report_IBA_Monitoring_Report_ICC_November_2007.pdf (accessed 2 December 2007).
15 See e.g. the London Charter for the International Military Tribunal (at Nuremberg); the statutes of the International Criminal Tribunal for the former Yugoslavia and the International Criminal Tribunal for Rwanda.
16 United Nations Security Council Resolution 1757, 31 May 2007 (S/Res/ 1757 (2007)), Statute of the Special Tribunal for Lebanon, art. 17, 25.

17 Rome Statute of the International Criminal Court, (UN document A/CONF. 183/9), 17 July 1998, arts. 75, 79.
18 David J. Scheffer, "International Judicial Intervention," *Foreign Policy* no. 102 (spring 1996): 34.
19 Landsman, *Crimes of the Holocaust,* 56–109.
20 Ibid., 65.
21 See generally, Desmond Tutu, *No Future without Forgiveness* (New York: Doubleday, 1999); Truth and Reconciliation Commission of Liberia, https://www.trcofliberia.org/ (accessed 14 November 2007); see also Priscilla Hayner, "Fifteen Truth Commissions—1974 to 1994: a comparative study," *Human Rights Quarterly* 16, no. 4 (1994): 597–655.

Selected bibliography

Payam Akhavan, "The International Criminal Tribunal for Rwanda: the politics and pragmatics of punishment," *American Journal of International Law* 90, no. 3 (1996): 501–10.

Jose E. Alvarez, "Crimes of State/Crimes of Hate: lessons from Rwanda," *Yale Journal of International Law* 24, no. 2 (1999): 365–483.

Gary Jonathan Bass, *Stay the Hand of Vengeance: the politics of war crimes tribunals* (Princeton, N.J.: Princeton University Press, 2000).

Bruce Broomhall, *International Justice and the International Criminal Court: between sovereignty and the rule of law* (New York: Oxford University Press, 2003).

Jonathan Charney, "International Criminal Law and the Role of Domestic Courts," *American Journal of International Law* 95, no. 1 (2001): 120–24.

Laura A. Dickinson, "The Promise of Hybrid Courts," *American Journal of International Law* 97, no. 2 (2003): 295–310.

Mark A. Drumbl, "Punishment, Postgenocide: from guilt to shame to 'Civis' in Rwanda," *New York University Law Review* 75, no. 5 (2000): 1221–326.

Richard Goldstone, *For Humanity: reflections of a war crimes investigator* (New Haven, Conn.: Yale University Press, 2000).

——, "The Role of the United Nations in the Prosecution of International War Criminals," *Washington University Journal of Law and Policy* 5 (2001): 119–27.

Priscilla B. Hayner, *Unspeakable Truths: facing the challenge of truth commissions* (London: Routledge, 2002).

Stephen Landsman, *Crimes of the Holocaust: the law confronts hard cases* (Philadelphia: University of Pennsylvania Press, 2005).

Martha Minow, *Between Vengeance and Forgiveness: facing history after genocide and mass violence* (Boston, Mass.: Beacon Press, 1998).

Naomi Roht-Arriaza, *The Pinochet Effect: transnational justice in the age of human rights* (Philadelphia: University of Pennsylvania Press, 2005).

Naomi Roht-Arriaza (ed.), *Impunity and Human Rights in International Law and Practice* (New York: Oxford University Press, 1995).

Cesare P. R. Romano, Andre Nollkaemper, Jann K. Kleffner (eds.), *Internationalized Criminal Courts* (Oxford: Oxford University Press, 2004).

Leila Nadya Sadat, *The International Criminal Court and the Transformation of International Law: justice for the new millennium* (Ardsley, N.Y.: Transnational Publishers, 2002).

Philippe Sands (ed.), *From Nuremberg to the Hague: the future of international criminal justice* (Cambridge: Cambridge University Press, 2003).

William Schabas, *An Introduction to the International Criminal Court* (Cambridge: Cambridge University Press, 2001).

Daphna Shraga and Ralph Zacklin, "The International Criminal Tribunal for Rwanda" *European Journal of International Law* 7, no. 4 (1996): 501–18.

Rebecca Wittman, *Beyond Justice: the Auschwitz trial* (Cambridge, Mass.: Harvard University Press, 2005).

Index

GLOBAL INSTITUTIONS SERIES

NEW TITLE
Institutions of the Global South

Jacqueline Anne Braveboy-Wagner, City University of New York, USA

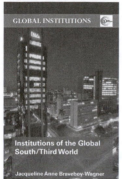

This is an accessible new introduction to organizations of key importance to the global south in the post-war period. It clearly assesses their achievements, performance and responses to global change.

Selected contents: Introduction 1 Tricontinental diplomacy 2 Tricontinental functionalism 3 Tricontinental single-issue functionalism 4 Regional visions: Pan-Americanism 5 Regional visions: Pan-Africanism 6 Regional visions: Pan-Arabism and Pan-Islam 7 Subregional communities: Latin America and the Caribbean 8 Subregional communities: Africa 9 Subregional communities: Southeast, South, and West Asia, and the Pacific 10 Summarizing global south institutionalism

September 2008: 216x138: 272pp
Hb: 978-0-415-36590-1: **£65.00**
Pb: 978-0-415-36591-8: **£14.99**

NEW TITLE
The International Organization for Standardization (ISO)
Global governance through voluntary consensus

Craig N. Murphy, Wellesley College, USA and
Joanne Yates, Sloan School of Management, USA

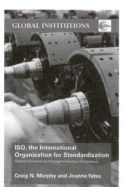

The International Organization for Standardization (ISO) is the first full-length study of the largest non-governmental, global regulatory network whose scope and influence rivals that of the UN system.

Selected contents: Introduction 1. Voluntary consensus standard setting 2. How ISO works 3. Infrastructure for a global market 4. From quality management to social regulation 5. Standards wars and the future of ISO 6. Conclusion

December 2008: 216x138: 160pp
Hb: 978-0-415-77429-1: **£65.00**
Pb: 978-0-415-77428-4: **£14.99**

Routledge
Taylor & Francis Group

To order any of these titles
Call: +44 (0) 1235 400400
Email: book.orders@routledge.co.uk

For further information visit:
www.routledge.com/politics